"Her Unexpected Second Chance"

Bulbs, Blossoms and Bouquets #2

By Laura Ann

HER UNEXPECTED SECOND CHANCE

First edition. March 10, 2021.

Written by Laura Ann.

DEDICATION

To my redheaded friend.
Without you giving me a chance,
I would have never stepped outside
my bubble.
This is for you!

ACKNOWLEDGEMENTS

No author works alone. Thank you, Tami.
You make it Christmas every time
I get a new cover. And thank you to my Beta Team.
Truly, your help with my stories is immeasurable.

CHAPTER 1

A little bell rang as Mel pushed open the door to the flower shop. She grinned at the familiar sound and hurried to the back room where she knew her friends would be waiting.

"Mel!" Caro called out, bringing everyone else's attention to Mel's entrance.

"Hey, Caro!" Mel called back.

"Hi, Mel!"

"Wassup, Chiquita Bonita!"

Mel grinned and greeted all her friends. She waved and hugged those she was closest to, smiling at the others that were more like acquaintances. Upon reaching her designated table, she sighed, then took in a deep breath of floral-scented air. Mel loved arrangement night.

Rose, the shop's owner, was a genius when it came to plants and had started a class where she taught arranging and the language of flowers. Surprisingly, it had blossomed into something more, giving Mel and the others her age a common interest that had built a group of friends stronger than anything Mel had ever had before.

"So...what are we making tonight?" Mel asked Genevieve, her table partner.

Genni shrugged. "I'm not sure." She fingered the petals of the flowers. "But the colors sure are pretty tonight."

Mel studied the array of shades. "You're right." She grinned at Genni. "It would clash horribly with that pink dining room of yours."

Genni dropped her head back and groaned. "Oh man...don't remind me." She brought her head back, a wicked grin on her lips. "I

3

almost left it that way, just to show Cooper who's boss, but I just couldn't bring myself to stick with the plan. Now it's a very tame taupe."

Mel laughed as she toyed with a leaf. Her heart stung as she thought of the wonderful couple Genni and Cooper made. Their story had started out difficult, but now they were happy as clams, almost sickeningly so. Jealousy thrummed inside Mel's chest, and it took a little more force then normal for her to push it aside. "I'm sure Cooper is grateful for your change of heart."

"It was true to the era," Genni grumbled, her bottom lip pushed out in a pout. The argument over room colors had occurred while Genni was renovating the old seaside mansion she'd inherited from her grandmother.

Mel patted her friend's shoulder. "I'm sure it was. But sometimes it's okay to go against tradition."

"Are we ready, ladies?"

Both women looked to the front, seeing Rose standing with a welcoming smile on her face.

"Let's do this!" Charli, another good friend, shouted.

The room rumbled with laughter and chatter before Rose got it back under control.

"Thank you, everyone, for coming tonight," she began. Rose's stunning red hair was pulled back into a high ponytail and her bright blue eyes seemed to glow in the fluorescent lighting. "I'm always so thrilled to have you here." Her smile grew. "Tonight, with fall on the horizon, I thought we would focus on an arrangement about saying thank you. Each flower...sweet peas, hydrangeas..." Rose fingered each bloom as she spoke. "White, pink and yellow roses...they all say thank you in unique ways. So, hopefully when you look at this arrangement, you'll remember all the wonderful things in your life. Or!" She put a finger in the air. "You can give it as a thank you to someone else." As usual, Rose's smile was radiant, causing others to reciprocate her joy no matter what mood they were in. "In any case, let's get going."

Mel paid close attention as Rose directed them on how to mix the colors and arrange the heights just so. When she was done, Mel stepped backed and eyed her vase carefully. "Not bad," she muttered.

"It's beautiful," Genni offered with a sincere smile.

Mel smiled back, an automatic reaction, but also an excited one. Before meeting Cooper, Genni had always been nice, but just a little aloof. Now, however, the pretty brunette had warmed considerably and Mel enjoyed her even more. "Thanks. So is yours."

Genni laughed. "Maybe that's because they're almost exactly the same."

Mel pursed her lips. "Nah. I mean, I have two pink roses, you only have one. They're absolutely, completely different."

Genni shook her head, her smile still wide. "Of course. How ridiculous of me to think otherwise."

Mel grabbed her vase and sniffed with fake arrogance. "I think I'll take my completely unique arrangement home, thank you very much."

"It's about that time, isn't it?" Genni responded, grabbing her own vase.

"You ladies heading out?" Rose asked, walking in their direction.

"Yep." Mel paused and looked around. "You want me to stick around and help clean up?" Most of the women had already filtered through the door, but a few were in clusters, chatting and gossiping the way small towns were known for.

Rose waved her off. "Lilly and I will take care of it. She loves counting all the stem pieces as she dumps them in the garbage."

Mel's smile softened. She adored Rose's daughter, Lilly. Lilly was a stunning beauty at only five years old, her only flaw being that she was deaf. But Mel and all the other women in their friend group didn't find that to be a flaw at all. Lilly's ability to sign and communicate was beautiful to watch and her expressive face could have even the hardest person captivated for hours. "Well, I definitely don't want to take away from Lilly's fun, so I'll leave them."

Rose chuckled softly. "She'll thank you in the morning."

Giving her goodbyes, Mel headed out the door, shivering slightly at the drop in temperature. Fall was definitely on its way. Hunching in on herself, she got in her car and put the vase between her legs in order to keep it steady, then headed for home. It took less than ten minutes for her to pull into her parking spot at the small row of condos.

But before getting out, Mel stared at the attached homes. Most of them had lights on and silhouettes of people or families moving about within. All except hers. The darkness of her house felt foreboding, unwelcoming and cold. *But where else are you going to go?*

The implied truth in that question made Mel reluctantly step out of the vehicle and trudge up her front steps. Once inside, she flipped on the lights and took the vase to her tiny kitchen. She set it in the usual corner and couldn't help but smile at the burst of color it provided for the white space. "Grateful," Mel murmured. "I'm supposed to be grateful."

She grabbed a Twinkie from the cupboard and headed back to her couch. Despite the enjoyable evening with friends, Mel wasn't feeling very thankful. More than ever, she was feeling lonely and left behind. Everyone had somewhere they were going in their life, whether in love or business, and Mel felt...stuck. "Knock it off," she scolded herself, wiping a stray tear from her cheek. "You have a wonderful business, good friends, live close to the ocean, a semi-nice brother close by, and now a vase full of flowers. What more could you want?"

To share it with someone.

She groaned and shoved the sweet treat in her mouth, hoping it would quell the longing inside of her.

To share it with Jensen.

"Well, you can't have him," she sneered, glad that no one could hear her talking to herself. "You're just a little girl to him, and that's all you'll ever be." She licked her fingers in dismissal. "You might as well aim to land on the moon."

Grabbing her Kindle, Mel forced her mind onto other things. Her life might not be perfect, but right now she could focus on someone else's who might be. *After all, landing on the moon is probably easier than capturing Jensen's attention anyway.*

"MR. TANNER?"

Jensen turned around from the white board he'd been writing on. "Yes, Hunter?"

The sophomore boy lounged back in his seat. "I'm confused. You said free verse poetry is basically just writing whatever you want. How is that any different than writing a story? If you're making stuff up, you just write whatever you want, right? What makes it poetry if it doesn't rhyme?"

Jensen snapped the marker lid back into place and turned around to fully face the class. "Does anyone know the answer to Hunter's question?" He looked around the room. "Andrea?"

The young lady tucked her hair behind her ear and shrugged. "I don't know. Poetry is...shorter. I guess. I mean, a free-verse poem wouldn't have all the descriptions of a story, right?"

Jensen nodded, grateful at least one person was on the right track. "Correct, but there's a little more to it."

"It's about the imagery."

Jensen's heart dropped as he turned to look at Micah Derringer. The young man was slouched so far down in his seat, he was almost a puddle on the floor. Dark, long hair covered most of his face and the hoodie of his jacket covered the rest. "Very good, Micah." Jensen tapped his desk. "Hood off, please."

Micah groaned, but complied, pulling his hair farther down his forehead as if the feathery strands could hide him from the eyes of the classroom.

"Thank you. Now...would you care to explain any more?" Jensen waited, hoping the boy would continue. He leaned back against his desk, folding his arms across his chest. Jensen tried hard to hide the fact that he was studying the boy's face, looking for clues. Micah was a good student when he decided to be, and actually had a pretty good gift with the English language. However, some of the poems coming across Jensen's desk had him worried. Talk of monsters, demons and other dark comparisons had him on edge.

He knew some teenage boys just went through stages where they were obsessed with dark things, but this felt like more than that. Micah was being raised by a single dad, who didn't have a good reputation. If Ken, the local police captain and Jensen's friend, was to be believed, Mitchell Derringer often had to be kicked out of the bars when they closed in the early hours of the morning. He was also known for picking fights, and it was that threat of violence that had Jensen keeping an eye on his student.

Micah shrugged at the question. "I don't know."

Jensen wasn't falling for it. "I think you do, Micah. You display it in your work often enough." He smiled encouragingly. "Should we share some of your writing with the class as an example?"

Micah shook his head rigorously. "No!" He sat up a little, then caught himself and slouched again. "I mean, nah. It's just about creating a picture in the reader's head. Poetry tries to use as few words as possible, each word becoming a symbol, whether the lines rhyme or not. But stories create a moving picture, like a movie in your head. The words work together, but aren't necessarily symbolic."

"Excellent." Jensen turned to the student who had originally asked the question. "Did that make sense, Hunter?"

Hunter shrugged. "I guess."

Jensen held in the desire to sigh. Just as he went to turn back to the white board, the bell rang and the kids started scrambling to get their things together. "Don't forget your poetry portfolios are due tomorrow! If you've forgotten what all should be included, please check the school portal!" Jensen waited a beat, then called out, "Micah?"

The teenager shifted his backpack and looked up from under his hair.

"Can I see you a minute?"

Micah looked around, appearing ill at ease before shuffling up front. "Did I do something wrong?"

Jensen shook his head. "Nope." He tilted his head, trying to see through the hair. "Actually, I just wanted to tell you how impressed I've been with your work. You really have a way with words."

The young man kept his gaze on the floor, but nodded. "Thanks." Long, slim fingers tightened on his backpack straps, one of which was attached with duct tape, and Jensen felt his worry ratchet up a notch.

"Have you ever thought of doing anything more with your work?" Jensen tried to prolong the conversation, his eyes searching for any signs of anything suspicious. It was so hard to tell, since it wasn't uncommon for a boy to be reserved or shrunken into himself. Right now, Jensen was running on a gut feeling, but that wasn't enough to give his principal.

Micah shook his head again. "It's just a bunch of words, Mr. Tanner. They don't mean anything." Without saying anything else, the young man bolted, making Jensen jump at the swiftness of the departure.

His head following the fleeing boy, Jensen's felt his eyes widen when Micah grabbed the doorframe and a distinctly blue color emerged from under his sweatshirt. Before Jensen could do much more than view the bruise, however, Micah was gone.

"Shoot," Jensen muttered, walking back around his desk. He sat down and tapped his foot impatiently. "But what can I do about it?" Again, a bruise wasn't real evidence. Micah could have done any number of things to receive that kind of wound. It's not like teenagers were known for staying out of trouble. Jensen sighed and rubbed his temples. He wanted so badly to help if one of his students was in trouble, but right now his hands were tied. There simply wasn't any evidence...yet.

He glanced at his watch. There was still plenty of time in the day before evening fell, so Jensen settled in to grade some papers, but his mind kept wandering. It was torn between a melody he'd been picking out last night and the problem with Micah. "I can't do anything about Micah right now," Jensen scolded himself. For now, it was better to just push that to the back of his mind. Unfortunately, only time would tell if Jensen needed to intervene. The song, however...

Looking at his watch once again, Jensen stuffed all his stuff together in his backpack and decided to head out early. If he hurried, he could get a track laid before dinner tonight. Something about this melody just kept speaking to him, and in his heart, Jensen knew it was good.

It might even be good enough to send to an agent.

The thought percolated in his brain not for the first time. When he was lonely or feeling more depressed than usual, the idea of trying his hand at a professional music career would rear its head. So far Jensen had never indulged the thought too much. Musician's lives were too unpredictable and flighty, or at least that's what he'd been taught. *Yeah...nothing like the wonderful monotony you have right now.*

He picked up his pace, struggling to ignore the fact that the idea of playing under the stage lights was intoxicatingly enticing. Jensen didn't share his music often. It wasn't like there was much opportunity in his small town, and he wasn't one to play just to show off. So his talents had been reserved for bonfires and other small social gatherings with his closest friends. Even those, however, had only been him strumming whatever was popular at the time. Nobody knew that he actually wrote his own stuff. Well...no one but his furniture anyway.

Jensen burst inside his home, his eagerness stronger than usual as he grabbed his beloved instrument and headed to the small spare bedroom he used as a recording studio. It wasn't fancy, but it got the job done.

Sitting in his chair, he let his fingers begin to move, that persistent melody line vibrating through the air as he built upon the tune. After a few minutes he grinned, pressed the record button and let himself go, every other worry forgotten in the excitement of knowing he was creating something worthwhile.

CHAPTER 2

"**M**r. Muscles! Your green, almond-milk, strawberry smoothie with a shot of wheatgrass is ready!" Melody sang out with a wide smile on her face. She waited while an elderly gentleman, Mr. Roy Smithers, shuffled to the front.

He grinned at her. "They get better every time," he rasped, taking his drink.

Mel laughed. "Glad you enjoy it!" She wagged her finger at him. "But I've seen those pics of when you were in the navy." Mel fanned her face and pretended to swoon. "I don't know how the ladies kept their hands off of you."

Mr. Smithers chuckled. "You do this old heart good, girl. Keep at it."

Mel winked. "See ya next Thursday," she said. If Mr. Smithers was anything, he was predictable. They went through this routine every week, like clockwork, and Mel loved it. She also loved her job. Starting "Smooth Moves" had been a leap of faith for her, but as a people person, it was perfect for Mel.

She'd come out of college with a degree in hospitality and a homesickness that brought her right back to her beloved Seaside Bay on the Oregon Coast. Her brother, Bennett, was here, and though her hippie mother had moved south to California, Seaside Bay had a wonderful small-town dynamic that Mel just hadn't been able to find anywhere else.

Plus, Jensen is here.

"Whoops," she whispered, grabbing the next ready Styrofoam cup. "Ms. Legs for Miles, I've got a Razmatazz with a dose of antioxidants with your name on it!"

Caroline, or Caro, rolled her eyes. "You're hilarious," she drawled in her Southern accent. Her tiny five-foot frame wasn't quite how Mel described her.

Mel grinned and handed over the drink. "Hey. We've got to have dreams. My job is to help encourage you toward yours!"

Caro gave her a look. "What if I don't want to be taller?" Her small hand went to her perfectly curvy hip.

A flash of jealousy hit Mel in the gut, but she quickly pushed it aside. She'd gotten good at that over the years, plus she loved Caro way too much to let jealousy get between them. "Then I'll work on talking about all your wonderful *perfect* characteristics rather than teasing you about your height."

Caro smiled and shook her head, her blonde hair swaying just right. "God couldn't give me *all* the good characteristics. He had to leave a few for other people, ya know."

Mel laughed as intended. "Thanks for stopping by, Caro."

Caro waved over her shoulder. "See ya later!"

"Absolutely!" Still smiling, she grabbed the next cup and stuttered.

Jensen.

Speak of the handsome devil...

"Teacher extraordinaire, I've got a blueberry, mint, and kiwi special just for you!" Her smile was too wide, as it always was when he was around, but Mel kept her feelings in check for the most part...another thing she'd gotten good at over the years.

Jensen Tanner walked up, that slight swagger in his step that had been a part of him for as long as Mel could remember. He chuckled, reaching out for the cup. "What's up, Mellie?"

Her smile drooped a little. She hated that nickname. It was much too "little sister" for the woman she was now. Unfortunately, as her brother's good buddy, Jensen would probably always see her as that scrawny little kid. "Not much. Just doing my best to help people have a good morning." She tilted her head, fluttering her eyelashes playfully. "You ready for another day of teaching?"

Jensen shrugged and stuffed a straw into the top of the drink, completely ignoring her flirtations. "Just another day," he said with his usual smile. He tipped the cup at her. "See ya later!"

Mel waved at him, deflating as his strong shoulders disappeared through the doorway.

"You got it bad, girl," Emily, one of the shift managers, whispered.

Mel snapped to attention. "I don't know what you're talking about," she said through a stiff smile, not looking at Emily. "Hot Stuff Junior? Here's your Smoothie Kabloozie!" Mel shared chin tilts with the sixteen-year-old boy who was the son of a local football hero. The young man was on his way to following in his dad's footsteps and the whole town was thrilled for him. "I added a shot of protein," Mel said in a loud whisper. "Wanted to help out that throwing arm."

Parker blushed. "Thanks, Mel."

She waved as he left. "He's a nice kid," she said to no one in particular.

"Yep. But not as nice as Mr. Teachy."

Mel sighed and turned to give her employee a look. "Mr. Teachy?"

Emily grinned. "Would you rather call him Hot Teacher? The love of your life? Your heart's desire?"

"Okay, okay, I get it." Mel hurriedly tried to shut her employee up. "But I'll say it again. You don't know what you're talking about."

Emily rolled her eyes. "I'm not blind, Mel."

Mel could feel heat rushing up her neck and she set her hands down on the cold stainless steel counter, hoping the temperature would help quell her body temperature. "I never said you were."

Emily blew out a breath and went back to the blenders. "If you decide you want to talk about it, let me know."

Mel didn't bother responding. There was nothing to talk about. Mel had been watching Jensen for too many years to think she had any chance with him. She'd been in love with her brother's friend since she was a teenager. She'd watched him graduate, go on to college, find another woman, get married, become a widower, then come home to teach. Nowhere in that life was there any indication that he viewed her as anything but Bennett's kid sister. The five years between them might as well have been a million.

Through the years, Mel had lost all hope that she could ever change his mind. She'd tried once, back in high school. The night had ended in disaster and embarrassment. Now as an adult, she knew she'd never get a second chance.

So, she'd resigned herself to being a friend, mooning from afar, and living her life trying to help others be happy instead of worrying about herself. Her smoothie shop helped her do just that, and it made Mel feel good...for the most part.

The one hole in her life would never be filled though, so there was no point in complaining to her friends, or gossiping with employees. Choices had been made, lines had been drawn and Mel's life was laid out for her.

Plus, she was content. Or at least, that's what she told herself when the nights were lonely or she'd had a difficult day. She had friends, family, and a successful business. Who needed anything more?

Not me.

"Eyes So Green They Look Like Jade!" Mel shouted. "Your kale and blueberries are waiting for you!" She laughed lightly with her customer as they picked up their drink.

Yep. I've got everything I need.

JENSEN SIPPED THE SWEET yet tart confection as he walked down the street to the high school. Stopping by Mellie's had become an almost daily routine for him. She was his best friend's little sister, so he'd first come to Smooth Moves in order to support her, but now he came because he honestly enjoyed the breakfast. He was convinced that drinking Mellie's smoothies was a better hit than coffee, and had been indulging in them ever since.

His new melody began floating through his mind as he walked and soon Jensen found himself humming the tune. His fingers twitched against his Styrofoam cup as if they could pluck the notes out of thin air. The song was off to a great start, but there was something about it that wasn't quite right... He just wasn't sure what it was.

Jensen scoffed and shook his head. *Music is just a pipe dream.* Ever since he was a young man, Jensen had been fascinated with the guitar and had taught himself to play in his teens. He had even entertained the idea of creating a band, but like many young dreams, the plan had never come to fruition.

Instead, Jensen had headed to college, gotten married and eventually become a teacher. All things that were safe and predictable. Everything his parents had taught him were the best parts of life. As the only child of two school teachers, his path had been laid out long before Jensen had ever taken his first step, and he'd gone along with it, not willing to rock the boat.

He sighed. "It's not like you mind any of it," he grumbled under his breath. "There's nothing wrong with teaching."

And there wasn't. For the most part, Jensen enjoyed the job. Only one part of Jensen's life hadn't gone according to plan, and that was the unexpected death of his wife. Jensen missed her, but if he was being truthful with himself, he wasn't as heartbroken as he should have been.

The thought brought on a burden of guilt he'd dealt with for a long time. The weight of that emotion felt second nature at this point, which just added to the monotony that was his life.

"Hey, Mr. Tanner!"

Jensen set aside his maudlin thoughts to wave at a student. "What's up, Ian?"

The young man grinned and wrapped his arm tighter around the girl at his side. "Not much. We were just discussing those poem thingies you were telling us about in class." His grin was pure mischief. "You know, the ones by that beard guy."

Jensen nearly choked on his smoothie. "Beard guy?" His eyes widened. "Oh, you mean *bard!* Shakespeare's sonnets?" His eyes darted to the girl and back. "I take it you mean the love sonnets?"

"Yeah...that's it." Ian gave a little thrust of his chin. "I was just sharing some of them with Nina here."

Jensen held back his laughter. "I'm sure she enjoyed that," he stated even as Nina rolled her eyes. "Good luck." Jensen grinned and shook his head as he heard the two teenagers begin to bicker behind him.

Jensen's humor faded, replaced by a ridiculous trickle of jealousy, as he passed more couples on his way to his classroom. *That's a new low. Being jealous of a bunch of teenage kids.*

He unlocked his classroom and headed straight to his desk, dumping his backpack to the side and plopping into his seat with a sigh. Glancing up at the clock, he noted that the bell would ring in less than five minutes, giving him little time to prepare for the morning's classes.

"Should just do a pop quiz and call it good," he muttered, setting his drink down. His phone buzzed and Jensen glanced at the text.

Dinner tonight? Mel's cooking.

Jensen grinned. Bennett was always inviting him over. "Yeah...but does Mellie know she's cooking?" It seemed the Frasier family was constantly worried about whether or not he was eating. Even when Mrs. Frasier still lived in Seaside Bay, he'd spent a lot of dinners at their house.

Sounds good. Thanks.

He sent the reply, not being one to turn down a good home-cooked meal, and then got back to work. Jensen could hear the kids starting to roam the hallways and knew he'd be inundated soon.

Hours later, when school was over, he sat back down, exhausted from being on his feet all day. Jensen leaned back, letting his head rest against the back of his chair. It was usually at this time of day that he felt way older than his almost thirty years.

His back ached, his feet hurt and his temples pulsed with a headache. To top it all off, the idea of going home to his empty cabin was about as appealing as eating raw geoduck. His phone buzzed, catching his attention again.

False alarm. Had something come up. How about tomorrow?

Jensen didn't take long to answer.

No prob. See ya then.

Jensen set his phone back down and let his shoulders slump. Truth was, it didn't matter what night Bennett invited him over, he'd be free. Other than teaching and the occasional night with his buddies, Jensen had nothing going in his life.

No excitement, no goals, no anticipation... Eevery day was exactly the same as the day before. *If only Melissa was still here...*

Jensen growled and shook his head, making his headache pulse harder against his skull. "That won't help," he reminded himself. During their one year of marriage, life had changed little. Melissa had been a nice, quiet girl he'd found in the library one day during a study session.

She was exactly the type of person his parents had wanted for their studious son. Focused on her academics, intelligent, easy to get along with and planning to become a teacher.

She'd been pretty in a very natural way. Her medium brown hair was long and straight and there was nothing unwelcoming about her features, but like everything else in Jensen's life, he hadn't found himself *excited* about her. She was just another step in the life that had been presented to him.

Maybe things would have been better if she was still alive, but Jensen didn't think so. Since there had been no exciting spark as newlyweds, how in the world would one have happened after they became working professionals? Jensen had been hurt and sad when she'd died, but not as devastated as he would have expected. Mostly he had felt guilty for how little time he'd spent with her during their short marriage.

He would never stop being sorry that her young life was cut short, but he struggled to continue to be sorry he wasn't married. None of it was Melissa's fault, he knew. She'd done nothing wrong. But there was a deep, mostly buried, part of Jensen that wanted...more. He wanted electric sparks, he wanted adventure, he wanted a woman in his life who inspired music and poetry and made him stupid-smile whenever he thought about her. He wanted something, *anything,* that was out of the ordinary, but he hadn't been raised to believe in fairy tales. He loved his friends, family and town, but they definitely didn't inspire the kind of excitement that he secretly craved.

Another heavy sigh escaped him as he gathered his papers for the evening and left the building. The day was still bright as they were in the early stages of fall, so the sun still set late into the evening.

The walk home was more painful then it should have been. It seemed like everywhere Jensen looked, there were couples. Couples walking their dog, couples holding hands, couples swinging a child between their arms. Every smiling face reminding him of the cold, dark house he was headed toward.

Jensen scowled and picked up his pace. *I must be the most boring thirty-year-old in existence. Go to work, go home, go to work, go home...nothing ever changes.*

He paused slightly upon reaching his little house, but a cool breeze rushed over his neck, forcing him to forgo the lonely trepidation he felt and step inside. He immediately dropped his backpack on the coffee table and proceeded to turn on all the lights. The sunlight through the windows was still enough to let him see in the home, but having the overhead bulbs glowing always seemed to help a little with the emptiness of the place.

A beautiful acoustic guitar stood in the corner, resting peacefully in its stand, and Jensen found himself walking toward it. "You've been waiting for me to come home, haven't ya?" he cooed, refusing to feel guilty for speaking to an inanimate object.

Lovingly, Jensen picked up the instrument and nestled it against his body, loving the perfect fit of the guitar's curves. He thumbed the strings, and closed his eyes at the soothing chords.

This...this was the one thing that never felt boring or useless or lonely. He never seemed to tire of creating music and loved the sounds filling every corner of the cottage, dispelling the starkness that seemed to permeate his life.

Deciding he wasn't hungry enough for dinner, Jensen walked over to the leather sofa and sat down, losing himself in the melody he'd been working. With just a little bit of work, he might turn it into something worth listening to. *Then at least there'd be one part of my life that was making progress.*

CHAPTER 3

M el paused and frowned at her brother's dining room table. "Why are there three plates?" she shouted over her shoulder.

"Because Jensen's coming," Bennett called back. He came out of the hallway bathroom, rubbing his head with a towel. "Didn't I tell you I invited him?"

Mel's body immediately flushed and she had to bite her tongue to keep from snapping at her brother. "No." *It's not his fault,* she reminded herself.

Bennett shrugged. "You cook for us all the time. What's the big deal?"

The big deal is that I have to prepare myself to see him because I'm a lovestruck idiot. She sighed, forcing her tense muscles to let go. "Nothing. It's not a big deal." She set down the fruit salad and turned to point a finger at him. "But that means that extra chicken is for him, not you."

Bennett groaned and rubbed his stomach. "I'm going to be starving by bedtime."

Mel shrugged. "Your fault. If you want me to cook enough for three people, which with you at the table really means like five people, you have to tell me ahead of time."

Bennett grumbled as he went to put the towel back in the bathroom.

Mel couldn't help but grin. Her brother's appetite was legendary among their friends. Even now that he was aging out of his twenties, he could eat a teenage boy under the table. "But where the heck does he put it all is the question," Mel murmured as she put the barbecued chicken on a platter and brought it to the table with the rest of the food.

The front door opened and Mel's head snapped toward the sound.

"Benny?" Jensen called.

"Wassup, man?" Bennett scrambled out of the bathroom and came to give his friend a shoulder slap. "Those kids burn down the school yet?"

Jensen rolled his eyes. "Not yet, but I don't know what they're doing in chemistry next week."

Mel grinned. She loved Jensen's dry sense of humor. "Dinner's ready, guys."

Bennet slapped his stomach. "Good thing, because I'm starving!"

Mel rolled her eyes good-naturedly. "That's your permanent status, bozo." Jensen chuckled and Mel felt her cheeks heat. She quickly ducked away so he wouldn't notice.

"She's got you there," Jensen said as he sat down.

"Yeah..." Bennett scratched the back of his head. "Now that she's all grown up, my little sister thinks she can talk to me like a mother hen or something." He winked at Mel, who stuck her tongue out at him.

Mel sat down, tucked a stray piece of hair behind her ear and put her napkin in her lap. "We all ready?" She turned to look at Jensen and her next words died on her lips. Jensen's eyebrows were scrunched together and he was glaring at her in an odd way. Mel leaned back, unsure of what was going on. "Uh, do I have something on my face?" She wiped at her cheeks, worried some flour or something was making her look weird.

"Jens!" Bennett barked. "What are you doing?"

Jensen blinked rapidly and jerked backward as if shocked at his own behavior. "Whoa..." He rubbed the back of his neck. "Sorry, I, uh...I got lost in a heavy thought there for a second." His eyes were on the table, like he was afraid to meet Mel's gaze.

She frowned. *What did I do? Was sticking my tongue out at Bennett really that big of a deal?*

"No worries, man," Bennett assured their guest. "We all get caught in our brains once in a while." Bennett rubbed his hands together. "But the important thing now is that we eat before it gets cold."

Jensen's answering laugh sounded forced. "Right."

After a short grace, the three of them dug in, silverware and chewing the only sounds for a few minutes. Finally, Bennett broke the silence.

"How was the smoothie business today, sis?" he asked just before stuffing a large mouth of potatoes in his mouth.

Mel shrugged. "Same as usual. Busy but good." She smiled. "Deliver any funny mail?"

Bennett grinned. "Nope. But I keep waiting for some weird package to come through. You always hear the stories of people mailing the craziest stuff and I haven't ever seen one!" He shook his head. "One of these days I'll be laughed out of town."

Mel gave him a look. "You're the only mailman here. Who's going to do the laughing?"

"Who cares? What's a mailman without any weird stories?"

Jensen huffed a laugh, sounding more at ease then he had a few minutes before. "I can't say I have *ever* thought of asking the mailman for funny stories."

Bennett shook his head and sighed. "You muggles. You know nothing about the wizardry I do."

"Oh my word..." Mel said with a groan. "Now you sound like Mom."

Bennett's eyes widened. "You do realize that was like, the worst insult ever...right?"

Mel shrugged, picking up another bite of chicken. "I don't know...like mother, like son, I always say."

Bennett slapped a hand to his chest and pretended to gasp for breath. "I knew it. Next thing I know, I'll be living on the beach in my skivvies, dumpster diving for breakfast."

"Better believe it." Mel snorted. "Please note that I'm not feeding you if you're running around in your underwear."

Bennett let out a loud sigh. "My family might turn their back on me, but you wouldn't leave me to go crazy on my own, would you?" He looked expectantly at Jensen.

Jensen shook his head, but took time to finish chewing and swallowing before answering. "No way. I know several teenagers that would probably love to live that lifestyle with you. I'll send them to keep you company."

Mel snickered when Bennett scowled. "Just what I need. A bunch of weirdos howling at the moon."

"Who knows..." Mel pressed. "One of them might be cute."

Bennett's face grew grim. "That's just wrong, even for a joke. They're little kids." He turned to Jensen. "Jens, my man. Help me out here. Mel is so tired of cooking for me, she's pushing teenagers at me. That kind of age gap isn't right."

Jensen's face was bright red and Mel frowned. "Jensen. Are you all right?" She started to reach toward him, but he scooted away from the table.

"I need water," he rasped, rushing to the sink.

"Back me up here!" Bennett called, not seeming to notice anything wrong with his friend's behavior.

"You're right," Jensen said more calmly as he walked back. "That kind of age gap is wrong."

"That's what I thought." Bennett slammed his hand down on the small table, making the dishes shake.

"Bennett!" Mel scolded. She tried to maintain her composure, but the age gap conversation had only furthered the permanent pain in her chest. *First, he treats me like I've got some kind of disease, and now he makes a point of talking about age gaps. Five years isn't that bad...is it?* She dropped her eyes to her plate, but her appetite was gone. The chicken and potatoes were completely unappealing. That secret stash of twinkies at home, however, was calling her name with a bullhorn. She'd secretly consumed far too many of them in her efforts to forget her crush on Jensen.

Bennett grumbled under his breath and the atmosphere at the table stayed slightly tense.

Feeling lower than dirt, Mel couldn't bring herself to try and fix it. She hated situations like this, but it was getting harder and harder to force a smile on her face when all she wanted to do was cry.

Later. Be brave now and you can crumble later. If someone guessed your secret, it would only make life worse, not better. She pushed her lips to either side, praying it resembled a smile. "Who's ready for dessert?"

JENSEN PUT HIS PLATE in the sink and almost shook his head again. Something was definitely wrong with him tonight. *Maybe I spent too much time in the studio...*

He'd been so excited to come and share his new song with Bennett, but something strange had happened at dinner. When Ben made that quip about Mellie being grown up, Jensen had felt something shift.

She IS grown up. How did I never notice that before?

With just a quick glance, he'd suddenly realized that her overly skinny teenage body had filled out and curved into that of a grown woman. Her hair was thick and long and framed her beautiful face perfectly. Skin that had been riddled with red pimples was now smooth and creamy, while her lips, which had once been too large for her face, now appeared luscious and inviting.

He gripped the edge of the sink. Just thinking about it was heating him up all over. *SHE'S BENNETT'S LITTLE SISTER!* his internal voice screamed. *You don't get to think she's attractive.*

"Move it, buster," Mellie said with a laugh. "Those dishes aren't going to wash themselves."

Jensen scuttled back with his hands up, then froze when Mel gave him a weird look. "Sorry. I, uh, wouldn't want to get stuck between you and cleaning."

Her frown turned into a small smile, but there was something in her gaze that said his behavior had hurt her deeply. A sharp pang hit his sternum and Jensen began to panic. *What is going on? Heartburn? Maybe? Yeah...that's got to be it. I just ate something that didn't agree with me.* He cleared his throat and pounded on his chest, nearly wincing when he hit the sore spot. "I guess I better, uh—"

"Hey, dude! You brought your guitar?" Bennett poked his head in from the family room with a wide grin. "What have you been working on?"

Jensen glanced at Mel, who had her head down as she worked in the sink, then back to Benny. "Uh, yeah, I brought it." He shrugged. "I thought maybe I could play for my supper." His smile was anything but genuine as he plastered it onto his face, but he had to do something to hide the turmoil bubbling inside of him.

Things were just too weird at the moment. Mel had never been anything but a kid sister and now, without warning, she was a beautiful woman. When had it happened and why was Jensen even noticing?

"Then come on!" Benny held out the instrument, beckoning Jensen into the other room. "You coming, Mel?"

Jensen automatically turned to see her response, but she didn't turn around.

"I need to get these in the dishwasher," she said with a shake of her head. "You two go ahead."

"Ah...come on," Benny whined. "Just leave 'em. I'll get those later."

Mel snorted, still keeping her attention on the sink. "Yeah, later as in a week or more. Your whole house will stink to high heaven if I don't take care of it."

Jensen slowly edged toward the room exit before he could do something stupid like offer to help her. That's all he needed at the moment was to be standing shoulder to shoulder with her, their hands in a sink of soapy water together.

"Come on," Benny urged in a whisper. "Escape while you still can."

A flash of irritation went through Jensen, but he held it back. Normally Benny's antics amused him, which is why he spent so much time at his house. But something about Benny being willing to leave all the work to his sister bothered Jensen tonight. *Let it go. This is a sibling thing. It has nothing to do with you.*

"I'm coming," he whispered back, grabbing his guitar from Benny's hands as he passed through the doorway. Jensen shoved all thoughts of attraction, growing up and too pretty little sisters to the back of his head. He'd definitely feel better after a long night's sleep. The weirdness tonight was probably just a reaction to the stress at work and worrying about his upcoming birthday... At least that topic hadn't come up yet. He wasn't ready to discuss changing decades yet.

Jensen sat on a chair and strummed the strings. The sound instantly soothed him and he let his fingers dance for a few moments. Without consciously thinking about it, the melody he'd recorded began to fill the room. He closed his eyes and sank into the sound.

"Wow..." Bennett interrupted. "I haven't heard that one before."

Jensen immediately stopped playing. He hadn't meant to play that song. He kept his own compositions for himself, only playing popular things for friends. But that song had been invading his mind for so long, it had just naturally come out. "Uh...I wrote it." His head jerked at a gasp from the doorway.

Mel had her hands over her mouth. "You wrote that?" she asked.

Jensen felt his neck heat up, working its way up over his jaw. "Yeah." Her hands went to her hips, which led to long, shapely legs... *Knock it off!*

"How did we not know that you compose?" she snapped, sounding truly upset.

Jensen forced his eyes away and repositioned the instrument on his thigh. "I don't know, I've never really shared anything before."

"You should have been a guitar player, man," Bennett said lazily from his place on the couch. "You're better than most of the ones I hear. Not to mention women dig that kind of talent."

Jensen stiffened. Just like with his own compositions, he'd never mentioned a desire to perform either. *Does he really think I could make it?* Maybe it wouldn't be such a bad thing to look into playing a little more in public.

"He's right," Mellie offered. Her voice had grown soft. "You should bring your guitar to your birthday party on Friday. You can play your song for everyone."

Was Jensen imagining it, or were her eyes slightly glassy? "You really think anyone would want to hear it?" he asked, feeling oddly vulnerable.

She nodded, her smile small. "Yep. Have you ever thought of sending out some of your stuff?"

Jensen dropped her gaze and shrugged. "I don't know. Sometimes."

"Well, play it for the group and then you can get everyone else's opinion," Benny drawled sleepily. "Maybe a few more crazed fans would be enough to make you think about it some more."

Jensen looked back up, but Mellie had gone back to the kitchen. He chose not to examine why her absence made the room feel colder. Instead, he put his thoughts back on his instrument and hummed as he played a few more familiar songs. The party next week was for his birthday, which he wasn't exactly looking forward to. Thirty years old and he'd done nothing important with his life. Maybe testing out his music would not only make the gathering more palatable, but be a step toward doing something that was out of the ordinary. Something that was more than the mundane life he lived right now. The idea settled in his mind and he found himself smiling slightly. He might be getting older, but maybe, just maybe, it wasn't too late to reach for something new.

CHAPTER 4

For two long, miserable days, Mel had pasted a smile on her face and pretended that nothing was wrong. Well...she'd been doing that for years, but somehow, these two days felt heavier than the rest of the time combined.

Something about the way Jensen had looked at her the night he'd come over for dinner had upset her equilibrium. She had no idea what had changed, but whatever it was...it wasn't good. He'd gone from his usual easy teasing to suddenly treating her like she was poison. He'd been very careful not to touch her and had made weird faces whenever she spoke. *What in the world did I do to offend him so badly?*

She bit her lip to keep the sting of tears away as she unpacked a cooler from her car. She'd convinced herself over the years that if she couldn't have a romantic relationship with him, she could at least continue to be his friend. And while her dreams had been filled with more, being near him had sufficed for the most part. But now, he didn't even seem to want her friendship.

"Hey, Mel!" Charli called out, rushing to her side. "Need some help with that?"

"Sure." Mel smiled, hoping it didn't look as fake as it felt. "I've got a fruit platter and some salad in here and it's heavier than you would think. Plus, I made Jensen's favorite, strawberry cheesecake."

Charli grinned. "Considering most of those are supposed to make a person *less* heavy, yeah...it does sound weird. Must be the cheesecake. Those things weigh a ton."

Mel snorted and they walked together toward the spot for the bonfire. "Like you have to worry about weight. You burn more calories in a single workout then the rest of us do in a week!"

Charli laughed, her tone lower and a little huskier than most women's. "Yeah, well, with all that calorie loss comes a crazy big appetite. I'm lucky I fit into my pants some days. I probably should lay off the cookies."

"Hmm...don't tell me my Twinkie stash is the reason mine were a little tight today..."

The girls were still laughing when they reached the group.

"What goody-two-shoes food did you bring today?" Bennett called out, jogging to his sister's side. "Ow!" He ducked and grabbed his head when Charli smacked the back of it.

"Geez, Benny. Your sister feeds you all the time. The least you could do is show a little gratitude. She's probably the sole reason you haven't had a heart attack yet."

Bennett grinned unrepentantly. "If living means I have to give up bacon and steaks, I don't think it's worth it."

"Hear, hear!" Cooper called out as he and Genni approached hand in hand. Those present greeted the arriving couple.

"See? At least one person knows what I'm talking about!" Bennett crowed.

Mel rolled her eyes.

"When's Jensen coming?" Charli asked as they pulled the food out of the cooler.

Mel stopped to look around, then shrugged. "I don't know. You'd think he'd be on time to his own birthday party."

Charli grinned. "Maybe he doesn't want to admit he's getting old."

"Thirty isn't old!" Ken, the police captain of Seaside Bay, called out with a scowl. "Just because we're more mature than you ladies doesn't mean we're old." Ken himself was the oldest of the group, coming in at thirty-four.

"Keep telling yourself that," Charli shot back. "I'll bet you all hear creaks when you rise from bed in the mornings."

"We can't all be Iron Man athletes," Bennett grumbled.

"Oooh, feeling a little less masculine, Bennett?" Mel teased, laughing when he glared at her.

"Here he is!" Ken called out, pointing into the distance. "The great English professor has graced us with his presence. Just in time for him to turn a decade older!"

"Hardy, har, har," Jensen said with a glare. "Real funny, Cap."

"Hey! That's my name," Felix argued. This was an old argument among the group. Felix was the captain of a fishing boat while Ken was captain of their local police station. Neither man ever wanted to give credit to the other.

"Here we go," Charli said under her breath. "Remind me again why we put up with these idiots?"

Mel's smile relaxed as she listened to the banter between the men. "Mostly because we're related to some of them," she whispered back. The group was a little bit of a ragtag team, but their history meant they couldn't help but be friends. Ken was not only the police captain in their area, but had grown up with Bennett and Mel, graduating a little ahead of them. Felix was Charli's older brother, and they were both locals as well. Genni had gone to school with Mel, but Cooper had only been in town a few months. Rose, who was home with Lilly, and Caro were also newcomers to the area, but had been around for a few years now. Brooklyn, who was missing the evening because she had a date, had arrived in town as a teenager, completing their little clan.

"Yeah, well, that might be all the more reason to ignore them." Mel snickered.

"Would you all shut your traps?" Caro hollered at the fighting men. "Some of us have better things to do than listen to you bicker like old women."

The arguing got even louder at Caro's complaint, and Mel sighed. "I think I'm gonna eat before things get too crazy."

"Count me in."

The women grabbed plates and loaded them high with food before finding their seats.

"What?" Bennett jumped to his feet when he saw them eating. "There's not going to be anything left!" He scurried to the table, getting his own dinner.

"It's you we have to worry about," Ken grumbled, climbing out of his beach chair and getting his own dinner.

Mel ignored the complaining and looked from under her eyelashes at Jensen. He wasn't getting food. Instead, he was playing with his phone, looking slightly lost. "Are you going to play for us tonight?" Mel tried to smile sweetly and nodded toward his guitar case.

He cleared his throat. "Yeah...maybe. If everybody wants to hear it."

"Do it," Bennett urged, plopping into a seat. "That song the other night was really good."

"What song?" Felix asked, licking his fingers.

"Eewww, bro. Use a napkin." Charli shoved one at her brother.

Felix rolled his eyes, but took the offering. "Yes, Mom."

"Maybe I should start calling you that," Bennett teased, looking at Mel. "What is it with you women and mothering?"

"It's a natural instinct," Charli shot back. "Mostly because you men never grow up."

Bennett grinned and pumped his eyebrows. "Life's more fun this way."

"Yeah, well, if we ever stopped taking care of you, you'd find out how fun life is," Charli threatened.

"Sure..." Bennett quipped. "Mel isn't going anywhere. It's not like she's got her own family to take care of." He sighed contentedly and leaned back lazily in his chair. "Nope. I'm afraid my dear sister will be taking care of her brother for a loooong time."

Normally, Mel would have laughed and joked right back with everyone else over Bennett's outrageous remarks. He loved stirring the pot, and she knew he did it all in good fun, but tonight, his words hurt. Maybe she was just more sensitive because something had gone wrong with Jensen, but no matter the reason, the comment stung.

Mel felt like she was losing her grip on her carefully controlled facade and life was falling apart. Shots like that from Bennett were just making it more difficult to maintain a happy demeanor when all she wanted to do was weep for the loss of something she never had.

"Don't listen to him," Caro said, leaning forward in her seat. "Just because he knows his ugly mug won't ever get him a wife, doesn't mean you won't find someone. You're far too wonderful to be stuck with this guy for the rest of your life." She jabbed a thumb in Bennett's direction.

Mel smiled when Bennett acted offended. "Thanks, Caro," she said over Bennett's sputtering.

"Anytime, sweetie," she said with a wink. "We girls have to stick together."

JENSEN LET THE LAUGHER and teasing of the evening roll over him. He'd been out of sorts ever since his dinner with Bennett and Mellie. All his spare time had been spent working on the new song and trying to drown out the fact that he was seeing little Mellie as not so little anymore. It just didn't seem right to view her as an attractive, available female.

He could smell the burgers and watched everyone eat for a few minutes, knowing they all expected him to get his own plate, but he wasn't hungry. His stomach churned, for more than one reason.

Since he'd successfully avoided Mellie this week, most of his nervousness had to do with sharing his song with the group. It felt intimate and personal to finally bring his music out of hiding, and that terrified and electrified him in equal parts.

"Aren't you going to eat?" Ken asked, his mouth full of fruit salad.

Jensen took a deep breath and shook his head. "Nah. I'm not hungry." He reached for his case, just to give himself an excuse to not get a plate, and pulled it out.

"Ooh, play that new song..." Caro snapped her fingers. "What's it called? That new country one."

Felix groaned. "Not country! No one wants to hear about an old pick up truck and his lost dog. Come on, Caro," he pleaded.

"It's not that bad," Caro argued, sitting up in her seat. "The newer stuff is much better—"

Jensen strummed the strings of his instrument before Felix and Caro could get into it any further. He loved his friends, but man...they knew how to argue, and his brain just couldn't take any more confusion at the moment. The group quieted down as he got going and at first, Jensen stuck with the classics. His fingers flew over the strings as he transitioned from one song to another, playing a good twenty minutes before he took a break.

"You forgot one," Mellie said softly from her spot in the shadows.

Jensen looked over, his eyes immediately finding her aqua gaze. Had they always stood out from her creamy skin that way? "What?" he asked, confused over her comment.

Her smile was hesitant and lacked Mellie's usual bubbly sparkle. "You forgot to play that one you wrote. You remember? The one you played the other night?"

"You wrote a song?" Felix asked. "Really? I didn't know you did that."

Jensen shrugged. "I mess around a little. I think most guys do."

"I've never written a song," Bennett said, scratching his chin. "Gotta leave some skills for the less good-looking guys, you understand. Hey!" He curled into a ball and put his hands over his head to protect himself when the rest of the group began throwing grapes and cups at him.

"Shut up," Felix said with a laugh. "Let the pro play."

Pro? Jensen had never been called that before and it added a little flame to his dream of stepping outside Seaside Bay. "You really want to hear it?" he asked, looking around at the crowd.

"Absolutely," Charli encouraged. "Ain't no holding out on this group. It can be your birthday gift to us."

Jensen smiled at her. "All right. It's not really finished yet, and if it's horrible…remember that you asked for it. Not to mention, I think this is backward as far as birthday gifts go."

He paused while the group laughed, then centered himself. Taking a deep breath, he began. There was just something about this song…it felt like an innate part of him and soon he was completely lost in the music. He closed his eyes, scrunching them as he tried harder to listen to every nuance of the sounds, determined to figure out why he couldn't quite finish it. His troubled mind calmed and soon nothing existed except him and the story at his fingertips.

For a man who made his living with the written word, it was amazing to let everything out without using a single bit of the alphabet. It felt primal, wild and yet comfortable. He could share himself without ever saying a word.

The last chord floated through the air, disappearing on the breeze, and Jensen held himself still, waiting until it was completely gone before daring to move. His eyes fluttered open and he finally noticed the shocked faces surrounding him. Feeling self-conscious,

Jensen cleared his throat and rubbed the back of his hot neck. "Was it that bad?" he joked, forcing an awkward laugh.

"What the heck are you doing in this podunk town?" Caro demanded, being the first to regain her voice. She leaned forward. "Jensen, you're amazing! Why did you ever become an English teacher when you have a gift like that?"

Relief flooded Jensen as similar words followed from the rest of the group. He relaxed back in his seat and let their praise wash over him. After such an emotional high from the song and the confusion and worry of the week, their excitement and encouragement felt good.

"This calls for birthday cheesecake!" Charli declared, jumping from her seat. "Good music always requires good treats!"

"What in the world does music have to do with sugar and dairy?" Felix asked with a scowl.

"Everything," Charli argued, unperturbed by her brother's condescension. "They go together like peanut butter and jelly."

"I never did like that combo," Ken said, standing up and stretching. "Why put fruit and peanuts together? Just seems odd."

"Are you kidding?" Benny asked with an open jaw. "Those two are classic."

A warm hand landed on Jensen's forearm and he nearly jumped out of his skin from the slight shock it gave him.

"Oh, sorry," Mellie whispered, pulling her hand back to herself. She bit her lip, once again looking wounded at his behavior.

This is so stupid. I'm a grown man. I've been married. I can handle talking to an attractive woman without freaking out. "Hey, Mellie," he said with a grin he didn't feel, pretending that he hadn't been avoiding her all week.

"Hey," she said, eyeing him a little warily. "I just wanted to tell you again how awesome your song is. Have you written many others?"

Jensen pursed his lips and nodded. "Yeah, a few."

"Awesome!" she said. "I mean, I always knew you were a good player, but that song is like, next level," she gushed. "You really should do some work in front of an audience."

He chuckled, forcing his body to relax. "What were you guys? Chopped liver?"

Mellie laughed. "No, but we're your friends. We don't count."

He picked at a string. "What would you suggest? It's not like Seaside has an abundance of entertainment venues."

She nodded, her eyes widening with excitement as she leaned forward and grabbed the side of his chair. "I know, but what if...well, what if we worked with what we had?"

Jensen frowned. "I don't follow."

"You need a place where people gather and would enjoy listening to your music, right?"

"I guess." Jensen turned his head slightly, feeling suddenly cautious of where she was going with this.

"And I have a shop where people do just that!" She threw her hands in the air. "You should come play a few shows." She frowned. "No...that's not the right word."

"Sets? Gigs?" Jensen supplied.

"Yes! Sets or gigs, whatever works.!" Her head bobbed, causing her long, blonde ponytail to bounce. "Come play some sets at the smoothie shop. I'm sure people would adore listening to you, and it would give you some real-time experience."

Jensen turned away from her sparkle for a moment and considered her offer. It was tempting. Being inside her shop sure beat playing out on the street corners or something. But the main problem was it meant that he'd be spending way more time with Mellie. And right now, too much confusion clouded his thoughts around her for that to be a safe thing.

"Do it man!" Ken encouraged. "It's a perfect starting point." He grinned. "Maybe in another year or so, we'll see your name up in Portland and say we knew you when."

Jensen laughed. "That'll be the day," he said. "I don't think the professional world works quite that way."

"You never know." Ken pointed a finger at him. "All it takes is being heard by the right person and a career can skyrocket."

Jensen nodded, still not quite convinced, but extremely tempted. *You've followed the rules your whole life,* he argued with himself. *Why not do something just a little different, just this once. It's not like it's going to hurt anybody.* He slapped the top of the guitar. "Okay. I'll do it!"

"Awesome!" Mellie jumped to her feet and clapped her hands. "This is going to be epic!"

Jensen nodded his agreement, but that small voice in the back of his head still argued that he would come to regret it. That the shift between him and Mellie needed to be dealt with before he spent so much time in her presence. *I'm an adult. I just turned thirty, for heaven's sakes. Not only can I control myself, but if I don't start taking chances now, I'll run out of time. Life is passing me by and I don't want to have regrets.*

CHAPTER 5

M el tapped her finger on her lips. "Maybe we can move it to the other side?"

Emily groaned, throwing her head back. "Not again..."

Mel threw up her hands. "Well, I don't know! I've never put on a music concert before!"

Emily grabbed Mel's upper arms. "You're freaking out for nothing, Mel. This is a smoothie shop. Anywhere to set him up is as good as the next."

Mel blew out a breath. "Sorry. I just want it to be set up the best it can be." She scrambled at Emily's knowing look. "You know...because he'll be more comfortable if it's set up correctly and be, uh, able to play better."

Emily nodded slowly. "Suuuure."

Mel stuck her nose in the air. Her employee saw way too much. "We better hurry and get back to helping with the customers."

Emily picked up her pace and the two of them went back behind the counter. "When's lover boy supposed to be here anyway?"

"You can't call him that," Mel hissed, scowling at Emily. She paused at Emily's shocked face and took a deep breath. "I'm sorry. I shouldn't have snapped." Some of the tension in her body drained slightly. "We don't have a relationship outside of being friends, no matter what you think I feel for him. So please..." She closed her eyes and took another deep breath. "No jokes about it."

Emily's lips were turned down. "I'm sorry, Mel. I wasn't trying to hurt you." She hugged Mel quickly. "And if he can't see how wonderful you are by now, then the dude's an idiot and doesn't deserve you anyway."

Mel laughed a little. "He's not an idiot, but thanks for the vote of confidence."

"Anytime." Emily turned back to the waiting group, grabbing a cup off the counter. "Who's the handsome devil with a shot of antioxidants today?"

Mel chuckled as a few of the tourists gave each other weird looks. She loved the tradition of calling out fun, complimentary names in her shop. Mel felt like that was part of her calling in life. She always felt good about herself when she was building others, and since her own life wasn't turning out quite the way she had hoped, she worked hard to make sure others did.

"Wheatgrass queen!" Mel called, holding the cup in the air. "Your royal presence is requested at the front."

"Do you guys do that for everyone?" the teenager girl asked, her eyebrows drawn together.

Mel's smile widened. "Only to royalty," she said with a laugh.

The girl grinned and laughed a little. "Thanks."

"I don't think she gets your humor," Emily said in an aside.

"It doesn't matter," Mel said easily. "She was smiling...and that's the whole point."

"Which is exactly why everyone comes here."

Mel whipped around, her heart nearly jumping out of her chest. "Good grief, Jensen," she said, putting a hand on her beating heart. "I didn't see you come in."

He shrugged, that perfect mouth quirked up in a delicious grin. "I'm on lunch break and in a hurry, so I snuck in the back rather than work my way through the front."

Mel nodded, immediately becoming serious. "Right. Let me show you the space we think will work." Jensen's presence at her back was stronger than ever, but Mel did her best to ignore it. The last thing she needed right now was to do something embarrassing. She'd done enough of that at the dinner where their relationship went haywire. "Did you have a good birthday?" she asked over her shoulder.

"Other than the bonfire, I didn't celebrate," he said with a shrug. "So it was fine, I guess."

Mel stopped at the spot for the stage and put her hands on her hips. "Why in the world didn't you do something else?"

He chuckled. "Are you saying your strawberry cheesecake wasn't enough of a celebration?"

Mel felt her cheeks flame. "I'll admit Caro's chocolate would have been more celebration-worthy, but I knew that cheesecake was your favorite."

Jensen stared at her for a moment, his laughter dying, before he cleared his throat. "Yeah...thanks for that. Sometimes it's great to have friends who know you so well."

"Right." Mel smiled and nodded, ignoring the usual pang of rejection the word "friend" brought. *You'd think I'd be used to it by now.* "Well..." She swung a hand toward the wall. "It's not much, but we thought if we cleared the tables to the other side and put a chair and speaker up here, you could go at it."

Jensen's eyes looked over the space and he nodded slowly. "Yeah...I'm sure it'll be great." He rubbed the back of his neck. "I've never really done anything like this before, so anything is great."

Mel wrapped her arms around herself. "I'm sure all the tile and stuff isn't the most ideal for acoustics, but hopefully once it's filled with people, it'll be okay."

"Yeah..." Jensen looked around, then back at her. "If there are people anyway."

Mel rolled her eyes. "Like there won't be people. They're gonna eat this thing up, Jensen! We never have this kind of entertainment."

He laughed softly, sounding a little uncomfortable. "I just hope no one has any high expectations. Other than you guys, I've never performed in public."

"You teach large groups everyday," Mel pointed out.

"That's not performing."

Her eyebrows went up. "Isn't it? You're in front of people, doing your best to keep them interested for a certain amount of time. The only real difference is when you're teaching, you're also trying to cram their thick skulls with knowledge." She shook her head. "That's got to be harder than playing your guitar in front of a few dozen people."

"Maybe so, but no one's judging my talent or lack thereof when I'm teaching." He shoved his hands into his pants pockets. "It really doesn't matter what the kids think of me."

"Hey, Mr. Tanner!"

They both spun and Jensen waved to a group of teenagers eating their lunch. Jensen looked sheepish when he turned back to Mel.

"And yet they love you anyway," she said, her voice softer than she intended it to be.

"I wouldn't go that far, but I suppose they don't hate me," Jensen admitted. He looked around the space again. "That's one of the things holding me back, actually."

Mel frowned. "Holding you back? From what?"

His brown eyes looked like melted chocolate. "Last night I had the stupid idea of auditioning for one of those national talent shows."

Mel's jaw dropped and her heart nearly stopped beating.

"But it would mean being gone for a long time." Jensen huffed. "Well, I should say, *hoping* I'd be gone for a long time. No one wants to be the first to get voted out. But anyway...I'm a little worried about missing the kids if I left." He huffed. "Not to mention whether or not I'd have a job to come back to."

Just the kids? Mel felt as if her whole world had shifted. She had accepted long ago that Jensen would never see her as anything more than a little girl, but at least she had been able to be near him. She'd been able to laugh with him, cook for him, and enjoy his companionship, even if it was mostly because of her brother. But if he left? She'd lose it all. He was good. *Really* good, and if the world got a hold of him, then Mel had the terrible feeling that he'd never come back.

JENSEN DIDN'T MISS the look of despair on Mellie's face, but he wasn't quite sure what she was so upset over. "I mean...I'd miss you guys as well, you know," he stumbled over his words, "the whole gang. But I figured as adults, it wouldn't be as big a deal, you know?"

Mellie swallowed hard and tightened her arms around herself before her usual sunny smile graced her face once more. "No, no, I get it. You're right, it would be hardest on the kids." Her ocean-colored eyes left his and seemed to dart anywhere but at him.

I hurt her. The realization made his stomach churn. Mellie was a rock in their friend group. She loved everyone and everyone loved her. While the others in the group teased each other, Mellie gave compliments. When someone was hurting, she was the first to arrive with a hug, and a listening ear. Really...it was amazing that she hadn't been snatched up by someone yet. Who could resist the sun in the land of perpetual cloud cover? "Hey, Mellie...I'm sorry—"

She put her hand up and he stopped his babbling. "There's no need to apologize. I understand."

Her smile looked slightly strained, but Jensen didn't want to push it. If she was willing to move on, then he wasn't going to stop her. His foot was far enough down his throat as it was. "Anyway..." he hedged. "The space looks good. If you don't mind having the chairs moved around and putting a couple of speakers up, then I think we'll be good."

She nodded. "Sounds great. I can have Bennett get the speakers from you so they can get here early."

"Great." He glanced at his watch. "Shoot. I've gotta run. Class starts in fifteen."

"Have you eaten yet?"

Jensen looked up, not the least bit surprised that she was worried about that. Benny was right. She mothered them both. "Nope. But I'm a big boy, I'll be fine."

Mellie shook her head. "No way. I know you too well. Your stomach will grumble for the whole last hour, making a mockery of your teaching skills." She briskly walked away. "Give me two minutes."

"Mellie...it's really fine," he said, not wanting her to go to any trouble.

"Nope." She ducked below the counter and began throwing fruit around. "I've got just the thing to get you through the afternoon."

Jensen couldn't help but grin and watch her work. As much as it threw him to suddenly notice how pretty she was, he couldn't deny that he adored being around her. Her bright, welcoming personality was the perfect antidote to their gray coastal town. Not to mention it was the exact opposite of a classroom full of depressed and angsty teenagers. No matter what, Jensen always felt better for having spent time with her. *Now if I can just enjoy her without thinking about her looks, life would be pretty great.*

"Here we are," she said, waving the cup in his direction. "It's Key Lime."

He raised his eyebrows as he walked around the counter. "Key Lime? Not Limarazzmatazzmahijinks?"

Mellie made a face, then broke into laughter.

Jensen felt another subtle shift inside of him at her response. Earlier it had pained him to know he'd hurt her, but now he felt a trickle of pride that he'd made her happy, especially enough to laugh with such abandon.

"Sorry," she said, her voice slightly higher than normal from her amusement. She wiped at the corner of her eye. "I haven't come up with a schnazzy name yet. It's a brand new flavor." She winked.

"You're one of the first ones to try it. Outside of myself and a couple of employees anyway." She shrugged a single shoulder.

"I feel so special," he said, taking the cup. His fingers brushed hers and that warmth from the other night invaded his nerves again. *This is getting out of hand.*

"You should," she shot back. "Not everyone gets to be a guinea pig."

Jensen made oinking noises, sending her into laughter again. He smiled and brought the straw to his lips, only to pause. He was flirting with her. Flirting. This wasn't just teasing and sibling comraderie like he usually did. This was full-on flirting.

After a moment, her face fell. "Is it that bad?" Her lips turned down on the sides. "I thought it was pretty good, if a little tart...but I thought you liked tart. I mean, you like raspberry and stuff, so I assumed tart was in your wheelhouse—"

"Mellie," he said, interrupting her rambling. "I haven't tasted it. Hang on."

"You didn't taste it? Then why the face?"

Jensen put a hand up, not willing to discuss his emotional discoveries with her. Things were weird enough as it was. He took a long draw of the drink. "Whoa..." He held the cup out and looked at it. "That's pretty good," he said, smiling to emphasize his point.

"Really?" she said breathlessly, the relief practically dripping from her tone.

"Yeah." He took another drink. "What's in it?" He rolled the slush around on his tongue. "It's sweet, but...not."

She shrugged and folded her arms over her chest. "Trade secrets. I can't be telling you."

Jensen put a hand over his heart. "What? I thought I was family!"

Her eyes drifted to the wall before widening. "Family who's late!" she scolded. She waved at him with her hands. "Get out of here before Principal *** fires me."

Jensen laughed as he left. "I don't think it's you he would fire, not to mention he's not your boss."

Mellie rolled her eyes. "Everyone thinks I'm the troublemaker in our group. Somehow I end up blamed for everything."

Jensen pushed open the back door, stopping for one more glance before he went back to work. "That's because Benny is your brother. Trouble follows the guy like a magnet."

She slapped her forehead. "Oh my gosh, truer words have never been spoken."

Jensen let his eyes enjoy the sight of her flushed cheeks and the couple of strands of hair that caressed her warm skin. However, before his heart could get any more weird ideas, he saluted her with the drink and walked out. "Thanks!"

She probably responded to his farewell, but he didn't hear it. Instead, he was practically running back to work, feeling lighter than he had in a really long time. He slowed his pace to a quick walk and took another drag of his smoothie, an easy smile playing on his lips. He couldn't seem to help it, even though inside he knew that Mellie had that effect on everyone. Each and every customer inside her shop always left with a smile and a laugh. She worked hard to make it so. Especially those she didn't know. Lots of tourists entered her cute little shop and all of them left feeling better than when they'd arrived.

His internal musings actually brought down some of the high he'd been experiencing. Mellie was so attentive that it was easy to feel her smiles were just for the person she was speaking to. That her laughter was reserved for someone just like him.

Jensen frowned. "But that's not how it is," he scolded himself. "She loves everyone and probably flirts and chats with people all day long. Your time together isn't anything special." He sighed, the depression he'd been struggling with coming back to the forefront. "Which is exactly why you should push aside the attraction you're feeling and focus on your guitar. It seems to be the only thing that might actually shake up your boring life."

He once again pondered on the idea of sending in a recording to one of those television talent shows. Surely it wouldn't hurt anything? *Nothing but my pride,* he thought. *But what if I got on?* The idea of excitement, stages, lights and cameras caused his heart to speed up a little. It was so different from what he was living right now and for that reason, he was more than a little intrigued. His birthday last week had made him feel as if a ticking time bomb was waiting over his head. He wasn't in his twenties anymore and felt he had so little to show for all his hard work. Regrets and monotony seemed to loom over his head, and he desperately wanted to change that.

The gig tomorrow at Smooth Moves. It'll be the perfect chance to see how I'd be received. If it goes well, then I'll do it. He made the promise to himself just as he walked into his classroom. Several students were already there.

"Hey, Mr. Tanner," Ian lazily drawled, leaning back in his seat with his legs stretched out. "Have a good lunch?"

Jensen set his cup down on his desk and turned to his class. "Yeah. I did," he said with a smile.

CHAPTER 6

M el couldn't seem to sit still. She wove through customers, wiping every surface, double-checking that the stage area was ready. Taking a deep breath, she forced herself to slow down. *Acting like a crazed fan isn't going to help anything.*

She stiffened. "Nothing is going to help at this point," she whispered, forcing back her usual feelings of rejection and unworthiness. After her little lunch with Jensen a couple of days ago, she'd found herself struggling more than ever with her feelings. If he left Seaside Bay, she'd lose him. She knew it. *Maybe in a way that would be okay,* she tried to convince herself. *Maybe it would help me move on.*

"Nervous?"

Mel spun, then frowned at Emily. "No."

Emily grinned. "Riiight."

Mel rolled her eyes. "I don't know what you think you know...but you're definitely wrong."

"That made perfect sense," Emily said, her lips pursed as she slowly nodded her head.

Mel glanced at the clock on the wall and her heart jumped. "He's going to be here any minute." She looked around the small space. They'd been advertising for several days that Jensen would be coming and word had obviously spread. There was barely space for the little set-up they'd created for him to play. Every couch and chair was full and people were standing in groups, chatting as they waited for the performer to arrive. Those of their friend group who were able to make it were sitting in the very back booth, hanging out and waiting for the man of the hour to arrive.

Mel wrung her hands together. She wanted everything to be perfect, but wasn't sure what that really meant. The idea to have him come perform was two-fold. It allowed Mel to have him around, something that was especially important since he hadn't been coming into the shop lately. And it also was a way to help him do something for himself. As wonderful as Jensen was, he was the tame one from the group of friends. He'd always been a little more of a rule follower and so when he'd expressed a desire to share his music, Mel desperately wanted to be a part of helping him achieve that.

The bell on the door jangled and her head shot up.

"Speak of the devil," Emily murmured.

Mel hadn't realized her employee was still at her side, but she couldn't take her eyes from the doorway to address her. Jensen had obviously dressed up for the night. He wore a collared shirt half-tucked into a pair of nice jeans. His dark hair was styled with just enough gel to keep it out of his face, leaving his warm brown eyes available for everyone to stare at. "Ow." Mel looked down to see Emily had elbowed her.

"You've got a little something...right here." Emily pointed to the corner of her mouth, her lips twitching as she held back a grin.

Mel's shoulders dropped. "I'm so obvious, aren't I?"

Emily's teasing look dropped. "No. Not unless someone's paying attention." She frowned, turned to Jensen, then back. "What I don't get is why you don't do something about it. I mean, you're gorgeous and fun, and any guy would love to be with you. Why don't you ask him out?"

Mel blew out a shaky breath, pushing her hand through her hair. "It's not that easy."

"Why not?"

Mel blinked back the sting of tears and tore her eyes from Jensen's appealing form. "Because to him, I'm nothing but a little sister who still wears pigtails."

"So help him see you as an adult." Emily smiled. "I have no doubt he'll fall head over heels in love with you if given the chance."

"That's just it," Mel murmured, giving her friend a sad look as she began to step away. "He already fell in love. And it wasn't with me." On that note, Mel walked toward the small performance area, pushing Emily's words aside and focusing on the present. The present where Mel did her best to help Jensen fulfill her dreams rather than worrying about the fact that she'd never have anything more from their relationship. "Hey," she said with a wide smile. "Is the set-up okay?"

Jensen glanced up from where he tuned his instrument. "Yeah. It's great. Thanks." His eyes wandered behind her. "A lot more people turned out than I thought would."

Mel nodded. "Yeah. I think everyone's excited to actually have some entertainment in our neck of the woods." She forced a laugh. "Normally we have to travel up to Portland or Vancouver for anything good."

"I wouldn't say I'm much of an improvement, but hopefully no one brought tomatoes with them either," he joked.

Mel could see a tightness around his eyes and she worried that he was nervous. "You're going to be great," she gushed. Her eyes drifted to the counter. "Hang on." Darting back behind her station, Mel quickly whipped together Jensen's favorite smoothie. She'd made it so many times, it only took a couple of minutes to have it ready. With a smile, she brought it to him. "For luck."

Jensen took the cup, eyeing it warily, then smiling when he read the message on the side. "Thanks, Mel. You're a great friend."

Mel was positive that Jensen had no idea how hurtful those simple words were. Her permanently bruised heart felt as if it had been kicked with a steel-toed boot, but she fought the desire to fold in on herself and protect the precious organ. "Don't you forget it," she quipped, pulling on her years of experience. "Break a leg, Jens." Not waiting for him to say anything else, she left his side and took refuge behind the counter. The long, stainless steel workstation put some much-needed distance between her and the man she wanted. It made it easier to stand tall and smile as he began strumming his first song.

Emily slipped up beside her, listening as the crowd quieted down and the sound of guitar music began to echo off the walls. "I'm sorry."

Mel looked down, noting the sympathy on Emily's face. Mel smiled sadly. "Me too, Em." She turned back to Jensen. "Me too."

JENSEN'S FINGERS SHOOK for the first ten minutes as he worked his way through a chunk of the popular songs he knew. He'd thought he was prepared for this evening, but even this small crowd of thirty or so people felt enormous compared to what he was used to. As soon as he'd walked in the door and seen Mel's stunning smile, his heart had begun to race and sweat began trickling down his back.

As people clapped after every song, however, he found himself calming down. His eyes drifted to the Styrofoam cup at the base of his chair, causing him to smile involuntarily. She had no idea the effect she was beginning to have on him. Try as he might, Jensen couldn't seem to make her go back to the sweet, little girl she had been. Now that he'd noticed her as a woman, that was what he saw every time he looked.

It took considerable effort not to glare at her every time she looked his way. It wasn't her fault he was going crazy, nor was it her fault she'd become a gorgeous adult. This was all on him. He just needed to get his mind out of the gutter and focus on more important matters. Like his music and whether or not he would audition for that show.

As exciting as a performer's life sounded, there was a part of him that was scared. He'd never stepped out of line before. He'd followed the exact same footsteps as his parents, just doing the status quo. Who was he to rock the boat and try for more? And would it be worth the cost if his dream did come true?

Clapping broke Jensen free from his tumultuous thoughts and he realized his fingers had stopped moving without him realizing it. *Good thing I've played that song a thousand times,* he mused as the crowd whistled and smiled.

"Play something new!"

Jensen jerked his head up and looked straight into Mel's oceanic gaze. They swirled with a mix of blue and green, the store's bright lighting bringing out the blue more prominently tonight. He shook his head before he lost himself in their depths. "What?"

Her red lips pulled into a blinding smile that had his pulse skipping a beat. "I said, play something *new.*" She put emphasis on the last word as if he should know what she meant, and then it dawned on him.

She wants the song I wrote.

Mel must have realized he finally caught onto her suggestion because her face relaxed and she nodded. "You can do it," she mouthed.

Trying to buy time, Jensen reached for the smoothie she'd brought, taking a long draw on the straw. The sweet, fruity flavors were more of a juice instead of a slushy at this point, but it didn't matter. It still tasted amazing, just like everything she made. He looked at the cup, her words written in bold black strokes.

Tonight's Headliner: Jensen Tanner, guitarist extraordinaire

The words made him grin again. She always knew exactly what to say to make someone feel like they could conquer the world. Setting the drink down, Jensen took a deep breath. He might not be able to do anything about his new attraction to her, but he could play one of his songs. There was no harm in that.

He resettled the guitar and struck the first note. It only took seconds for him to get lost in the music. Playing hits was fun, but there was just something about playing stuff that had come from inside of himself that took him away. It was as if he was free. Free from his job and from the constraints of his parents. Free from expectations and the boringness of day-to-day life.

In his music, he felt like anything was possible. Even that headline that Mel had teased him about.

When the last chord struck, Jensen blinked and came back to the room as he was swarmed with good wishes and congratulations. Many of the people who had shown up were ones he knew, while others were obviously tourists stopping by for a bit of fun. The common theme, however, was how much everyone seemed to enjoy the music.

"You're amazing, Teach!" Ian said, offering Jensen a fist bump. Nina was at his side, just like she had been the week before outside the school.

Jensen chuckled and put up his knuckles. "Thanks, Ian. Glad you enjoyed it."

"How come you never told us that you play?" Ian folded his arms over his chest. "You've been holding out on us."

Jensen rubbed the back of his warm neck. "Until recently, I didn't really tell anyone. It's just a hobby."

"A hobby that could make you famous," another girl from the high school gushed. She was holding arms with another young woman. Jensen had seen them before but they weren't in any of his classes. "We want to be the first ones to get your autograph."

Jensen's smile was starting to hurt his cheeks, but he couldn't seem to stop. He was definitely on a high from how well the performance went. "I'm not sure it'll be worth the paper you put it on," he said with a laugh. "This is fun and all, but I doubt I could make a career out of it."

"The real question is...do you want to?"

Jensen and the high-schoolers turned to see Mellie standing close by. A warm, citrusy scent washed over Jensen and he realized it was her. *Now I'm smelling her? Perfect. That's exactly what I need. Another thing to have to fight.* "That's a hard question to answer," he finally muttered.

Mel's smile was sweet as sugar and twice as addicting. "You're a smart guy, I'm sure you can figure it out." Her words were right, but Jensen could see something in her eyes that seemed...off.

"Ooh," Ian said in a low tone. He grinned and nudged the boy next to him. "You and the smoothie lady, Teach? I didn't know that."

Jensen quickly shook his head. "No!" He winced when Mellie jumped at his harsh answer. "I mean, no. She's my friend's kid sister." He tried to give an easy smile. "She just likes to tease me."

Ian sauntered closer to Mellie. "You don't look like a little sister to me," he said, tilting his head in a playful manner.

Mellie's eyes nearly disappeared as she laughed at the flirting. "I can tell you're a dangerous one," she quipped back. "All those ladies at the school better watch out." She glanced behind Ian to Nina. "Or maybe just one girl?"

Ian put a hand to his heart. "Be still my heart." He glanced slyly at Jensen. "Isn't that how it goes, Mr. Tanner?"

Jensen's smile was brittle, but he kept it in place. "Yep. Good one." The teenager's flirting shouldn't have bothered him so much. It's not like Mellie would entertain anything with a kid his age, but it did. *Why? Why did Benny have to go and say anything about her being all grown up? Why did I have to notice?*

Mel glanced over her shoulder. "I actually better run." She winked. "Looks like your playing is good for business."

Jensen looked over to see a long line forming at the counter. "Oh, yeah. Glad it helped."

She took a hesitant step forward, then rested a hand on his forearm, nearly searing him with her heat. "Thanks for doing this. We'll have to set up a regular schedule." Her smile widened, but it didn't seem to reach her eyes. "At least until you head for greener pastures."

Jensen pushed a shaking hand through his hair. "That would be something, wouldn't it? Can you imagine me living it up in the big city?"

Her smile faltered for just a split-second before it was back in its usual place. "I guess that answered my earlier question." She squeezed his arm. "I have no doubt you'll get your wish someday."

Before Jensen could correct any of her assumptions, she disappeared through the crowd and his attention was taken by more patrons wanting to chat about his music. He could see all his friends waiting in the back of the shop, but they seemed content to wait until he was free.

Jensen met Benny's eye and Benny grinned before pumping his eyebrows. Jensen gave back the same greeting, then turned his attention to the guest speaking with him. *I'll go over and say hi when I'm all done here.*

Being all done took a lot longer than Jensen thought it would. Mellie had turned the shop sign to **Closed** over an hour before the last customer finally walked out, the little bell overhead ringing at their departure.

CHAPTER 7

"Whew," Mellie said breathlessly, wiping dramatically at her forehead. "I thought they'd never leave."

Everyone laughed.

"That's what happens when you have someone famous hanging around," Caro called out from her place in the back booth. She winked at Jensen. "Celebrities always bring in the crowds."

Jensen rubbed his neck. "That's a little premature, don't you think?"

Bennett jumped from his seat and wrapped an arm around Jensen's neck. "I want in on the action, man. Bring me along as emotional support or something so I can meet all the ladies that'll be throwing themselves at you."

"Are you saying you're a dog?" Felix drawled with a raised eyebrow.

"Hey!" Bennett put a hand over his chest. "Buds were the first emotional support companions before those dang animals got in the way."

"Give me a break," Charli groaned, rolling her eyes. "Trying to pick up someone else's admirers isn't emotional support. It's stealing."

The bantering continued with lots of laughter and smiles, but Mel could barely keep hers in place. All this talk of Jensen being famous was just another knife to her gut that she was losing him. *You never had him*, she reminded herself, but the reminder wasn't enough.

Why don't you do something about it?

Emily's earlier question swirled through Mel's head. *But what?* That was the real question. What could she do that would keep

Jensen by her side, even if they were only ever friends? *Is it fair to do that though? Is it fair to keep him from pursuing a career just because of my feelings?*

There seemed to be no good answer to her struggles. She instinctively knew that if he left, she'd lose him forever. However, keeping him here would ruin his shot at a dream and she didn't want that for him either.

"So...what's the next step?" Bennett asked, sipping on the last bits of his smoothie. His straw made an annoying slurping noise and Charli smacked the back of his head. "Ow. Geez. You guys are always hitting me," he whined, rubbing the spot.

"Maybe if you'd stop being the annoying little brother for once, we wouldn't have to," she shot back, folding her arms over her chest with a scowl.

Bennett grinned. "Aw...come on, Charles...you know you love me." He gave her a charming grin and Mel found herself giggling quietly. Bennett was the only one who got away with calling Charli, Charles, and he did it with the sole purpose of knowing it drove her crazy. Charli had a fierce personality and didn't put up with attitude from anyone, which was why her relationship with Bennett was so entertaining.

"Yeah, like I love a barnacle on the bottom of Felix's boat," she said with an evil grin.

Bennett made a face. "Wow. I thought you hated those. Who'd have thought you thought of them as family?"

Charli rolled her eyes. "Idiot," she muttered.

"If by idiot, you mean handsome devil, then yes. Yes I am an idiot."

"Oh my word!" Caro cried out, slapping the table. "Would you two stop?"

"I really hate to say it, but for once I agree with Caro," Ken said with a smug grin.

Caro nodded at him. "That probably is a first, but thank you nonetheless."

"Anytime." Ken saluted her, then glanced at his phone. "Shoot. I'm on night duty this week and gotta run." He stood from his chair and headed toward the door. "But don't forget to let me know what we're doing next. I want in on the 'Make Jensen Famous' act."

That churning sensation grew in Mel's stomach again and she put a hand over it, as if the touch could stop the turmoil.

Caro's wide eyes looked seriously at Jensen. "The proper thing to do here would probably be to ask what you want to do," she said, tilting her head to the side. "You're amazing, but do you actually want to try and be a performer?"

Jensen rubbed the back of his neck, a gesture that Mel had seen hundreds if not thousands of times. It was his go-to when he was anxious or uncertain. "Sort of?" he said with a shrug and scrunched nose. "I have to admit I'm kind of torn."

"Why's that?" Felix asked, settling further into his seat. His eyes drooped a little and he yawned. "Sorry," he said when his mouth closed again. "I had an early charter today."

"Maybe we should all sleep on this and meet again another night," Mel said eagerly. "We're all tired and it's probably not a good time to try and make plans." She turned to Jensen. "You must be exhausted from performing, so let's all just think about it for a bit."

Jensen smiled at her. "And there she is," he said with a soft laugh. "The little sister who's always worried over everyone."

Mel bit her tongue, positive that she would taste blood if she pressed any harder. She shrugged, unsure how to respond to a compliment that cut like a knife.

"That's her," Bennett agreed. He tapped the table. "But she's probably right. Ole Cappy over here is going to start snoring soon if we don't tuck him in."

Felix scowled. "You try and tuck me in and I'll show you who's old."

Bennett made a movement as if he would follow through, but then sat back and laughed. "Nah, we'll save that title for Mr. Guitar over here." He waved at Jensen. "Isn't he the one who just crossed decades?"

"True enough," Felix said with a grin. Sighing, he stood. "Come on, Charli. Let's go get some shut-eye."

His sister stood and began to follow him to the door. "Think about it, Jensen," she called over her shoulder. "We're all here to help you."

Jensen nodded, but his earlier humor seemed to have fled. Mel caught the tightness around his mouth and eyes and she frowned a little, wondering what he was upset about.

"Guess that's my cue," Caro said, rising to her feet. She gave Mel a hug. "Thanks for letting us crash your store."

Mel stepped back and grinned. "Anytime."

"Rose, Brookie and everyone else is going to be sad they missed it," Caro said, her eyes going to Jensen. "Guess that just means we'll have to do it again."

Jensen's smile returned. "I might be up for that."

"Good man," she cooed, patting his shoulder as she passed. "See y'all later!" Her long, blonde hair disappeared into the night.

The room was quiet for a minute before Bennett let out a snoring noise. He snorted and bounced around in his seat. "Oh, I'm sorry. Did I nod off?"

Mel rolled her eyes and began putting all the chairs back in place. She was off in the morning, so she could sleep in if she stayed up late to clean up the place. "Must be because you're as old as Jensen," she teased her brother.

Jensen snorted and stood. "Here. Let me help."

"Oh no, I got it," Mel hurried to assure him. Truthfully, she was about at her emotional end tonight. She needed everyone gone so she could have a few minutes to cry before pulling herself back together. It was exhausting to always be the peppy one, no matter your own feelings, and right now she was more worn down than usual.

Mel paused when a heavy hand landed on hers. She looked up into warm brown eyes that made her knees weak.

"Let me help," Jensen said softly, his eyes boring into hers as if he could see very secret.

But you can't let him see your secrets, Mel's internal voice reminded her. She blinked rapidly and looked down at the chair. "That'll be great. Thanks." Swiftly she moved away, hoping her eyes hadn't given away her feelings. That was the last thing she needed right now. Knowing she was in love with him would probably only drive Jensen to leaving faster.

JENSEN WAS QUIET AS he put away the first few chairs. He couldn't exactly say why, but Mel's dismissal of him hurt, and Jensen didn't like it.

"You never did answer the question," Benny said, standing from his seat to start helping put things back in order.

"What question was that?" Jensen asked.

"What you *want* to do."

Jensen squished his lips to the side, the room going very quiet as his friends waited for his response. The pressure in the room seemed to increase as Jensen fought an internal battle, not quite sure what to say. "I did say I was unsure," he hedged.

"So tell us what you're unsure about," Benny pressed. "We're family. That's what we're here for."

Jensen's eyes drifted to Mel, but her head was down as she wiped down the countertops. Her shoulders seemed tight and Jensen realized she'd probably worked all day. *Hopefully she can sleep in tomorrow.* "I've stayed here my whole life," he started.

"Except for school," Benny corrected.

"Bennett," Mel groaned. "Let the man speak."

Jensen grinned. Was there ever a time when Mel hadn't stood up for him? He couldn't think of one. "He's right though. I did leave for school."

Mel huffed, but nodded.

Jensen chuckled. "*Except for school*," he said in an exaggerated tone, "I've been here my whole life. I've done everything I was supposed to do." He sighed and pinched the bridge of his nose. He wasn't sure he wanted to continue. He loved his parents and wasn't trying to make them sound bad, but most of the decisions in his life had been based on what they wanted for him.

"It's okay," Mel said softly, her small hand landing on his shoulder, giving Jensen a jolt. "You don't have to explain things you don't want to." Her understanding gaze was bright under the fluorescent bulbs and for a second Jensen struggled to remember what they were talking about.

Shaking his head, he shrugged. "No. It's okay. I mean, I don't want to speak badly of anybody. It's not like I was an unwilling follower, but I've..." He made a face.

"You've done everything your parents said to," Mel finished softly.

Jensen's head snapped back to her. "Yeah. How did you know that?"

Mel smiled softly and walked away, presumably to begin working again. "You forget I've known you forever, Jensen. I watched my brother and the other guys break all the rules while you were always in the background. You didn't stop them, but you didn't usually participate." She grinned at him. "Considering your quiet, studious parents, I always just assumed you were just like them. But now that I'm older, I realize you were probably just trying to make them proud."

Once again, something began shifting in Jensen's chest. It was the same sensation that had started at Benny's home the other night, but it was getting stronger. There was something about truly being seen that had Jensen's heart pounding and his body warming. The fact that it was by a beautiful woman only seemed to heighten the emotions. "That's exactly right," he said in awe.

Benny snorted. "Leave it to Mel. I think she knows us all better than we know ourselves."

Benny's joke brought Jensen out of his reverie. He cleared his throat and tugged at his collar. "Probably," he said, his voice cracking slightly.

"One of us has to," Mel called to her brother. "If I didn't know you so well, I wouldn't know how often you don't clean or skip dinner."

Benny paused. "True. Maybe it's not such a bad thing."

Mel huffed a laugh. "You need a wife," she grumbled, sweeping the floor more vigorously.

"What?" Benny's jaw dropped and he gave her an incredulous look. "You really think I need a woman to slow all this down?" He waved an arm over himself. "A lady would only cramp my style."

Mel gave him a disbelieving look and Jensen put a fist to his mouth to try and hold back his laughter but some of it crept out anyway. He laughed harder when Benny sent a glare his way.

"Got a problem...friend?" Benny asked in a dark voice.

Jensen held up his hand. "Nope. No problem here."

"Melody?"

Mellie gave her brother a dry look. "Mother always said if you can't say anything nice to not speak at all." She smiled sweetly. "I think I'll actually listen to her advice for once."

That was it, Jensen lost it. He doubled over as he laughed, feeling wonderfully light at the familiar atmosphere surrounding him. It was a well-known fact that Mellie and Benny's mother was certifiably insane. The woman had always been a little loopy, but a few years ago, right after Mellie finished high school, Celeste Frasier had decided it was time to pursue her passion, and she moved down to California so that she didn't have to be bothered by the responsibilities of life anymore, and so the government couldn't track her. Last the siblings knew, their mom was living on a beach, her hair in dreadlocks and preaching about the conspiracies of government manipulation. To take anything the woman said seriously was tantamount to a miracle.

A paper cup hit his head and Jensen calmed himself enough to stand upright.

"It's not funny," Mellie said, but her smile contradicted her words.

"It so is," Jensen argued.

"Anyway," Benny drawled, rolling his eyes, "you better finish explaining why you're too scared to try anything new, or I'm outta here." He yawned and scratched his head. "The mail still has to be delivered, you know."

Jensen's humor dropped as their previous conversation topic came back. He shrugged, not really feeling up to sharing it all. "I've always just done what I was supposed to, I guess," he admitted. "Trying to create a career as a performer definitely isn't what I was taught would pay the bills."

"But how will you know if you don't try?" Benny argued. "I'm pretty sure there are plenty of artists who pay their bills."

"And there are plenty more who don't," Mellie countered. "The term 'starving artist' was created for a reason."

Jensen nodded and sighed. "Exactly. But..."

"But?" Benny pressed.

Jensen shook his head. "Never mind."

"Oh no, you can't stop now," Benny said with a glare.

"But I'm afraid if I don't try it now...I'll never do it."

The words were met with silence. Even Benny didn't have a snappy comeback.

The screech of a chair being pushed back into place sounded extra loud when Benny finally broke the awkwardness. "I think it just comes down to what you want," he said, unusually serious. "If you want to give it a try, you might as well do it before you have other responsibilities to tie you down."

Jensen caught Mellie's wince at those words, but his focus was mostly on Benny.

"If you don't really want to, then don't." Benny put his hands on his hips. "You're grown. Your parents are nice, but it's your life. Do what you want."

The craving for excitement began to build in Jensen's chest at his friend's words. Almost as if he'd been waiting for the green light from someone other than himself. *What do I want? The status quo? Or to try something new?*

The idea of auditioning came to his mind again. It would be a way to really see if he had something worth pursuing without having to risk too much. *But if I got on the show, would it be worth the cost of my life here?*

Jensen wasn't sure yet, but the idea was sounding better and better by the moment. "You're right," he told Benny. "I'll do what I want."

CHAPTER 8

Mel hid a yawn as she walked into the shop the next afternoon. She'd taken the morning off knowing the evening would be late, but her sleep hadn't gone quite as planned. Instead of getting extra rest, all she got was extra nightmares.

Her bed had been a mess this morning from all the tossing and turning that had occurred during the night.

"Whoa," Emily said with wide eyes. "What happened to you?"

Mel glared at her employee from the corner of her eye. "Don't say a word."

"Too late," Emily said with a shake of her head. She glanced at her watch. "I'm off in fifteen minutes. Why don't you and I have a chat before I go home?"

"Don't you have homework?" Mel asked. Emily was doing online college and was only a couple years younger than Mel, which meant they got along well in the work environment, but their separate stages of life meant they didn't really get together outside of the smoothie shop.

"It can wait a bit," Emily said, handing a drink to a customer. "You look like you could use my attention more than Ancient Civilizations."

Mel sighed and rubbed her throbbing forehead. "Yeah...maybe that'd be okay." She looked around. The shop was fairly empty, which was normal late in the afternoon. It would pick up again after dinner for the dessert crowd.

"Go wait in your office," Emily instructed. "I'll be there in a few."

Mel glared again. "Who put you in charge?"

"You did," Emily said with a grin. "I'm the shift manager, remember?"

Mel rolled her eyes. "Whatever."

Emily laughed softly and shooed Mel away. Frustrated, but not knowing what to do about it, Mel let her friend push her away and she went to her office for a bit of quiet. The space was small, but cute. A short couch took up one wall, while a desk with a vase of flowers took up the other.

Mel allowed herself to feel the soft petals of the flowers and sniff their delicate scent before tumbling onto the couch. She was too long to lay on it, but she tucked up her knees and did her best to get comfortable. Throwing an arm over her eyes, she lay still, focusing on her breathing.

It seemed like an eternity before the door opened and Emily snuck inside. "Lorraine arrived, I've clocked out, and the place is still slow."

Mel nodded, not opening her eyes. "Thanks," she croaked. The sound of a chair on carpet told Mel that Emily was turning one of the seats around to look at her. She peeked from under her arm to see Emily watching with a concerned expression on her face.

"Mind telling me what happened after I left last night?" Emily asked softly.

Mel's whole body deflated as she let out a long breath. "Not much. Jensen, as you know, was amazing. Everyone loved him. The crew stuck around to chat a bit, with everyone encouraging him to go for the big time." Her voice grew slightly thick at the end of her speech and Mel forced herself to stop. This wasn't like her. She was the eternal optimist, even if she didn't always feel like it inside. Mel never appeared in public without a smile and a ready compliment. It was like some women with their make-up. It helped her feel good about herself and gave her confidence to handle any situation. But right now she didn't have the energy. Everything seemed to be going up in smoke and Mel's endurance was at an end. Jensen had reminded her she was a friend too many times lately, on top of the fact that he was thinking about leaving.

She'd never felt so low.

"This isn't going to work," Emily said succinctly.

"What?" Mel frowned and moved her arm away from her face. "What isn't going to work?"

"This." Emily waved her hand at Mel. "You moaning and moping around. You'll never catch Jensen that way."

Mel scrambled to sit up, then paused and held her head. "I don't think you're being fair," she said softly, trying not to make the migraine worse.

"Probably not," Emily said with a shrug. "But whether or not it's fair, it's not going to help the situation."

"There is no situation," Mel said, her eyes filling with tears. "He wants to leave. He's thinking about trying for a professional career, which would take him away from Seaside Bay...and me. End of story." She swallowed the lump in her throat. "And we both know that if he leaves, he'll never come back. He's good, Em. You heard him last night."

Emily nodded thoughtfully. "You're right, he is. People would definitely pay to hear him play, but that doesn't mean that's what he wants to do for a living."

Mel jumped to her feet and began to pace. "But he does. I heard him last night say that he was worried he would regret it if he didn't act now. That life was passing him by."

Emily shrugged. "Maybe that had to do with his recent birthday. Turning thirty would make anyone feel old."

Mel rolled her eyes. "Thirty isn't old, Em. Just because you're barely twenty doesn't make the rest of us ancient."

Emily smiled and laughed softly. "True enough, but it still might explain his sudden desire to do something else with his life. Maybe he's hitting his midlife crisis early."

"So...what?" Mel asked, plopping back down. "I just wave good-bye and watch him leave?" She sniffled. "I don't know if I can survive that."

"I know." Emily's voice dropped. "But it's not like it's any better right now. Don't you think a clean break would be better? Either make his time here worth it, or let him go."

Mel frowned. "What do you mean, make his time here worth it? How do I have anything to do with that?"

"Make him see what he's missing out on," Emily said. "Show him your hand. If he's feeling like he's missing life, then show him what it would be like with you."

"Are you saying I should pursue Jensen?" Mel's voice squeaked and she slapped her hands over her mouth. "I've never pursued a guy before. Isn't that their job?"

It was Emily's turn to roll her eyes. "How old are you again? That kind of archaic attitude is ancient history, Mel."

Mel put her hands in her lap. "Maybe so, but I don't know if I would have the courage to go after him. Not to mention he's always telling me what a good friend I am. Don't you think that makes it pretty clear about how he feels about me?"

"Then forget him and move on."

Mel slumped. "I've tried."

"Then try again."

Mel laid her head back. "You make it sound so simple. Either do or do not," she said in her best Yoda impression.

"It is," Emily said. "Either go after him or let him go. Make a choice and stick with it."

"But what if I go after him and he still leaves?" Mel's voice was barely audible and the fear quivering in her chest made her voice shake.

"Then you're no worse off than you are now," Emily said. Even without looking, Mel could hear the sympathy. "I don't know for sure if Jensen will regret not trying for a music career," Emily said. "But I can tell you for sure that if I were in your shoes, I would regret not trying to catch his attention."

"I don't know if I'm brave enough." Mel sat up straighter, looking her friend in the eye.

"Mel...I've known you for three years, and for every single day except today, I've never seen you with anything but a smile on your face, no matter what was going on." Emily shook her head. "You might actually be the bravest of us all."

Mel took a quiet moment to think about Emily's sweet words. She didn't even know where to start. Maybe waiting for a man to make a move was old-fashioned, but it just seemed like the way things were done. *Can I ask him out? Would he think I was crazy?* She blinked a few times. *Would it matter? If he's leaving anyway, thinking I'm crazy probably wouldn't make a difference.* Her hands tightened into fists and she felt her jaw clench. Slowly, Mel brought her eyes to Emily's waiting one. "Okay," she said, her voice quiet but strong. "I'll give it a try."

HEY, WE NEED A VOLUNTEER tomorrow for a reading group. Are you available?

Jensen pinched his lips together after he sent the message. He really wasn't sure it was wise to ask Mel to help, but he wasn't sure who else to turn to. She was always the first to volunteer for everything and had always been his go-to partner in the past. At least until he started getting weird ideas around her. Now, he wasn't sure he should spend any more time with her than necessary.

Sure. What exactly do you need?

He sighed, a mixture of relief and anxiousness. Mel was always great with the kids, but he'd have to work hard to control himself around her. A couple nights ago when she'd been so kind about his worries, he'd known he was in trouble. Jensen had always been aware she had a heart of gold, but the outside of her was coming into focus in a way that proved her face was as beautiful physically as she was on the inside.

He chuckled under his breath. "I think it's supposed to be the other way around," he murmured. But not with Mellie, and Jensen felt like an idiot for not seeing her for who she was earlier.

"Jensen?"

His head snapped up to see Principal Nielsen in the doorway. "Hey, Ethan. What's up?"

"Just wanted to make sure everything was good for tomorrow?" Ethan's eyebrows were high on his forehead. "You said you had a friend who could help?"

Jensen nodded. "Yeah. Mellie will be here."

Ethan tapped the doorway a couple times. "Melody? Perfect, we've already got her volunteer paperwork on file so that'll work out fine. Make sure she knows we appreciate her help."

Jensen nodded again. "Will do."

Ethan paused. "Did you, uh, manage to get Mr. Derringer to agree to attend?"

Jensen felt his concern shift. He'd been keeping an eye on his student and though there hadn't been any blatant signs of abuse, Jensen's gut still bothered him when he looked at the withdrawn student. "I did."

Jensen had spoken to Principal Nielsen, hoping to get more eyes on the boy. Inviting Micah to the reading group had been a way to try and get closer. It was one of the reasons Jensen had invited Mellie. She seemed to have a knack for bringing down anyone's barriers.

"Great." Ethan nodded firmly. "Let me know if you notice anything else."

"Have any other teachers said anything?" Jensen asked before his boss could leave.

Ethan sighed and took his glasses off to pinch his nose. "No, though a couple have admitted he's a loner." His dark eyes met Jensen's. "I think everyone assumes it's just one of those phases."

Jensen leaned back in his chair, the hinges squeaking. "And you? Do you think I'm crazy?"

"No one thinks you're crazy, Jensen," Ethan said with a scowl. "Maybe slightly overprotective, but not crazy."

"You didn't answer the question, Ethan."

The principal's eyes dropped to the floor. He was probably ten years or so older than Jensen, the hair above his ears just starting to turn gray. Jensen knew Ethan had a wife and three children at home, and was a strong family man. He was counting on that to help him out when it came to protecting Micah.

When Ethan looked back up, his face was tired, looking older than his actual age. "I don't know," he admitted truthfully. "I understand what you're seeing, but I've been around long enough to know that sometimes kids just go through odd things."

"And his dad?" Jensen asked tightly. That was one of the biggest reasons Jensen felt his worries had merit. If Micah came from a loving family, abuse would have been the last thought on Jensen's mind. But with a man who had been violent before and had a history of drinking too much? It made Micah's behavior worrisome.

"You're right. His dad is difficult." Ethan pulled a cloth out of his shirt pocket and began to clean his glasses. "I'm perfectly happy to support you in helping the boy, but unless we have some real, solid proof of abuse...I can't do anything. Bringing a false accusation like that down on someone's head wouldn't help anybody, least of all Micah."

Jensen's gut clenched. He knew Ethan was right. They needed proof, but short of a confession from Micah, or spying on the Derringers, Jensen had no idea how he was going to get that.

"Maybe Melody will perform one of her miracles tomorrow and Micah will open up to her," Ethan said. He patted the doorway again. "See you later."

Jensen waved, but didn't speak. He was afraid he would snap at his boss and that wasn't a good plan. As the only principal in the town of Seaside Bay, Ethan handled everything from crying five-year-olds to rebellious eighteen-year-olds. He knew how to be firm when necessary, and that included handling his staff. Right now, Jensen just needed to be grateful that Ethan was letting him push ahead with the reading group. It would have to do.

His eyes slid back to his phone and he realized he hadn't finished his conversation with Mellie. Picking up the device, he texted her the details for the next day, and she responded with a thumbs up emoji.

With that settled, Jensen gathered his papers, stuffed everything in his backpack and headed for home. The ocean breeze was chilly and the overcast clouds were threatening rain, making Jensen grimace and walk faster than normal. He pictured his umbrella sitting next to the front door where he had forgotten it this morning.

"Thirty years of living here," he grumbled as a few drops hit his forehead. "You'd think I'd learn."

His hair and clothes were fairly soaked by the time he arrived, giving him a chill. After drying off, Jensen headed straight to his guitar, the one thing he knew would help calm his mind.

Letting himself get lost in the music for a few minutes helped ease his anxiety and Jensen was soon relaxed, and he began to hum along to his new song. As his mind drifted, he came back to the thought of auditioning.

The pull of stage lights and performing seemed stronger than ever. It seemed the more he became stressed about work and Mellie, the more the idea of getting out of town appealed to him.

What's it going to hurt?

He watched his fingers as they plucked out the now familiar tune. There was no guarantee that he'd be able to help Micah, and despite his new attraction to Mellie, she was still his best friend's little sister, making her off-limits. "If she was even interested," he huffed. Her brilliant smiles and kind words were given to everyone. She'd never treated him differently, giving him no reason to think she'd welcome any advances from him.

He looked at his phone. For a minute, he felt a great weight sitting on his shoulders. *Do I? Don't I?*

Finally, with a growl, he grabbed his phone and turned on the camera. "It's not life or death," he grumbled as he set everything up. "It's one song and I'll probably never get picked." He put the phone just right in order to video himself. "There's nothing holding me here and I'll never know what I can do until I try."

Settling the guitar, he took a deep breath and pressed record. He might not have a real shot at getting chosen, but at least he wouldn't have any real regrets either.

CHAPTER 9

M el pushed through the front doors of the Seaside Bay school, the rush of air-conditioning making her shiver. "Why do they keep schools so cold?" she murmured, rubbing her upper arms when goosebumps broke out all over her skin. Her light, long-sleeved shirt wasn't much help against the direct blast of air.

Walking into the office, Mel waved at the front desk secretary. "Hi, Mrs. Windsor. How are you today?"

"Well, Melody Frasier," the older woman said with a wide, toothy smile. "I haven't seen you in an age, honey."

Mel leaned onto the desk. "It has been a while. I don't think I've volunteered since last spring at Sadie's."

Mrs. Windsor nodded. "That sounds about right. So what brings you in today?"

"Jensen asked me to help with a reading group." Mel glanced at the clock on the wall. "They start right after school, so I'm here a little early in order to help set up the room."

"I'm sure Mr. Tanner will be grateful for your assistance." The secretary held out a clipboard. "Just sign in and I'll take care of the rest."

"Got it." Mel filled out the row of boxes and waved before heading farther into the school building. The classroom was easy to find since the school wasn't very large, and after a quick glance, Mel saw that the meeting room was empty. She pressed the long silver handle down and walked in, flipping the light as she went.

Just as she was moving around the chairs, a loud shrill screech rent the air, startling Mel before she caught herself. "Geez. It's like you've never heard a school bell before." Shaking herself, she went back to rearranging.

Her nerves were definitely on edge. Ever since promising Emily that she would try her hand at capturing Jensen's attention, Mel had been as nervous as a young girl on her first date. While she'd flirted with boys over the years, Mel had never purposefully tried to gain someone's attention. And to make it worse, this wasn't just any old someone. This was the man she already loved, and the possibility of rejection nearly suffocated her.

But what do you have to lose?

It was that exact thought that had gotten Mel through the night and into the school today. She didn't have anything to lose. Jensen was already threatening to leave, so Mel wasn't truly out anything by seeing if she could convince him to stay.

The door opened behind her. "Hey, Mellie."

She tensed, still hating that nickname, but trying not to care. She spun with a smile on her face. "Hey, Jensen. How was school?"

Jensen rolled his eyes. "My honors class had a test today. You'd think I was asking everyone to give up their first-born child with how much moaning and groaning there was."

Mel laughed. "I always hated tests."

Jensen shrugged. "You and every other kid, apparently."

Mel bit her tongue, but decided was as good a time as any to get started. She straightened her shoulders. "But I'm not a kid anymore." She tried to lower her voice a little, hoping it came across as mysterious and not a chain smoker.

Jensen's head snapped in her direction and he paused.

She held still while his eyes dropped a little before snapping back up. It looked like he was having an internal battle, and Mel was more than happy to let him have it. She was nervous enough as it was.

"No..." He said warily. "You're not."

Mel nodded, then turned back to her work as if nothing was wrong. Her neck felt like it was on fire and she knew that Jensen was watching her, but Mel did her best to appear unaffected. She was trying to get his attention, yes, but she absolutely would not throw herself at him. Her plan was to be more subtle about it. Touch his arm, smile, flirt...and if that didn't work, she would ask him to dinner or something equally as daring.

The door opened again and Mel turned, her smile already pasted on her face.

"Hello, Jack...Eliza..." Jensen nodded at the kids coming in. "Glad you could make it."

The tension from earlier dissipated as students filtered into the classroom. Mel greeted each student with a little wave, but waited in the back, knowing Jensen would let her know what he needed her to do.

Soon they had around ten teenagers in the group, but Jensen kept watching the door, as if he was waiting for someone else. Finally, he sighed, sounding disappointed, and turned to the group. "Welcome, everyone. We're glad to have you here." He moved to the front of the group. "For anyone who doesn't know, I'm Mr. Tanner and this is Melody Frasier, or Ms. Frasier to you," he explained, eyeing the students.

Mel bit her lip to keep from cracking up. Jensen was such a sweetheart, so to see him acting in charge was fun to watch.

"The purpose of this group—"

The door opened and every head in the room spun toward the sound. Mel frowned slightly when a boy in a black hoodie, his face obscured by not only the jacket, but his long hair, came slinking into the room. His clothes didn't fit his growing body very well and Mel felt a momentary sense of fear at the "stay-away-from-me" aura he exuded.

She shook her head slightly, pushing the dark thoughts from her brain. *He's a teenage boy. So he's a little goth. If he's part of this group, he can't be all bad.*

"Micah," Jensen said a little too quickly.

Mel realized this was who Jensen had been waiting for.

"Awesome, man. Thanks for coming."

The boy nodded, but didn't speak. He slipped into a seat that was just outside of the circle, as if he didn't quite want to be part of the group.

Mel couldn't seem to keep her eyes from watching him. She couldn't decide if Micah was going to pull out a knife and steal everyone's wallets, or if he was simply awkward. At his age, it could easily be either one.

"Today, we're going to break into pairs," Jensen continued. "Let's get to know each by talking about our favorite books, poems or stories. Whichever you want." He smiled, his hands gripping the desk as he leaned back on it. "Feel free to break down why you enjoy something as deeply as you want. This is going to run a little like a book club, so eventually we'll all read stuff together and pick it apart. I'm hoping to use this as a way to not only teach how an author does what he does, but how we can do it in our own writing." His eyes roamed around the room. "You've all been invited because you showed exceptional skills in writing, though you each have different strengths. I want to help you build those strengths, but also find your weaknesses and change them." He smiled and Mel almost sighed at how wonderful it was. "Any questions?"

"Yep." A big kid in the back leaned his chair on two legs. "Who gets to chat with Cute Smoothie Girl?"

Mel felt her cheeks flush. Compliments always seemed to have the same effect on her.

"Apparently not you," Jensen shot back, causing most of the group to laugh and the boy to scowl. Jensen stood and folded his arms over his chest. "Her name is Ms. Frasier and she's to be treated with respect." He raised his eyebrows. "Got it?"

The teenager rolled his eyes and nodded. "Yeah, yeah."

"Great. Okay, go ahead and start pairing off." After he finished speaking, Jensen took a few steps to arrive at Mel's side. "Sorry about that."

Mel smiled. "No worries. Every woman likes to hear she's cute."

Jensen chuckled and rubbed the back of his head. "Yeah...anyway." He cleared his throat. "Would you mind pairing with Micah?"

Mel's eyebrows went up. "Micah? Really?"

Jensen nodded, his eyes darting from the boy in question and back to Mel. "He's a bit of a loner if you can't tell, and I'm hoping your incessant sunshine will help break through his barriers. He's really gifted."

Mel studied the boy for a minute, who remained in his seat, watching the other kids pair up, but not participating. Her heart went out to him and she nodded, turning back to Jensen's beautiful pleading gaze. "I'm on it."

JENSEN WATCHED MEL walk confidently toward Micah. Her body language was open and honest, and her smile blinding. *There's no way he can resist that,* Jensen thought with a smile. Micah was going to be putty in Mellie's hands, Jensen was positive of it. Not even the surly loner could resist her warmth.

His smile faded as he thought about their moment before the students had arrived. He'd made a comment that she'd corrected. It was the second time in a couple of weeks that he'd been told she wasn't a young child anymore. It had been hard not to let his eyes wander to her curves as visible proof that she wasn't a teenager anymore. The attraction he'd been fighting for days had come roaring back and Jensen had been unable to look away, though Mellie had gone about her business as if she hadn't just flipped his world upside down.

Now who's putty?

That small sarcastic voice in the back of his head was way too close to the truth sometimes.

"Mr. Tanner?" Jensen turned to the girl who was trying to get his attention. ""Eliza, what can I do for you?"

"What do we do if our favorite books are in completely separate genres?" she asked, folding her arms over her chest.

Jensen almost laughed at the pout in her tone, while the boy next to her, Darrin, was grinning smugly. He was the one who wanted to talk to Mellie and Jensen immediately knew the boy was going to enjoy playing devil's advocate. "There's nothing wrong with reading different genres. We can learn to appreciate all of them in one way or another," Jensen said.

Eliza rolled her eyes. "Better tell that to Big Head over here." She pointed a thumb in her partner's direction. "He claims that romance is only for women who can't get a guy on their own and isn't worth the paper it's printed on."

Jensen whistled low. "Romance is the biggest genre in the world. If what you're saying is true, then that tells me the problem isn't with women, but the fact that men don't know how to romance them properly, leaving the women to look for fulfillment elsewhere."

Eliza crowed, pumping a fist in the air, and the other girls in the room clapped and added their own two cents.

Darrin sulked and pointed a finger at Jensen. "Where do you fall into that category, then?" He grinned. "Are you romancing your woman the right way? Or does she read books in her spare time?"

Jensen's collar felt tight and he had to fight the urge to look over at Mel. "Considering I don't have a 'woman,'" he used his fingers to emphasize the word, "I don't fall into either category."

"You're not dating anyone, Mr. Tanner?" Eliza asked, her eyes wide. "Why not?"

Jensen put his hands in the air in surrender. "This club isn't about my love life...or lack thereof," he added with a grin he didn't feel. The move worked, and the students laughed at his joke. "Get back to discussing your books, please."

Grateful they hadn't given him any more grief about dating, Jensen walked around the room, listening in on conversations and offering his own opinions when helpful. Through it all, his eyes kept drifting back to Mellie and Micah.

At first, the entire conversation had been one-sided with Mellie talking animatedly, her hands waving and soft laughter floating through the air. Each bit of that seemed to strike Jensen's chest like an arrow. He wanted to step closer, to listen to what she was saying and let her speech wash over him, but he held himself in check. *She's beguiling me more than she is Micah.*

This situation might be more problematic than he thought. He had assumed he could keep his attraction in control, but fifteen minutes in, and he was already struggling. He stepped up to another group, sitting down in order to force himself to pay attention to the conversation.

"All I'm saying is that Frodo was weak," one of the boys said. "If you can't handle the heat, you gotta get out of the way."

"Are you kidding me?" his partner asked in shock. "He won. He got the ring back to Mordor."

"Yeah...but barely. He almost gave in a dozen times."

"But he didn't, which is exactly what makes him so strong."

Nope. Jensen quickly stood back up and walked away. There was no way he was getting in the middle of that conversation. The pairs spoke for another half-hour before Jensen finally called the group to a close.

"Thanks so much for coming!" he said, making his voice louder than usual in order to be heard. When everyone quieted down, Jensen also dropped his volume. "I hope you enjoyed talking and debating." He smiled, knowing some of the conversations had been more like fights, but nobody had walked out, so he would count it was a win. "Do we want to assign a book for next time, or should we keep things random for now?"

The kids looked at each other and several shrugged.

"Random."

Jensen looked over to see Mel smiling widely.

"I think it's great to hear what others are enjoying," she said, glancing to Micah, who was studying a hole in his hoodie.

"Does that work for everyone?" Jensen asked the group.

Most of the heads nodded.

"Are we doing partners next time, again?" the big kid, whom Jensen found out was Eric, asked.

Jensen pursed his lips. "We'll see how everyone feels. It might be good to bring up a topic to the whole group and have a full discussion."

When most of the kids nodded, Jensen clapped his hands. "Okay. That sounds like a plan. See you next week." Once a week wasn't quite as often as Jensen wanted the group to meet, but it's all he'd been able to get permission for. The group was mostly an excuse to keep an eye on Micah, but it still had to follow the rules.

It only took a few seconds for the classroom to be emptied of students, leaving just Mellie and Jensen. He stood from where he'd been leaning on the desk and began straightening chairs. "So...how'd it go?"

Mellie made a noncommittal noise. "Tell me about Micah," she said softly, helping him clean up.

Jensen squished his lips to the side and paused. "That might take a while." His eyes widened when Mellie sashayed in his direction.

With that kind of walk, there was definitely no mistaking her for a young girl. Jensen felt his neck heat as she got into his space. His heart began to pound and he had to clench his fists to keep from reaching out for a strand of her silky hair. *LITTLE SISTER! LITTLE SISTER!* His mind was screaming at him, but his body wasn't listening. Her lips looked plump and her eyes intense as she held his gaze.

"How about you eat dinner with me and you can tell me the story?" she asked, her head tilted slightly to the side.

"Dinner?" He gulped. Why did she make it sound like more than a business meeting?

Mellie shrugged and backed off a little, letting Jensen breathe. "Only if you—" she started, then she stopped and straightened her shoulders. "Yes," she said firmly. "Dinner."

That darn shift happened again as Jensen kept eye contact. Things were changing within him and he was struggling with how to handle it. It was impossible to miss that Mellie was inviting him on a date and a large part of Jensen wanted to say yes. She was beautiful, she was kind, she was the happiest part of his life...but she was also his best friend's sister and that should trump everything. At the moment, however, it felt less important than it should. "Okay," he said, praying desperately that he wouldn't regret this decision.

CHAPTER 10

Mel looked in her rearview mirror and applied some lip gloss with a trembling hand. She was going on a date. A real date. With the man she loved. She had no idea if Jensen was viewing it as a date or not, but Mel certainly was. It was just the two of them and they would be at a restaurant. It was definitely a date.

A shadow came up to her window and she looked out, swallowing hard. Jensen looked larger than life as he waited for her. Grabbing her keys and purse, she opened her door and stepped out, clicking the lock on the door as she went.

"Ready?" Jensen asked, a soft smile on his face.

Mel nodded, not trusting her voice to stay steady. Jensen walked at her side with his hands stuffed in his pockets. He brought one out to hold the door open for her and Mel gave a quiet thank you as they walked inside.

"Table for two, please," Jensen said.

It only took moments for them to be seated.

Mel kept her eyes on the table, toying with her menu, unsure how to break the ice. She'd gotten him here and now she had no idea what to do with him.

"Why don't we order and then we can talk about Micah?"

She snapped her head up. Mel had almost forgotten that Micah was the reason for their little meeting. She'd been so excited, yet terrified of having dinner with Jensen alone that the mysterious student had completely slipped her mind. Her cheeks flamed with embarrassment and she thanked her lucky stars that she hadn't done something too crazy like reach for his hand or something. "Sounds good," she said, forcing a calm she didn't feel. Those all too common feelings of rejection were slithering down her spine, but Mel pushed them away.

We're at a restaurant. That's a step in the right direction. It's not like Rome was built in a day.

Her thoughts helped calm her a little. This was more than she'd ever had before, so she would count it as a victory. Besides...Micah's story really did intrigue her. The boy seemed brilliant, but something was holding him back, and Mel wanted to know why.

Five minutes later the menus and their waitress were gone, leaving them to their awkward silence.

"So..." she started, tapping her fingers on the table. "Tell me about Micah. He seemed like a nice boy."

Jensen huffed. "He is...most of the time."

Mel raised her eyebrows.

Jensen sighed and leaned his arms on the table, closing the distance between them. "Since I pulled you into this whole literary group thing, I'm going to trust you with a secret, okay?"

Mel frowned but nodded. "Go ahead."

"Micah is the whole reason I started this club."

Mel waited, but Jensen had paused like this should be really significant. "Okay..." She tilted her head a little. "Is that supposed to mean something to me?"

Jensen grinned. "Not necessarily. But I figured you'd have a question."

Mel tapped her lip. "Is this where I say, 'Why would you start a club just for Micah? Especially since he didn't seem very excited to come'?"

Jensen chuckled. "There's that curiosity I was waiting for."

Mel laughed softly. "Okay, you got me. Why did you?"

Jensen's humor dropped and he leaned in even farther. "Because I'm suspicious that Micah's home life isn't very...safe."

Mel's eyes widened and her jaw dropped. "What?" She winced at the volume in her tone, bringing her voice down and leaning across the table to meet Jensen. "You think he's being abused or something?"

Jensen looked dead serious when he nodded. "I do."

"How do you know?" Mel felt like she might cry. The idea of any child being hurt was enough to give her nightmares, but Micah seemed like such a decent kid. Having a personal connection to someone struggling seemed to make it all the harder. If he was having a hard time at home, it would certainly explain some of his appearance and behavior.

Jensen grimaced and dropped her gaze. His eyes stayed glued to the shiny wooden table between them. "I don't for sure, but I've seen a couple of things that make it suspicious."

"So you what? Built the club so he'd have a good place to go to after school?" Mel tilted her head down, trying to catch his gaze. "Why don't you just tell Principal Nielsen?"

Jensen brought his eyes up to hers. "Not exactly, and I have." He scrunched his nose and pushed a hand through his hair. "I spoke to Ethan a couple weeks ago so he could ask Micah's other teachers to keep an eye out. Not only has Micah become more withdrawn this year, but some of his writing has started to get fairly dark, making me think he's battling some difficult demons."

"That's horrible," Mel whispered, her heart breaking for the boy.

"But no one else has seen anything suspicious," Jensen continued. "Without solid proof, we can't call in Child Services or interfere in any way."

"So you're trying to find that proof," Mel said with a slow nod, everything becoming clear. She frowned after thinking for a moment. "But why ask me to help? Surely he'd be more likely to open up to a teacher he already knows?"

Jensen grinned and shook his head. "Do you really have no idea?"

Mel leaned back, feeling like he was insulting her in some way. "About what?"

"About how you make people feel," Jensen said. He grinned like a little boy, tugging at Mel's heart and making her less frustrated. "Mel-lie, everyone *adores* you. Even the people who have no idea who you are. Your bright personality just draws people into your orbit and they always walk away a better person."

She blinked rapidly, trying to stop the impending tears. *If that's the case, why doesn't it work on you?* She wanted to ask, but she held her tongue. Jensen might not have any designs on her romantically, and obviously hadn't caught on to the fact that she was trying to ask him out, but he at least thought good things about her, and that had to count for something.

"I asked you to help because I hoped that you being *you* would help open Micah up."

Mel could barely see the table as she nodded. "Thank you," she choked out. "That's really sweet of you."

Jensen chuckled, and Mel nearly jumped out of her seat when his warm hand landed over her bouncing fingers. "Don't thank me," he said. "I pulled you out of your own life for my own selfish reasons. I'm just hoping that it'll pay off enough that you won't hold it against me."

"I could never hold it against you, Jensen," she said, daring to look up at him. "I'm flattered that you think I help people feel better. It's one of my goals to build up those around me, so your words mean that I'm succeeding in some way, and that's one of the best compliments I've ever gotten." *The BEST one would be to hear that you have feelings for me, but for now...this will do.*

Jensen sat back in his seat, his posture relaxed as he smiled at her. She immediately missed the weight of his hand on hers. "Well,

I only speak the truth." He paused for a second. "Anyway, do you mind telling me how your conversation with him went? Maybe he said something that'll give us an idea as to what's going on."

Mel pursed her lips. "Sure, but I'm not sure it'll be of any help. Although now that I know the true objective, I'll be sure to do a better job next time."

JENSEN NODDED HIS UNDERSTANDING, then waited. She was so beautiful sitting there in the waning light. The window behind her was turning orange and pink, casting its brilliance on her blonde hair, which swished enticingly around her shoulders today. She often wore it up in a high ponytail, which matched her exuberant energy level. Today though, she looked softer and more approachable. The blonde locks curled just slightly at the ends, though the rest was straight, and was the perfect canvas for the colors coming through the window.

The dwindling light also caused some light shading on her face, highlighting high cheekbones, a thin nose and soft pink lips. In a word, she was stunning, and Jensen wished he was brave enough to make this something more than a business meeting.

He had thought she was inviting him on a real date back at the school, but during the break they'd had between school and dinner, he grew doubtful. Why would Mellie suddenly ask him out? She'd never given any indication that she had feelings for him. *I must just be projecting my own emotions toward her.* It all seemed too sudden and he decided he had to proceed with caution. They had a good friendship and Jensen didn't want to mess that up, especially the one with her brother.

"We definitely didn't talk about home," Mellie said before taking a sip of her water. "At first he didn't really seem to want to talk at all, but he lightened up after a bit." She gave him a sheepish grin. "I probably bored him silly with my talk of romantic suspense novels, but Micah took it all in stride." She pushed her lips out, a move she did when thinking. "After I finished, I began to ask him questions and he finally broke down and started telling me about his favorite story."

"What did he talk about?"

Mellie laughed softly. "He's a fan of Edgar Allan Poe."

Jensen nodded. "Makes sense. The dark themes of humanity definitely would appeal to Micah based on what he's been writing in his poetry portfolio." Jensen tapped his fingers against the table. "Maybe that means he really is just going through a phase." He shook his head. "Maybe he's just going goth at the moment and there's nothing to worry about."

"Do you know his parents at all?" Mellie asked. She stiffened and leaned back when their waitress came by. Neither of them spoke while their meals were being delivered. "Thank you," Mellie said, smiling at the worker.

Jensen did the same and then they waited until they were alone again before restarting the conversation.

Mellie gave him an expectant look. "His parents?"

Jensen nodded. "Yeah. His mother is gone, but he lives with his dad." Jensen glanced around to be sure no one could hear, then leaned in a little further. "Mitchell Derringer."

Mellie's eyes widened. "Really? That's Micah's dad?"

Jensen nodded. Apparently the man's reputation had spread farther than the school and the bars. "Do you know him?"

Mel made a face and shook her head. "Not really, but the couple of times he's come into the smoothie shop, he always..." She bit her lip. "Never mind."

"What?" Jensen asked, setting down his fork. His stomach curdled, knowing he wasn't going to like what she had to say.

Mellie shook her head. "I don't want to say anything. It was more a feeling anyway."

"Mellie."

She looked at him and sighed. "I really wish you'd stop calling me that."

Jensen jerked back a little. "Wait...what?"

Mellie made a face and looked down at her food. "Mellie. I want you to stop calling me Mellie."

"Why?" Jensen completely forgot about the other topic. He'd always called her Mellie. Why was this an issue now?

She took a couple of deep breaths before meeting his eyes. Her greenish-blue gaze was mesmerizing and he felt captured. "Because Mellie sounds like a little girl. It's what you called me when I was younger, Jensen, and I'm not a little girl anymore."

"I know that," he automatically said, defending himself. Oh boy, did he know it. He just wouldn't tell her it was a recent revelation.

"Do you?" she pressed. "Because you still treat me like I'm a young girl and as much as I don't want to hurt your feelings, I'm tired of it. I'm an adult. I've got a degree and I own my own business, for heaven's sake." Her breathing was heavy and Jensen could see her fingers shaking slightly as she reprimanded him.

Having known her as long as he had, he knew those words couldn't have been easy for her. Mellie...Melody...never rocked the boat unless she was teasing her brother.

"I mean...you call me in to volunteer, thinking I can help one of your students who might or might not have an abusive situation at home, but you can't address me as an actual adult?" She leaned back, pressing away from the table. "This was a bad idea. I shouldn't have come. I'm sorry."

He could see a sheen in her eyes as she began to stand and Jensen panicked. "Wait." He lunged across the table and grabbed her hand. "Please. Sit."

Mellie...he mentally slapped himself. It was going to take some work to think of her as anything else. *Melody* was right. He treated her as a young girl, but still asked adult things of her. It wasn't right. He needed to get his act together.

Melody sighed and sat back down. "I'm sorry," she began, but Jensen stopped her.

"No...I'm sorry." He frowned. "You're right. You're not little and I can't treat you one way and expect you to behave a different way. I'm sorry." He made sure he kept eye contact with her the whole time and he was glad he did. Otherwise, he would have missed the shock and following warmth in her eyes.

That look had him reassessing his earlier doubts. Melody was definitely not looking at him as a friend. There was visible excitement and an invitation in her gaze. Jensen had seen it many times before, but it had never been coming from a woman who piqued his interest. The last couple of weeks, however, had definitely had Jensen's interest shifting.

His little friend was all grown up and was turning heads...his.

"It's all right," she said softly, relaxing in her seat.

"Think you can handle a little bit more of my company?" he asked, giving her a hesitant grin.

Those beautiful jewels of hers twinkled in mischief. "I think I can handle that."

"Good." Jensen dug into his dinner. "Let's finish up here and then maybe I can talk you into feeding me those Twinkies you always keep hidden in the cupboard."

Melody gasped. "How did you know about those?"

Jensen winked at her, feeling much bolder than he had earlier. He was now confident she was interested in him, and that gave him a boost he had been lacking. If the attraction went both ways, then surely Benny couldn't object. At least Jensen hoped that was the case. "Do you really think you could have Benny and me over for dinner so many times and he wouldn't sniff out anything with sugar in the house?"

Melody snorted. "I should have known. That big lug has the nose of a hound dog."

Jensen laughed. "Too true." He raised his eyebrows. "Think I can talk you into letting me in?"

Melody twirled her spaghetti and peeked at him from under her lashes. "I think we can work that out."

Hope blossomed in Jensen and suddenly life wasn't quite so boring anymore.

CHAPTER 11

Mel's hands shook as she unlocked her door and let Jensen in behind her. He'd been in her home a thousand times, but tonight was different. For the first time ever, there was no brother standing between them as the connecting link. Jensen had come over only for Mel and she was terrified.

"Have a seat," she said, waving to the couch. "Can I get you something to eat?" *Oh my gosh, I did not just say that...* She wanted to smack herself upside the head. They'd just come from dinner, but her nerves had her acting like a dolt.

Jensen chuckled. "Other than the promised Twinkie, I think I'm good."

Mel forced a smile and hurried to the kitchen. "Just for the record, I think it was you who promised yourself the Twinkie." She stood on her tiptoes in order to reach the tallest cupboard where she kept her stash. Experience had taught her that if she had to work for it, it kept her from overindulging. "Ahh!" she squealed when large hands landed on her waist. She spun, gasping for air, not knowing that Jensen had followed her into the kitchen.

Jensen's look was smug as he held her captive against the counter. "Need some help?"

More than you know...

She cleared her throat. "Uh..."

Jensen's grin grew and his hands flexed on her waist. "I didn't know you could be speechless."

Mel laughed, feeling slightly awkward. "You're making it hard to think straight," she admitted in a whisper.

Jensen's face grew serious and his hands fell away. "Mellie..." He gave her an apologetic look. "Melody...I..."

Rejection hit her chest so hard that Mel was sure it left a bruise. Biting her cheek to hold back a sigh, she started to move to the side, the dessert forgotten.

"Wait."

Mel paused her escape, but didn't turn to meet his gaze. When he didn't speak again, she shook her head. "No worries, Jensen. I get it."

His long fingers wrapped around her arm, the grip firm but gentle. "No...I don't think you do." Slowly he spun her around, but Mel kept her head down. The tears in her eyes were embarrassing enough, she definitely didn't want him to see them. His free hand began to run up and down her arm in gentle caresses. "I never realized just how beautiful you were," he said, his voice sounding surprised.

Mel blinked rapidly, trying to clear her vision. She wanted to see the expression on his face, wanted to know if he was sincere or just placating her for a more gentle let-down, but the liquid stubbornly refused to go away.

"You were right in front of me all this time and I...I never saw you." His knuckle went under her chin, tugging a little when she resisted bringing her face up. The word 'but' hung heavy in the air, waiting to be spoken but not truly needing to be said. The crushing silence was enough.

Her neck and ears felt as if they would burst into flames at any moment and her eyes stung with the tears she was holding back. The pulse beating against her neck had to be visible if he bothered to look, and her shallow breathing nearly matched the pace at which it raced.

"Look at me," he said softly, his knuckle moving from one side of her jaw to the other, tickling the skin and leaving giant goosebumps in its wake.

Mel pinched her lips together and shook her head. She was too afraid to see the pity that would be swirling in his chocolatey gaze. "Maybe it's better if you just go," she said, her throat thick and slightly hoarse.

"Not until we talk this out."

It was high school all over again...sort of. This time, Jensen was far more aware of her feelings than he had been back then. When she'd tried to tease him into a sweet, Christmas kiss, he'd laughed, rubbed her hair and gone on his way, never catching on that she was dead serious in her desire for affection. Instead, she'd been placed firmly back on the "little sister" shelf and she'd run away with her tail between her legs.

This time, however, Mel feared she'd never recover. He wasn't oblivious this time around. She *knew* that he could see her crush, and for just a small moment in time...he'd responded, but apparently his good sense had taken back over before anything could happen.

"I get it," she said, her voice sounding weary. Part of her wanted to be angry, but she couldn't. It just wasn't in her nature to be angry with people. She was the one who smiled and then backed away when things got crazy. Fighting back didn't work for her. She tried to pull away again, but sighed when he held on. "Jensen, let me go. We can just pretend this never happened."

"No."

The unexpected answer had her eyes automatically snapping to his of their own accord. Her swift movement finally broke her tears free and they began to slowly slide down her scalding cheeks, freeing her vision, but giving away her heartache. "Why not?" she demanded. The least he could do was to be a gentleman about all this. It was embarrassing enough as it was. Years of her life spent in useless infatuation. Such a waste.

"Because, no matter how freaked out I am about the whole situation, I'm not ready to walk away yet."

She felt her eyes widen. A kernel of hope tried to blossom in her chest, but Mel held it in check. It was too early to count any victories. "I don't understand."

His dark gaze roamed her face, only adding to the heat she was already experiencing. "If your brother had any idea of how badly I want to kiss you, he'd strangle me with my own guitar."

Her knees shook and Mel grabbed his shoulders to keep from collapsing to the floor. "You want to kiss me?"

His nod was somber. "I have for a while now."

"Then why haven't you?" Her breathing sped up again and the sharp edges of her pain began to dull.

His grin was not a happy one. "Did you not hear what I said?" he asked, releasing her. Mel stumbled a little when he stormed away, his hands going to his head. "You've always been a young girl," he said, his voice a little louder than usual, letting Mel know he was really frustrated. Jensen never raised his voice...ever. "Benny's little sister. You weren't supposed to ever be more than that."

"And why not?" she asked, a foreign anger trickling in her chest. Why was it such a big deal that she was someone's sibling? Why, in the world of romance, did it matter who her brother was? "Am I supposed to be shut away or something for the rest of my life simply because I have an older brother?"

Jensen glared at her. "That's not it and you know it."

"Then what is?" she asked, throwing her arms in the air. "My brother is a decent guy..." She rolled her eyes. "Most of the time anyway." The words didn't relieve any of the tension, falling flat on the floor with an embarrassing clatter, and Mel pushed forward. "Point is, the guys he hangs out with are also bound to be good guys. Is it really that crazy to think I would have a crush on one of them?"

Jensen shook his head. "No. It's not crazy for you to like them...it's crazy for one of them to like you."

She sucked in a breath, which inadvertently flamed that little spark of hope. If she wasn't careful, it would become a roaring fire and she'd be burned when he turned her down, because right now, he didn't look like he was anywhere close to doing anything else.

THE EMOTIONS INSIDE of Jensen could have powered the entire city of Seaside if he'd been hooked up to the right machine. He felt as if a tornado was tearing through his chest, leaving nothing intact in its wake.

Her hurt was breaking him, yet the worry of ruining a friendship not only with her but with Benny was just enough to stop him from acting on his feelings. He and Benny had been friends for almost all of Jensen's life, and the idea of letting that go was terrifying.

But Melody's red eyes, tear-streaked cheeks and resigned face were just as difficult. He could feel his body straining toward her, wanting to hold her in his arms and hush her worries, kissing those soft red lips that were trembling with emotion.

"I don't understand what you wanted to talk about, then," she rasped. "You aren't willing to act on anything between us, so why draw this out? Just go home and we'll go back to the way things were."

Jensen slowly shook his head. He could understand her anger, though it felt odd to have Melody scolding him. She was the encourager of their group and this sad, hurting woman in front of him wasn't right. "I can't do that."

Melody looked away, pinching her lips into a straight white line.

You have to try, he told himself. *Just like the guitar thing, you'll always regret it if you don't see what could be.* Cursing the fear in his head and shoving it as far back as possible, Jensen stepped forward, determined to see this through. "Would you like to know why?"

Melody shook her head, her arms wrapped tightly around her torso, as if she were holding herself together.

Slowly, he reached out and rubbed his hands over her upper arms. Her skin was cold but soft and he felt it slowly warm under his touch, leaving him with a small smile of success. "Your brother is like *my* brother," he said softly, sliding his arms to her upper back and gently pulling her toward his body. "But I don't know how to ignore what I feel for you."

Those glistening ocean eyes snapped to his. "What?" she asked breathlessly. "What are you saying?"

"I'm saying that if we don't give this a try, I think we'll both regret it."

Her small hands landed on his chest and the touch sent a jolt of energy through his body. "Are you sure?"

Jensen nodded, his eyes dropping to her lips. They were slightly swollen from her crying, but that only made them all the more tempting. He drew their faces closer together, her quick breathing washing over his face as they closed the distance between them. "Melody..." he murmured, his lips just brushing hers as he spoke. "May I kiss you?" He closed his eyes and breathed her in, swallowing her lemony scent as if it were a drug. She was still shaking, but her grip on his shirt had tightened, anchoring the two of them together.

"Please," she begged, sending away the last bit of reluctance that Jensen had been nurturing.

Without letting himself debate for another second, he pressed his mouth to hers. If he'd been struck by lightning, Jensen didn't think the feeling could have been any stronger. As if two magnets had been kept just out of reach from each other for too long, the space between them snapped shut. Her arms wrapped around his neck and he felt her rise up on tiptoe in order to make their connection more solid. His arms tightened around her back, holding her to his chest, refusing to entertain the idea of ever letting her go.

Every bit of depression and loneliness he'd been drowning in lately was a distant memory as he held this lively woman in his arms. *It never felt like this with Melissa...* He knew he shouldn't compare the two women, but it felt impossible to keep the thoughts from surfacing. Melissa had been a good woman, but never had she stirred something so strong in him.

Melody's light reached corners of Jensen that he hadn't known existed and only made him pull her in even tighter. He couldn't get enough. She felt so perfect in his arms, as if she was always meant to be there.

He tilted his head, changing the angle in order to deepen the kiss and reveling in her light gasp at his actions.

"Jensen," she whispered, her voice hoarse.

"Hmm?" He brought his mouth down to just under her ear. He took the opportunity to suck in another lungful of her perfume. He wasn't sure if she actually put on the smell of lemons and berries or if it was a permanent part of her because of her work, but he wouldn't complain either way. It suited her better than any floral or musky scent ever could.

"We have to stop."

Jensen paused just long enough to realize she was right. His head was so clouded with her smell and the feel of her against his chest that he was losing all control over his thoughts and actions. He straightened, keeping his arms around her low back, unable to completely lose touch. "Sorry," he muttered, making a face.

She smiled at him, the happiness radiating from her lighting the small home from top to bottom. "Don't be," she said softly. Her fingers touched his cheek as if she couldn't believe he was real. "I absolutely refuse to admit how long I've been waiting for that kiss, but it was well worth it."

Jensen chuckled and tucked her under his chin. She snuggled in, wrapping her arms around his torso, and he sighed into the rightness of the contact. *This is where she belongs.*

"So where do we go from here?" she asked, her voice slightly muffled from being pressed into his shirt.

"Wherever we want," he quipped. He pressed a kiss to her hair. "Though it won't include more kissing at the moment, since I obviously can't control myself, so it better include Twinkies."

She shook against him, only this time, Jensen knew it was amusement rather than nerves. "I'll admit to being sad about the kissing, but Twinkies have been my go-to for years." She leaned back to smile at him. "They certainly do in a pinch."

He stole one more firm but short kiss. *Way too short.* "Then let's get me one before I lose my good sense...again." He let go of her, immediately feeling the loss, and walked back to the open cupboard. "Top shelf?" he asked over his shoulder.

"Mm-hm," she answered back.

Jensen felt around until he had a couple of packages in his hands, and pulled them down. He turned to face her, leaning his seat against the counter top, and held them in the air. "What will you give me for it?"

Melody's eyes widened before she gave him a sultry grin.

That might be even better than her regular smile.

She sashayed in his direction almost exactly like she had at the school this afternoon. Putting her hands on his chest, she kissed all along the bottom of his chin from one side to the other. "Will that do?" she asked against his skin.

"Yep," Jensen choked out. He quickly handed her one of the packages, tore his open and stuffed it in his mouth. If he didn't feed his addiction right this second, he knew he'd pull her back in and never let her go. Somehow, the thought wasn't nearly as terrifying as it should have been.

CHAPTER 12

"You made it," Jensen said from behind her. Mel spun around, grinning widely at his handsome face. She'd come early for the book meeting in order to set up the classroom again...and in order to see Jensen for a minute or two. They'd both been busy with work during the past week and hadn't seen each other much. She sucked in a surprised breath through her nose when he grabbed her head and brought their mouths together.

The touch was intoxicating and a little rough, which only made it more exciting. When he pulled back a minute later, Mel didn't open her eyes right away. Instead, she took in a deep breath, enjoying the feel of him near her and the tingling on her lips from his assault. When he chuckled, she reluctantly fluttered her eyes open, enjoying the happiness in his brown gaze. "Literature group needs to be every day if that's how I'm going to be greeted," she quipped.

Jensen's grin was smug and carefree, two looks that had been absent from his face for a long time. "If only that could be arranged," he said, running a knuckle along her jawline.

The door opened and they jumped apart like guilty teenagers. As students began to trickle in, Mel glanced at Jensen, who had walked to the teacher's desk and was leaning on it lazily. He winked at her, then put his eyes on the students and turned all business.

Mel grabbed one of the seats at the edge of the group. She left a seat next to her open, hoping that Micah would show up and be willing to chat with her again. By the end of the last session, she had been enjoying his insights, but now that Jensen had shared his concerns with her, she wanted more than ever to see if the young man needed help.

Mel's own mother wasn't exactly parent of the year, but at least she'd never hurt any of her children. Mel didn't want to see the teenager suffer and prayed that Jensen's suspicions were wrong.

Just like the week before, the group started without Micah, but five minutes in, he slunk into the classroom, slipping into the seat near Mel. She threw him a soft smile and wave, trying to be friendly without coming on too strong. Knowing she had an ulterior motive for speaking to him made her feel like some kind of spy and while that was a fun thought, she also felt a little guilty.

This is for his safety, she reminded herself. *He has no one else to look out for him, so it's not wrong to try and dig a little bit.*

"Ready? Break!" Jensen said, ushering the kids into groups.

Mel blinked. She'd missed his entire lecture. A dark chuckle to her right had her looking at Micah.

He grinned under the shadow of his hood. "You don't have any idea what he said, do you?"

Mel grinned sheepishly and shrugged. "Nope. I was lost in my thoughts."

The young man nodded. "Yeah...I do that too sometimes."

She turned to face him better. "Care to share, then?" She tilted her head and waited for him to speak. They were already off to a better start than last week.

Micah picked at a hole in his jeans for a moment. "It's pretty much the same thing as last week. Only this time, Mr. Tanner asked us to talk about something we wrote."

"Oh." Mel chewed her lip. "What if we haven't written anything?"

Dark eyes met hers. "You don't write?"

She shook her head. "Nope. I'm a reader, but not a writer."

Micah frowned. "Huh. Then why are you volunteering with this group?"

Mel grabbed a chunk of her long hair and began playing with it. "Because Je-Mr. Tanner asked me to."

The boy's lips began to twitch. "Are you, like, together with Mr. Tanner?"

Mel sat up straighter and dropped her hair. "That's not important at the moment. Let's get back to the topic at hand." They hadn't publicly shared their relationship yet and Mel certainly wasn't ready to spill the beans with a student first. But the young man was exactly how Jensen described him. Brilliant.

"Got it," he drawled, winking at her. "Who are we afraid to tell?"

"What?" Her jaw dropped and her eyes widened.

Micah rolled his eyes and grunted. "I'm not blind, Ms. Frasier. Just because I'm a teenager doesn't mean I can't read between the lines."

She forced herself to smile at him. "Actually, I think you're a little too observant."

He grinned mischievously.

"Why don't we put that brain of yours to work picking apart a piece of writing, hmm?"

He rolled his eyes again and folded his arms over his chest. "Fine. We can talk about you and Mr. Tanner later. But I'm not talking about my writing."

"Why not?"

Micah went quiet again and Mel worried she'd lost him.

"Because."

That's not a reason. The words came unbidden to her mind. An automatic response from her childhood. Bennett was forever giving that excuse and their mother never bought it, just like Mel wasn't buying it now. "Okay..." She decided she didn't have the right to pry deeper yet, but she hoped to earn it. "How about a book you read this week? It doesn't have to be your favorite, just something recent."

Micah tilted his head back and scratched at his chin. His hood fell slightly and Mel gasped.

"Micah. What happened?" The blue rings around his wrist could have only come from one thing. Mel put a hand to her churning stomach.

Micah jerked his hood back up and tucked his hands into his sleeves. "Nothing." He reached for his backpack, his movements jerky and frantic.

"Micah..." she pleaded, trying to grab his arm. She could feel the eyes of the entire room on her back, but Mel ignored them. "Wait, please."

Despite being thin, the boy was much stronger than Mel and he moved quickly to the door, yanking it open.

"Micah!" Mel shouted, running after him. She jerked the door open and ran after him. "Please stop!"

"Leave me alone!" he shouted over his shoulder, breaking into a run. His worn down sneakers squeaked on the linoleum floor.

"We can help you!"

Her call went unanswered and Mel skidded to a stop when he disappeared around a corner. She knew she'd never keep up with him—his longer legs ate the distance much too quickly. Tears pricked her eyes and soon trickled down her cheeks. Mel put a hand to her chest, a physical reminder that her heart was still beating, though it felt as if it was shattered.

"What happened? Jensen asked, coming up behind her.

With an anguished cry, Mel spun and threw herself into his arms. She cried heavily for several minutes while Jensen rubbed her back, waiting patiently for her to get control of herself. "He needs our help," she managed to squeeze through her tight throat.

"Come on." Jensen ushered her back into the classroom and put her in a chair. Grabbing another one, Jensen set it in front of her and sat down, grabbing her hands in his warm, comforting grip. "Now. Tell me what happened."

Mel glanced around, realizing the other children were gone. She hiccupped and took a deep breath. "You were right," she started. "Micah's being abused." Mel's tears began in earnest again. "And he needs us."

JENSEN'S HEART STUTTERED a little at the words he'd been dreading. When Micah ran and Mel followed, Jensen knew something bad was happening, but he hadn't been privy to their conversation to understand what. He gripped Mel's hands tighter. "What did he tell you?"

Mel shook her head, letting go of him and wiping at her tears. "He didn't tell me anything."

Jensen frowned. "Then how do you know?"

Her eyes drifted down to her wrist and she turned it this way and that, seeming lost in thought for a moment. "His wrist," she finally whispered. "His wrist was covered in a blue ring." She brought her fingers around her own and held it up. "That line could only have been caused by a tight grip."

"But he didn't tell you that's what happened?" Jensen asked. Disappointment hit him. Bruises were easily explained away and he worried that Child Services couldn't do anything on conjecture.

"No," Mel said, wiping her cheeks again. Her mascara was a mess and her cheeks blotchy, but her soft heart made Jensen all the more attracted to her. She barely knew this kid and here she was weeping over his home life. Most people became uncomfortable when something was out of the ordinary and it caused them to ignore signs and symptoms until it was too late. But not Melody. She loved everyone on sight, and that was just one of the reasons that Jensen loved her.

Well...not love. It was too early to think like that, Jensen knew. He had loved Melody as his friend, but things were shifting between them. The move from platonic to romantic hadn't been as difficult for Jensen as he would have expected, but he wasn't ready to say he loved her that way. And whether or not he could see himself falling in love with her wasn't a topic he wanted to worry about right now. Melody was overwrought and they needed to speak to the principal to see what could be done.

Jensen stood up. "Come on," he said, holding out his hand. "Let's go see what Ethan has to say about this."

Mel looked up at him, then slipped her hand inside his. "We have to do something," she said as they headed toward the door.

Pausing, Jensen dropped her hand and wrapped his arm around her, kissing the side of her head. "I know," he whispered reassuringly. "I want to help too, but I'll be honest. I don't know that a bruise will be enough. We need Micah to say he needs help."

Mel's eyebrows shot up. "You can't be serious! If it was just a bruise, why did he run out of here like a monster was trying to eat him alive?" She turned and put her hands on Jensen's chest, her fingers curling tightly into his shirt. "He's scared, Jensen. Didn't you see his face? He was terrified when he realized what I saw."

Jensen put his hands on her shoulders. "I get it, Melody. I do. I want to help as much as you do, but I'm not sure the school is going to take action. They need something more solid than what you're discussing."

"So...what?" she demanded, stepping back and putting her hands on her hips. "We just let him keep being abused because we don't have enough proof otherwise?" Her blonde hair flew through the air as she shook her head. "I can't live with that. I won't."

Jensen stepped forward and pressed a gentle kiss to her forehead. "Me either," he reassured her. "But right now we have to do things the right way, or we'll end up making things worse." He stepped back and opened the door for her. "For right now, let's talk to Ethan and see if this is enough to get started on."

Melody sighed, but nodded and walked into the hall. It only took two minutes to arrive at the office, where they were ushered back to see Mr. Nielsen.

"Jensen," the principal said, standing up from his desk and shaking Jensen's hand. "Ms. Frasier." He nodded and shook her hand as well. "Have a seat."

"Thanks, Ethan," Melody said softly, perching on the edge of her chair. Her knee bounced erratically and Jensen tugged his chair a little closer to her, resting a hand on her chaotic limb.

She smiled sheepishly and her leg stilled.

"What can I do for the two of you?" Ethan asked, his hands clasped on his desk. The middle-aged man frowned and glanced at his wall clock. "Aren't the two of you supposed to be in the reading club right now?"

Jensen cleared his throat and nodded. "Yes, but I let them out early."

Ethan's eyebrows went up.

"We had a run-in with...Micah."

Ethan's face fell and he leaned forward. "Did you find something out?"

Jensen looked over at Melody and nodded, giving her the floor.

Mel's bottom lip trembled again, but she took a deep breath and shared the story like a champ. Jensen held her hand the whole time, grateful for her strength and concern.

"So..." Jensen said once she was finished. "Is there anything we can do?" He held his breath. Realistically, he knew they probably didn't have enough to go on, but he prayed he was wrong. He was staying calm and logical for Melody, but there was a carnal part of him that wanted nothing to do with logic. The more he watched Melody cry, and the more he thought about what it would take for someone to squeeze a boy's arm so hard he bruised, the more the anger inside of Jensen built.

He wasn't a violent man by nature, but a part of him wanted to hit something. As if a punch to a wall...or a face...would help release some of the building pressure inside his chest.

Ethan slowly shook his head. "Honestly? I don't know. It might be enough to send someone by his house for a check, but unless Micah told you he wanted help, I'm not sure if we can do more than that. Obviously, no charges can be brought against Mr. Derringer without more than what we've got."

Jensen let out a long breath. It wasn't much, but it was better than nothing.

"That's a start, I suppose," Melody said weakly. She leaned forward. "Are you sure we can't do something more? Can we talk to the police at all?"

Mr. Nielsen shook his head. "Not until we have more. But if a home visit comes back suspicious, then the police will be definitely be brought in."

Jensen nodded. "Okay." He rose and held out a hand to Melody. "You'll let us know how that turns out though, right?"

Ethan stood and nodded. "Of course. As soon as I know something."

Jensen nodded his thanks again and led Melody out of the office door. He held her hand all the way out to the parking lot, walking toward her car. "You going to be okay?" he asked, taking her keys to open her door for her.

Melody shrugged. "Yeah. It's not like I'm the one being hurt."

Jensen cupped her cheek and rubbed his thumb over her cheek bone. "We'll get this figured out," he promised.

Melody put her hand over his his, nuzzling into his touch. "I sure hope so. I hate the thought of him being hurt, especially by his own father."

Jensen nodded. "Me too. But maybe it's not his dad. Or maybe it's something we haven't thought of yet."

"Maybe..." she hedged, but it was easy to hear she didn't believe it. "Anyway..." She looked into her car, then back at him. "I better run. Are you coming over for dinner?"

"Wouldn't miss it." Jensen leaned in and gave her a quick kiss. "Is everyone still planning on the bonfire tomorrow?"

Melody nodded. "Yep. Probably one of the last ones this year since it's getting too cold." She chewed on her lip. "Are you ready for everyone to know about us?"

"I think the whole school knows, so we might as well be the ones to break it to our friends." He smiled reassuringly, putting on a confident face he didn't really feel. Facing Benny tomorrow wasn't going to be fun, but it was necessary. Today's troubles just added to his already heavy burden. *At least by tomorrow night, one of the problems will be over...I hope.*

CHAPTER 13

"You okay?"

Mel nodded, but the movement felt jerky and she knew her nervousness probably shone off of her like a beacon in the night. She and Jensen hadn't really been trying to keep their relationship a secret, but they hadn't gone out and publicized anything either. Which meant that tonight's gathering was the first time her friends, and more importantly her brother, would see her and Jensen together. "Yes...no...maybe."

Jensen chuckled and tugged on his T-shirt collar. "I understand a little too well. I'm hoping I don't have to go to work Monday with a black eye...or two."

Mel stopped walking. "You don't really think Bennett will hit you, do you?" She searched Jensen's handsome face in the darkness.

He gave her a quick kiss. "No. But that doesn't mean he won't have something to say about it."

She nodded. "I know. I really don't want this to come between you two." She kicked off her flip-flops as they stepped from the rocky area into the clean sand. The grains were chilly between her toes and Mel snuggled into her sweatshirt a little deeper. She was grateful the wind wasn't very heavy tonight, which would have forced them to cancel the dinner. As anxious as she was about the upcoming confrontation, it was better to get it all out in the open as soon as possible.

Jensen squeezed her hand as the fire came into view. "Ready or not..." he murmured.

Mel tried to swallow the lump in her throat, but it was stuck tighter than a mussel on a rock.

"Jensen! Mel!"

The group turned when Caro called out their names and greetings immediately began ringing through the air.

Despite her anxiety, a smile spread across Mel's face. These were her people and she loved them. Surely it would all be okay. She waved and answered the hello's as she and Jensen walked into the light of the fire, their hands tightly clasped together.

Words died as everyone noticed their connection and the space grew quiet. Mel's heart began to beat fiercely against her ribcage and she leaned into Jensen's strength a little more, seeking comfort from the awkward staring.

"Well, well, well..." Caro drawled in her sweet Southern tone. Her bright blue eyes glowed in the firelight. "It's about time."

Mel's jaw dropped. "What?"

"Honey, you've been drooling over that man since long before I ever got into town," she said smugly. Caro leaned forward as if keeping their conversation private, though it was anything but. "I wondered if he'd ever wise up enough to see what was right in front of him."

Mel was still in shock that her crush had been so apparent when Jensen tugged her into his chest and wrapped his arms around her. "It took a bit, but I've managed to wake up." He grinned. "It might have taken a few knocks to the head, but..."

Most of the group chuckled, but Mel's eyes drifted to one person in particular. Bennett was slouched in his chair, leaning sideways so his chin was resting in his hand. He hadn't spoken yet and wasn't laughing with everyone else, so Mel had no idea what her brother was thinking. "Hey, Bennett," she said softly. She felt Jensen tense up behind her.

Bennett nodded. "Sis." His soft blue eyes drifted up and over her shoulder. "Jensen."

"Wassup?" Jensen asked, his voice quieter than usual.

Everyone grew quiet again and the air grew thick, oppressive even. Mel waited and waited for her brother to say something. To shout, scream, cuss them out...anything. But instead, the silence reigned and it was the worst form of punishment her brother could have given her.

After far too long with no movement, Ken reached out and whacked Bennett's arm. "Dude, you're killin them. Knock it off."

Bennett glared at Ken before breaking into a smile. "I'm the brother." He hit Ken's shoulder. "I have to give them grief. It's in the job description."

"Maybe so, but your poor sister over there is about to break down in tears, and Jensen looks like he's going to have a heart attack," Charli quipped from her spot at the food table.

Mel felt Jensen relax behind her, but she wasn't quite ready to let down her guard yet. However, she also wasn't positive she wanted to get into it in front of everyone.

"Come on," Jensen whispered in her ear. "Are you hungry?"

Mel shook her head. She wasn't sure she could eat anything right now without it coming right back up. Bennett still hadn't really addressed anything, though the bantering had picked back up among the crew.

"He's right," Felix agreed. "Brothers giving grief is in the job description. Says it right on page ninety-one of the manual."

"Manual?" Brooklyn asked. "Where in the world did you get a manual?" She folded one leg over the other. "My brothers obviously missed that part of their training."

"Your brothers are fifteen years younger than you," Felix shot back. "They probably can't even read yet."

"I'm more concerned about the fact that you said it was on page ninety-one," Ken said with a smirk. "I'm pretty sure Benny, here, didn't get past page ten."

"There were ten pages?" Bennett asked, bringing the laughter up a notch in the group.

"Thank you," Mel said softly after Jensen unfolded a chair for her. She perched on the edge, not quite ready to relax yet.

"Congrats," Genni said from Mel's right.

Mel looked over and let out a long breath. "Thanks." She smiled at Genni. "Could you also tell I had a crush on him?"

Genni shrugged. "That might not be a fair question," she hedged and Mel's heart fell.

Knowing her feelings had been available for everyone to see made her feel foolish and dumb.

"We've known each other a long time." Genni peeked sideways at Mel. "It's hard to hide feelings when you're a young teenager."

Mel groaned and slapped a hand to her forehead. "I'm such an idiot."

"Hey..." Genni soothed, leaning over to pull Mel's hand away from her face. Her smile was encouraging and understanding. "Don't worry about it. We were all rooting you on, but Jensen tends to be the quietest of the guys, so it was hard to tell what he was thinking." She pumped her eyebrows. "But I'll bet it's nice to have such a history with each other. You don't even have to go through that get-to-know-you-stage."

Mel laughed softly. "I wouldn't say that. Everything feels old and new at the same time. I mean...I know him, but I'm discovering I didn't *know* him. There's way more to a person than what they might show in a friend group like ours."

"True enough." Genni leaned back and she turned to look at her boyfriend, Cooper, before coming back to Mel. "Even though he lived in the house for a while, I'm still learning things about him every day." Her eyes twinkled with happiness. "And it's the best part of my life."

Mel smiled back, grateful to have someone who seemed to understand. "Mine too." She chewed her lip. "Now I just have to hope Brother Dearest won't give us a hard time, or make Jensen choose between us."

Genni shook her head. "He'll definitely give you a hard time." She shrugged. "I mean, come on, it's Bennett."

Mel nodded in grudging agreement.

"But he won't make Jensen choose." Genni patted Mel's hand. "He loves both of you too much for that. The teasing, on the other hand, might be epic."

"Great," Mel said dryly. "Something to look forward to."

JENSEN COULD FEEL BENNY'S eyes on his back. His hands felt clammy and he worried he would drop the plate he was filling, but miraculously, it stayed put. Taking a deep breath, he turned and met Benny's intense gaze. *Best to just get this over with.*

His strides were determined as he skirted the group and came up behind Benny's chair. "Ken?" Jensen asked, waiting for the police captain to catch his meaning.

Ken looked over his shoulder, over at Benny, then back up. "Good luck." The large man stood and walked over to the seat next to Mel that had originally been Jensen's.

Jensen sat down, feigning a confidence he didn't feel, and forced his body to relax into his seat. Once settled, he looked at his best friend again. "Go for it," he said.

Benny's head was tilted and his eyes narrow, but Jensen couldn't tell if he was angry or not. "I'm not sure where to start," Benny said.

Jensen shrugged. "Anywhere."

Benny sighed and pushed a hand through his blond locks. He'd been growing them out lately and they fell right back into his eyes, giving him a surfer-boy vibe. "I mean...I've always known that Mel had a crush on you." He glanced sideways at Jensen. "She annoyed us to death when we were younger and it was completely obvious."

Jensen nodded. He'd known that too, but what he hadn't known was that the feelings had lasted past middle school. *She must have just gotten better at hiding them,* he mused.

"But I always figured it was just an infatuation and that she'd grow out of it." Benny sat forward, his elbows on his knees, his eyes focused on the fire. "Care to tell me how it happened?"

Jensen twisted his lips into a grin. "Actually...it's kind of your fault."

Benny's head snapped in his direction. "What?"

Jensen took a moment to finish chewing before he answered. "Remember a couple weeks ago when you made some joke about Melody being all grown up and mothering you?"

Benny shrugged. "I don't know. I tease like that all the time."

Jensen nodded. "Okay, well after that comment, I had a strange epiphany." He made a face, knowing they were reaching the awkward stage of this chat. "I realized she *was* grown up." He poked at his food, his appetite starting to diminish. "I had always kept a picture of her in my head of the young, bouncy girl with pigtails. Bright smile, spreading sunshine and cheer everywhere she went." Jensen huffed an amused laugh. "You know what I'm talking about."

"Too well," Benny agreed. "The only part that's gone is the pig-tails."

"That might be the only part that's gone, but it's not all she is anymore," Jensen muttered. He took a moment to open his water bottle and wet his dry throat. "That night, my mental image was shattered." He shook his head. "Ever since, I just haven't been able to get her off my mind."

Benny put his hands over his ears. "Dude, if you start to wax po-etic about her womanly attributes, I'm gonna curl up and die. Then I'm gonna beat you up."

Jensen grinned, and the tension in his chest eased. This was the kind of teasing he understood and could handle. "Don't worry. I won't tell you about those things. But it wasn't just the physical part of her growing up that caught my attention."

"Good thing," Benny grumbled, settling back onto his knees.

"She's a good person, Ben. She's kind, generous, happy, and intelligent. I was kind of feeling stuck when we had that dinner, and now it's like the sun has come out from a long winter."

"No poetry!" Benny said, making a face. "Did you not hear me earlier?"

Jensen laughed. "Sorry. No more."

Benney growled and shook his head, then stilled. "In all seriousness," he said softly, "I know my sister is awesome and it only makes sense that you would see that too." He turned, his eyes softer than normal. "But what I want to know is...are you willing to protect her?"

Jensen frowned. "From what? Is she in trouble?" Micah flashed through his mind, but Mel wasn't in danger from that. That was a school issue that she was privy to, but wasn't technically involved.

"No." Benny shook his head and sat back in his seat. "But she does have a bigger heart than the rest of us combined. And that means it gets broken a lot easier."

Jensen gulped as he finally realized what his friend was alluding to. "I'll be honest, Ben. I can't promise I won't break her heart. I have no idea how our relationship will go. It's brand new, nowhere near being ready to make any kind of long-term commitment." He paused to swallow. "But I can promise that I'm not going into this lightly. It's not a game, she's not a plaything and I'm not planning to just have fun and leave her hanging. I like her. A lot. And amazingly enough, she likes me too. As long as we're both happy in this relationship, I hope to continue it."

Benny's face didn't change. "And Melissa?"

"What about her?"

"You've already been married. You're more experienced than she is."

Jensen shrugged. "I don't see how that has anything to do with Melody, other than the fact that I'm past the point of dating simply to date."

"You're not going to be comparing the two women and making Mel feel bad about it?"

"No." Jensen's answer was a little more harsh than it needed to be, but he wanted there to be no misunderstanding. Melissa had a place in his life, in his past. But he wasn't in the past, Jensen was in the present. And not only was Melody a part of that, but he thought she might also be a part of his future.

Benny studied him a little longer, then nodded. "Great. I'm glad to hear it." He grinned. "And I give you my blessing."

Jensen scoffed. "You make it sound like I'm marrying her or something. We're just dating."

Benny grinned. "I'm gonna have so much fun with that conversation, if we ever get to that point."

Jensen rolled his eyes.

Benny frowned. "I might have to go out and buy a gun. I mean, how can I intimidate anyone without a gun? My good looks won't keep men from wanting her hand."

Jensen groaned. "This is exactly why we didn't talk to you before."

Benny put a hand to his chest, feigning offense. "What? You purposefully kept this from me? It's like you think I might overreact or something."

"Or something," Melody's sweet voice broke through their chat and she stepped up behind Benny, kissing his cheek. "We okay?" she asked quietly.

Benny grinned and winked. "Yep. But you bring a boy home again and I really will pull out the shotgun. Maybe I'll prop a shovel in the corner, you know...just for fun."

"We don't have a gun," she said wryly. "And I don't live with you."

Benny scoffed and waved a hand through the air as if swatting a pesky fly. "Details."

Melody turned to Jensen. "Feeling better?" she asked.

Jensen nodded. "I'm just upset he called me a boy." Jensen winked at her. "I'm not even close to being a boy at all."

Melody laughed and Benny scowled. Grabbing a carrot, Jensen took a bite and grinned while he chewed. The conversation had gone better than he expected and it was nice to have things settled. *One problem down, one to go...* Now if only the situation with Micah could be resolved as easily.

Jensen pushed the worries aside. Tonight was for fun and friends. School problems would come easily enough on Monday. He'd worry about it then.

CHAPTER 14

Mel's foot bounced as the teenagers in the room chatted. Micah hadn't shown up and Mr. Nielsen was still waiting to hear from Child Services on how the home visit went. It was supposed to have happened yesterday, but the report hadn't come in and without Micah here, Mel had no way of knowing what was going on.

Waiting is going to be the death of me.

"Hey, Smoothie Lady!"

Mel snapped out of her thoughts and smiled at the young man calling her. "Hey. What's up?"

The boy grinned and jerked his head back to flip his hair out of his eyes. His smile was the kind that said *I know I'm good looking* and Mel had to hold back a laugh. Some of the teenagers in the shop would flirt with her when they came through and she always enjoyed giving them a bit of attention to build their confidence.

Although I don't think this guy needs any more confidence.

"I'll bet I can guess your favorite book," he said.

Mel swallowed her laughter. "Oh, yeah? What is it?"

He leaned back on the two rear legs of his chair, his grin widening. Before he could answer though, Eliza tossed in her two cents.

"I'll bet yours is *All My Friends Are Dead*," she snapped at him, folding her arms over her chest.

Darrin snapped his fingers and pointed at her. "You know, there's one called *I Can Make You Hot*." He tilted his head. "Want me to find it for you?"

Eliza rolled her eyes. "Only if you agree to read *How To Raise Your IQ*."

Mel's body was shaking as she tried to keep from giving into her amusement. The rest of the kids were breaking into sides and egging Darrin and Eliza on. It was the most entertaining thing Mel had seen in a long time.

"Okay, okay!" Jensen shouted, putting his hands in the air. Mel could tell he was trying to be serious as the leader of the club, but even he couldn't hide the twitching of his lips. "I think we need to call a timeout," he finished.

"Mr. Tanner?"

"Yes, Eliza?"

She smirked, her head tilting from side to side a little. "I think we should study Shakespeare for the next couple of weeks." She directed a sly gaze at Darrin, who looked completely unruffled by their verbal argument. "Maybe we can expand everyone's vocabulary a little. And...that way when I call Darrin a leathern-jerkin, crystal-button, knot-pated, agatering, puke-stocking, caddis-garter, smooth-tongue, Spanish pouch..." The hooting and hollering in the room had grown to epic proportions. "He'll at least have a chance of knowing what I'm talking about."

Darrin slammed his chair to the floor, his face turning red.

"Uh-oh." Mel jumped to her feet, but Jensen beat her there.

"And this class is over for the day," Jensen said in an authoritative voice. All humor had fled his face. "Thank you, Eliza, for showing off your memorization skills, but I think we've had enough for the day."

"This isn't over," Darrin said, jabbing a finger at Eliza's face.

She blew on her nails and buffed them on her shirt. "Got it, you luxurious mountain goat."

Mel had to turn away. She couldn't keep a straight face. The girl knew how to dish it out and obviously didn't let looks or popularity bother her, which was a point in her direction, according to Mel.

"Break it up," Jensen said. "In fact...just go home. We're done."

"But we still have ten minutes," one of the kids whined.

"Then use that ten minutes to figure out how to speak civilly to each other," Jensen said. "Now go home."

The chattering and continued banter was loud and obnoxious as the group moved into the hall. Once the door closed, it brought the volume level down immensely and Mel took a deep breath. "Wow," she said, moving to Jensen's side. "Remind me not to get on her bad side."

Jensen chuckled. "Yeah. She's pretty quick-witted. I have no doubt Darrin will be spending the next week building ammunition against her."

"Eh...they won't wait until next week to go at each other." Mel pumped her eyebrows at him. "My guess is they'll be kissing by tomorrow."

Jensen jerked back. "What? Did you not just hear that fight?"

"Nope. I heard some insane flirting." She smiled. "Ten bucks says they date."

Jensen scratched his chin. "I hope not. He's got a reputation as a playboy."

"I can see that," Mel mused, leaning against the desk and folding her arms over her chest. "He seems pretty confident in his women skills."

"Oh, are you referring to the fact that he was trying to flirt with you first?" Jensen glared at the door as if it would have some impact on the teenager who had already left.

Mel rolled her eyes and leaned over to kiss his cheek. "Don't worry. He's too young for me."

Jensen huffed. "If that's the only thing holding you back, then by all means..." He waved toward the hallway.

Mel laughed. "What in the world has you so upset?" She scooched closer to him and nudged his shoulder. "Care to share why you've been grumpy today?"

Jensen sighed and pushed a hand through his hair. "Sorry. I spoke to Ethan before club today."

Mel straighted. "And?"

Jensen stood and began to pace. "And nothing. Child Services said everything looked fine and Micah didn't give them any reason to think he was being hurt. Said the bruises on his wrist were from doing a house repair."

Disappointment dropped into Mel's stomach like a lead balloon. "I know what I saw, Jensen," she said firmly. "Only a hand could have made bruises like that."

Jensen nodded, but wouldn't meet her eyes. "I know, and I believe you, but Ethan is refusing to do anything more."

"Well, what do we do now? We can't just leave him there!"

His brown eyes finally met hers. "We can't take him away either."

"Says who?" Mel scowled.

Jensen's look softened and he came over, rubbing his hands on her upper arms. "I'm worried about him too, Melody, but it's not like we can take him home or something. We'd probably be accused of kidnapping. He's still underage."

She blew out a long breath and her muscles slumped. "This is so frustrating. The law is there to protect people, not force them to stay in a bad situation." Jensen's hands felt so good as they moved against her skin. Warm, strong, and capable were all terms that came to mind as he stood in front of her. She was falling farther and farther under his spell as they dated in earnest.

It wouldn't take much for her to feel like she could officially tell him she loved him, but she knew their relationship was much too new for those words yet. Not to mention, her concern over his desire for a guitar career was always in the back of her mind. She didn't know if he'd ended up sending in an audition or not, since the topic hadn't come up for a while.

She could only hope that if the situation did arise, he would prove to love her as much as she loved him, and that it would be enough to keep him in town and by her side.

"IT STINKS WHEN GOOD intentions backfire," Jensen agreed. He sighed. "All we can do is keep an eye out and report anything more suspicious."

"But if he doesn't come to the club, then how are we supposed to do that?" Melody asked, her eyes slightly watery.

Jensen leaned down and brought their foreheads together. "Don't forget I still have him in my ELA class. We'll figure this out." He jerked upright when the door opened and they both turned to see who had come in.

"Micah," Melody breathed. She jumped to her feet and rushed over to the young man. The young man winced and folded into himself, causing Melody to skid to a stop. "We missed you in the group today," she said, her voice trembling slightly.

Jensen slowly walked over, eyeing the teenager. He'd been teaching long enough that Jensen knew trouble when he saw it. Micah looked like a snake ready to strike. He was turned sideways from them, keeping his face in the shadows of his hood. His weight was leaning on his back foot and his entire body was shaking. "You need to stay away from my family," he said. His voice was gravelly, making him sound like a smoker.

"Micah..." Melody took another step forward, her hands up as if he was a skittish colt. "We just wanted—"

"No!" he shouted.

Melody jumped and Jensen pulled her backward, tucking her slightly behind him. For the first time ever, he was concerned that Micah might hurt someone. The boy was obviously scared, but if he lashed out, Melody would be caught in the crossfire. "Micah," Jensen said in a low, calm voice, "tell us why you're here."

"You sent someone to my house," he said, his voice having dropped to a whisper. "I know it was you."

Jensen nodded. "We were worried about you."

"You need to stop worrying about me," Micah sneered, his dark eyes glaring from under his hood. "My dad doesn't want you guys coming around anymore."

"Did he hurt you?" The question was out of Jensen's mouth before he could think better of it. He closed his eyes and sighed. Poking the wound was not usually the right way to go about getting answers.

"Look, I only came to warn you," Micah said, not answering anything. "We don't need your help. Stay away."

Melody shifted around Jensen's body and refused to be pulled back. "Let us help, Micah. Take us to your dad."

Jensen felt like his eyes would pop out of his head. "What?" he shouted, his reaction landing at almost the exact same time as Micah's.

"Let us talk to him," Melody pressed. "Maybe we can get him the help he needs."

Micah was shaking his head and even from under his hood, Jensen could see the tears in his eyes. Melody was getting through to him. "I can't," the teenager whispered, his voice breaking at the end.

Melody stepped forward, gently resting a hand on Micah's forearm. "What does it hurt to try?" she asked. "You're such a good boy. You deserve more."

Micah stiffened for a moment. "Talking won't help," he finally said, and the tension in his body faded some.

Melody's lips pulled into one of her sunshiney smiles. "How about we just walk you home, then? That way we can make sure you're okay before we leave?"

Micah's eyes darted from Melody to Jensen and back and several times. Jensen held himself still, trying to portray compassion and strength at the same time. He needed Micah to trust him. This was exactly the type of situation they trained for as a school teacher. If a student felt like they could trust their teacher, it made all the difference in helping get them out of a bad situation. "We'll just walk," Jensen assured him.

"Nothing else? You won't confront my dad?"

Jensen shook his head. "Not this time." Jensen refused to make a promise he couldn't keep. He would absolutely confront Mitchell if he had the opportunity. Despite the findings of Child Services, Micah's coming to them confirmed all their earlier suspicions. Home wasn't safe, and Jensen was determined to do something about it.

But he would start small, and right now, that meant making sure Micah knew he would keep his word.

Micah paused as if weighing what Jensen had said, then acknowledged the words with a nod before saying, "He won't like it."

"It'll make me feel better," Melody gushed, her hands clasping over her heart. "Just let us walk you home and see you safely there." She widened her smile, but Jensen could see the tension in her cheeks. "That way we can tell you what happened in class today! You missed the most epic insult battle ever."

Micah's right eyebrow slowly rose. "Who was it?"

Jensen relaxed when he realized Melody had gotten through to Micah and he was no longer a threat.

Melody clasped her hands behind her back and leaned in conspiratorially. "Darrin and Eliza."

Thin, dry lips twitched and Micah stuffed his hands in his front pockets. "This I gotta hear."

"You really do." Melody put out an arm, barely touching his shoulder as she guided him to the hallway.

Jensen quickly grabbed his backpack and followed behind them, keeping a slight distance between them. Right now Micah's connection was with Melody and that was just fine. If Jensen pushed, he might break the tenuous thread and now more than ever, that wasn't a good idea.

The wind had picked up during their time inside the school building and Jensen winced when it cut through his clothes, nearly freezing him where he stood. His jacket was still at his desk, but he didn't dare go get it. *This'll only take a few minutes. I can warm up later.*

He followed behind Melody and Micah, listening to their chattering as they walked several blocks down the street. Once outside of the main drag of town, they turned off to a small dirt road, which Jensen knew led to a trailer park. It wasn't a large neighborhood, but the mobile homes were filled with people from all stages of life. A few beach bums, older widows and single mothers, and of course Micah and his father, lived in the small, rundown units.

A burst of wind hit Jensen in the face and he realized that Micah's hood had blown back before he could stop it.

Melody gasped, her hands flying to her mouth. "Oh, Micah," she whispered thickly.

Jensen quickly stepped so he could see the boy's face, but paused when he saw the purple bruise high on the boy's cheekbone.

Micah scrambled to get his hood on, ducking his head away from the adults. "I have to go," he said, rushing away from them.

"No! Micah! Come back!" Melody started after him and Jensen had no choice but to follow.

CHAPTER 15

"Melody!" Jensen's voice called after her, but she ignored it, too intent on catching the fleeing student. When Micah's hood had fallen off, exposing that bruise on his cheek, Mel's heart had nearly stopped. She couldn't let him go back to his home. She just couldn't!

Micah leapt up a set of wooden steps just as strong arms banded around Mel, stopping her from running.

"What's going on out here?"

Everyone froze as Mitchell Derringer burst out of his trailer. A dark bottle hung from his fingertips, while his hair and shirt looked like they hadn't been washed in over a month. The potent smell of alcohol slapped Mel in the face and she shrunk backward, burrowing into Jensen's hold.

"Mr. Derringer," Jensen said, his voice as tight as his grip.

Mr. Derringer blinked a couple of times as if trying to get his eyes to focus. "Well...if it isn't Mr. Tanner," he drawled snidely. His dark head turned toward Micah. "What trouble did you get in now, boy?"

Micah shook his head and opened his mouth, but Melody couldn't seem to keep herself quiet.

"None, Mitchell," she said, straining against Jensen's hold. "We just wanted to see Micah get home safe."

Mitchell stared at her for a moment, then burst out laughing. "None?" His upper lip curled. "Don't you know this boy is nothing *but* trouble?" He turned and pushed Micah inside. "Get in there. You're late."

Micah's chest caved in as he made himself smaller to avoid his dad's swinging arms and Melody covered her mouth to keep back a sob. *We can't leave him here.*

"Calm down, Melody," Jensen whispered in her ear. "There's nothing we can do today. Just keep track of what you see."

Mel nodded her understanding, but she hated herself for it. She wanted to pull Micah out of that house and take him to her own. She wanted to feed him and give him a warm, safe place to sleep where no one could ever hurt him again. The thought of leaving him here was making her sick to her stomach and she prayed she wouldn't throw up.

"So…" Mitchell's voice was low and raspy. "I already had visitors yesterday, which makes me wonder just why I have more today." His bloodshot eyes narrowed. "You wouldn't know anything about those people snooping around my house, would you *Mr.* Tanner?" Mitchell's inflections told Melody just how the man felt about Jensen.

"I'm afraid I don't know them," Jensen said easily, pushing Melody to his side and behind his back ever so slightly.

She was impressed with his way to answer truthfully without giving anything away.

Mitchell's answering chuckle was deep and a little dark. It sent a shiver down Mel's spine. His face suddenly grew serious. "Get off my property and stay away from my boy."

"He's in my class, Mr. Derringer," Jensen said. "And he's an amazing student."

Mel straightened her shoulders at Jensen's defense of the boy. She wanted to yell, *"So there!"* but figured keeping quiet was her best move right now. Only her brother seemed to be able to get away with talking back that way.

The middle-aged man snorted. "I'm sure he is." His head slowly tilted. "But you need to know the boy's a liar. Any stories that he's been sharing with you are just that...stories." He grinned smugly. "Boy's got an imagination that could rival Disney's."

Mel didn't even realize she'd stepped around Jensen before it was already done. "He's a good boy, Mitchell. Don't tell me any different."

"Aha...pretty little Miss Frasier has come out to play, huh?"

Mel fought the desire to slink away from the way Mitchell made her feel. Even just speaking to him left her feeling dirty. Usually at the shop or in town, she'd make sure she kept a good distance from him, but today she was fighting for Micah, and showing weakness wouldn't help. "I've been helping him in an afterschool club," she said, stepping forward once more. She shook off Jensen's hold and smiled as kindly as she could. "He's really good with books and his writing—"

"So that's what he's been doing in the afternoons," the man huffed. He tossed his bottle to the ground, the trash thudding heavily in the dirt. He folded his arms over his barrel chest, then dark eyes raked over Mel, scaring her more than anything else up to this point. "Can't say I blame him."

"That's enough," Jensen said, his voice strong and demanding. He took Mel's arm again and tugged her back. "Look, Mitchell. We walked Micah home because we were worried about him. Our job is done, so now we'll leave."

"Want her all to yourself?" Mitchell yelled cheerfully at their backs. "Are you afraid she'll take a look at me and decide she wants something a little more...exciting?" That low chuckle filtered through the air again.

Mel noticed Jensen stiffen and slowly turn.

"Jensen," Mel warned. "Don't listen to him. You know he's just trying to rile you."

"What do you want, Mitchell?" Jensen asked, not responding to Mel's words. He faced the trailer, folding his arms over his chest, and puffed himself up a little. "We came to be neighborly, not for you to speak about Melody as if she's some kind of object."

Mitchell's eyebrows rose. "I didn't want anything. You came to me, remember?" His eyes went back to Mel and he made a point of licking his lips. "But now that you're asking..."

"Go near her and you'll regret it," Jensen growled, stepping between Mel and Mitchell.

Without his jacket on, Mel could see the outline of every muscle in Jensen's back and she was grateful he wasn't the type to sit around and grow soft. However, his anger was an emotion she wasn't used to, and it frightened her a little. "Jensen," she whispered, putting a palm between his shoulder blades.

Mitchell laughed at the display. "Looks like she's got you under her thumb."

"Jensen, let's go." Mel grabbed Jensen's hand, sighing in relief that he let her, and began to tug him away. "Let's just go."

"And don't worry about coming back," Mitchell called after them. "If any more of you school people come snooping around, they might find more than they can handle."

Mel had to tug harder on Jensen's hand, but he finally turned her way and began to storm out of the trailer park. His long legs ate up the distance too quickly for her to keep up and Mel found herself jogging every few steps. Considering how much she wanted to put distance between her and Mitchell's gross comments, she didn't mind the rush.

It wasn't until they turned the corner onto Main Street that she was able to take a deep breath and relax just a little. "I can't believe that man," she whispered. Her vision began to blur. "And we had to leave Micah there." She sniffled. "We just left him..." Her voice trailed off as she began to cry. All the emotions of the last few minutes came rushing into her all at once and her body began to shake.

Disgust, fear, anxiety, worry, anger, frustration...it all swirled into a vicious tornado that stole her breath and caused her to stop walking. Putting her hands on her knees, she stopped, trying to breathe through lungs that felt wooden and stiff. When her vision began to turn black, Mel knew she was in trouble.

"MELODY!" JENSEN LUNGED forward, wrapping his arms around her torso as she swayed on her feet.

"I'm all right," she whispered, her eyes squeezed shut as if in pain.

"Just breathe, sweetheart. That's it...in and out." His eyes darted all over her. The goosebumps on her skin let him know she was cold, which was to be expected, but otherwise, he couldn't figure out what was wrong. Mitchell had made some horrible comments, but he hadn't actually touched Melody, so what was causing her to grow faint?

"Sorry," Melody said, her voice a little stronger. She straightened her body, but he kept his hands around her waist, nervous that she would fall over if he let go completely. "I think I just got overwhelmed once we got out of there."

Jensen pulled her into his chest, tucking her head under his chin. "You were so brave back there."

Melody laughed, the sound a little wild. "I wasn't brave at all. I was shaking in my boots." She leaned back to look at him. Her nose and eyes were red and Jensen couldn't stop himself from wiping away her tears. "It breaks my heart to think of leaving Micah there," she whispered, her eyes darting back and forth between his.

Jensen sighed and rested his forehead against hers. "I know. But it wasn't safe for you to be there any longer." Just the thought of what Mitchell had said to her had Jensen's blood boiling. The man was revolting. They definitely needed to get Micah out of the house, but

Jensen wouldn't have been able to stay calm if anything had happened to Melody.

"Don't."

He looked down, his eyes wide. "What?"

"Don't even think about it," she declared, her hands fisting his shirt. "Mitchell isn't going to touch me. He was just saying those things to rile you up." She snorted. "He probably was hoping you'd throw a punch so he could call the police."

Jensen smirked. "Ken would have been on my side."

Melody wasn't amused. "I'm a big girl, Jensen. I'll be fine. It's Micah we need to worry about."

"And I will worry about him," Jensen agreed. "As long as you stay out of the equation." He stepped back, took her hand and began leading her back through town. Despite the fact that their footsteps were hurried, Jensen found himself shivering by the time they got back to the school. Pulling his keys from his pocket, he opened the car door. "Get in."

"I need to get my own car," Melody protested, but Jensen shook his head.

"I'm not letting you out of my sight for the next while, so hop in."

Melody put her hands on her hips, and it was easy to see her protest on her lips, but Jensen stepped forward and kissed her before she could speak.

"I know you're amazing," he whispered against her mouth. "But the way Mitchell looked at you has me ready to kill someone. So think of this as a favor for myself. I *need* to be with you for the next while, to make sure you're safe." He held his breath to await her reaction. What he'd spoken was true...he just hadn't mentioned that if Mitchell decided to come after Melody, she would have no chance of holding him off. The drunkard was large and heavy, two things that were the exact opposite of Melody.

"Fine." She sighed, stepping back to sit in the passenger seat. She looked up. "But you're going to have to let me go home at some point."

Jensen nodded, acknowledging that she was right. He wouldn't be able to keep her overnight and they both had lives to get to tomorrow, but this evening, he was going to hold her and reassure himself that she was safe.

It only took minutes to pull into his cabin and Jensen ushered her inside. "There's a blanket on the couch," he said as they got inside. "Let me change my clothes and I'll be right out." When he came back out in a sweatshirt and wool socks, he found Melody curled up on the sofa, staring out the window. "Find anything interesting?" he asked, gently sitting down beside her.

Her smile was gone and her eyes vacant as she turned to him. "I'm just worried about Micah. Is he warm? Hungry?" She swallowed. "In pain? Scared?"

Jensen nodded, a sick feeling in his stomach forming at her words. Reaching out, he gathered Melody into his arms and lap, tucking her into his chest. "I know...life sucks sometimes."

She shook slightly with laughter, but the amusement gave way to sniffles. "How do we just go about our lives knowing that he's being treated this way?"

Jensen sighed again. He seemed to be doing a lot of that lately. "It's not like we're just going to ignore the situation," he reassured her. "We'll tell Ethan what's going on, maybe even Ken. A few extra patrols won't hurt anybody, and if we can get a witness to Mitchell's behavior, we just might have a shot at getting Micah out."

Melody nodded and her slender fingers began to play with the string of his sweatshirt. "Tell me something I don't know about you," she said softly.

Jensen shifted to get more comfortable. "Something you don't know? With as long as we've been friends, I would have thought you'd known everything by now." He tilted his head down to grin at her and the answering smile warmed him far better than a blanket could have.

Her smile fell for a split-second before coming back again. "There are all sorts of things I don't know, and I want to." She straightened, resting her hands against his chest. "Tell me something," she begged, kissing his cheek.

"Plant one right here, and I might agree," Jensen flirted, tapping his lips.

Melody laughed and leaned in to follow his directions. Instead of just a peck, however, Jensen grabbed the back of her head and kept her there. She squeaked and jumped, then relaxed into him and Jensen wrapped his other arm tightly around her back. It didn't seem to matter how many times he kissed her, Jensen found that he wanted more.

His fingers worked on the back of her head until he managed to pull out her ponytail holder and let that glorious blonde hair free. He almost moaned as the silk slid through his fingers. He wasn't sure if it was the newness of the relationship or Melody herself, but his attraction and emotions had never been this strong for a woman...including back when he'd married Melissa.

"Jensen," Melody said, pulling away a little.

"Hmm?" He followed her, not ready to let go just yet. His mouth went to her neck and he began to explore her soft skin there.

"Jensen!" Melody said with a laugh. "You have to stop!"

"Why would I do that?" he asked, continuing to enjoy his exploration.

"Because you haven't answered my question."

"If you're still thinking about that, then I'm not doing my job very well," he grumbled, leaning back just enough to look her in the eye. Bright blue and green happiness looked back at him and Jensen smiled.

"You're doing your job a little too well," she said with a laugh. "That's the problem."

"And yet here we are...talking..." Jensen raised his eyebrows and gave her a look.

Melody sighed and ran a hand through his hair. "You're too tempting for your own good, Mr. Teacher."

Jensen closed his eyes, enjoying the sensations of her touch. "And yet again...here we are *talking* instead of kissing." When her hand stopped moving, he cracked open one eye. Her face had gone serious.

"I've waited so long for this that I'm afraid if I kiss you too much, I won't be able to stop," she admitted in a quiet voice.

Jensen kissed her forehead, her cheekbone, her nose and finally left a soft, lingering kiss to her mouth. "I can't predict the future, Melody, but right now...I'm all yours. Instead of letting fear get in the way, why don't we seize the moment and make the most of what we've got?" He could practically see the debate going on inside her head. "I kept a cricket in my room for three weeks when I was eight."

She gave him a weird look. "What?"

Jensen shrugged. "You wanted something you didn't know. I kept a pet cricket for three weeks before my parents figured it out and made me release it."

Melody smiled. "Really? Why?"

"Because as a kid I was allergic to cats and dogs and I desperately wanted a pet."

Melody laughed, grabbed his cheeks and planted a firm kiss on his lips. "I love that, thank you for sharing."

And I love you. He bit back the words. *Not yet.* "If I tell you another story, can I have another kiss?"

Melody laughed again and shook her head. "You really are about seizing the moment."

Jensen nodded. "Who wouldn't be if they had you in their arms?"

Melody wrapped her arms around his neck. "Then, deal. Every story gets a kiss." She kissed him again. "The better the story..." She kissed him longer. "The better the kiss."

"Challenge accepted." Jensen tightened his hold. It was going to be a fun evening.

CHAPTER 16

"Thanks, Smoothie Lady!" Darrin grinned and winked as he took the drink from Mel's hands.

She smiled back and laughed softly. Since she'd begun volunteering with the reading club, a few of the students had begun to stop by the smoothie shop before school. Mel enjoyed saying good morning and the extra boost to her business was always a nice plus. "Have a good day!" she called out as he left. Just as she turned back to her next customer, the bell rang above the door and Mel automatically glanced back, only to freeze in her footsteps. *Mitchell.*

It had only been two days since Mel and Jensen had tried to speak to the man. According to Jensen, Micah wasn't at school yesterday and no one had answered any phone calls from the school. The encounter with Mitchell had been shared with Ethan and he was looking into further action, but they still lacked solid evidence of wrongdoing and it had made Mel anxious and troubled.

Mitchell's dark eyes caught her and he winked. Unlike Darrin's playful action, this one sent cold shivers down Mel's spine. She forced a quick smile and then put her focus back on the cups she was handing out. Her pile was growing bigger by the minute. She needed to get the crowd moving.

"Grandmother of thirteen!" Mel called out, smiling when Mrs. Thompkins came up. "I'd heard there was another one," Mel said. "Congrats. How are mom and the baby?"

Mrs. Thompkins was practically preening as she accepted her drink. "Wonderful," she gushed. "Annabell Louise Wathers. Seven pounds, four ounces," the grandma announced proudly.

"Have you seen her yet?" Mel asked.

"Not yet. Annabell arrived two days ago and I had a couple of things to finish up here." Mrs. Thompkins leaned in. "But I'm flying out tonight. I'll be there for a full two weeks!" she squealed.

Mel chuckled at the woman's enthusiasm. "Well, have fun! And give Anna a hug of congratulations from me, and Anna*bell* a kiss."

"Always," Mrs. Thompkins said. She waved and hurried out the door.

For the next five minutes, Mel handed out drinks, smiling and greeting her usual customers and making friends with tourists. It wasn't until a certain cup was in her hand that she found herself frowning.

Lumberjack extraordinaire.

Mel opened her mouth, but couldn't do it. Setting the cup down, she began to untie her apron. "Hey, Emily. I need to run to the back. Can you take care of this one?" Mel tried to keep her voice calm, but her heart was punching her ribcage so hard that she was sure it would come out at any moment.

Emily gave Mel a weird look but nodded. "Sure. Go ahead."

"You're not leaving, are ya?"

Mel froze, her back to the dark voice speaking to her. Slowly, trying to keep her face under control so as to not show the disgust she held for the man, Mel turned. "I need to take care of something," she said evenly.

"You can't even give me my drink first?" he asked with a smirk. "It'll only take a second."

Mel could feel sweat beading on her forehead. His presence was really creeping her out and he seemed to know it. "The drink is right in front of you, Mr. Derringer. Go ahead and grab it."

Mitchell slowly shook his head, his arms folded over his large chest. "And take away the fun of your call-out?" He tsked his tongue. "I don't think so. I paid just like everyone else. I want my fun." His eyes seemed to darken at those words and Mel's body began to shake.

Not that anyone else would notice, but the way he was watching her, Mel felt certain he was sending a different message through his words, and she wanted no part of it. "Like I said, I have something to do. Please excuse me." Mel turned, but a loud slap on the counter had her jumping back.

"I won't excuse you," Mitchell said in a harsh whisper. "Now. I paid. I deserve to be treated just like everyone else."

Emily began to step forward, a determined look on her face, but Mel grabbed her friend's arm. As scared as Mel was, she was more worried about the others around her. Keeping Emily, her employees and customers safe was more important than taking care of herself. Slowly, Mel stepped forward, her hand fumbling blindly for the cup. "Lumberjack extraordinaire," she said softly.

"Aww...come on," Mitchell pressed. "You can do better than that."

Mel felt a muscle begin to twitch in her jaw. *Just get him out of here. Give him what he wants and get him gone.* She opened her mouth and took a deep breath. "LUMBERJACK EXTRAORDI-NAIRE!"

Mitchell's triumphant smile was enough to make her puke. "There now, that wasn't so bad...was it?" It wasn't really a question, more of a statement, but Mel nodded anyway.

She thrust out the cup.

Mitchell reached to take it but his fingers grabbed her hand and kept her from letting go.

The noise of the room seemed to disappear, despite the chattering and ringing of the front door bell. All Mel could see was Mitchell's leer and heavy gaze. Her breathing began to grow shallow and she squeaked when he jerked her forward, causing Mel to lean over the counter.

"Listen up, Miss Do-Gooder," he said quietly. "Unless you want—"

"Let her go."

The words weren't as deep as Mitchell's threatening tone, but the steel behind the order was every bit as strong. Mel's eyes tore from Mitchell's and she almost cried in relief when she saw Jensen's handsome, if livid, face. "Jensen," she breathed. "Oh!" Mel stumbled and had to catch herself on the counter when Mitchell shoved her back. The drink splashed onto the counter and floor, soaking the entire area with a bright red slush.

"Get out." Jensen pointed to the door.

"I have every right to be here," Mitchell said smugly. He folded his arms over his chest, his biceps bulging in a way that let Mel know the move was done on purpose. "You don't hold any authority here."

"Mel?"

She blinked, trying to catch her bearings. "Yes?" she asked in a hoarse voice.

"Is this your property?"

Mel nodded, then spoke up when Jensen's eyes glanced at her and back to Mitchell. "Yes."

"Do you wish for this man to be here?"

"No."

Emily's arm wrapped around Mel's waist and Mel felt herself relax a little at the supportive contact. It wasn't Emily's arms that Mel wanted, but right now she would take what she could get.

"There. The owner has the right to kick you out, and she has. Let me escort you." Jensen turned and held an arm toward the door.

Mitchell turned to Mel. "We'll talk later," he said, then his eyes went to the floor and back up. "And I'll be back for my refund." His heavy boot kicked the now empty cup. "The service in this place has really gotten shoddy lately."

Mel bit her tongue as she watched Jensen escort Mitchell out, not breathing until both men were outside.

"What the heck was that about?" Emily asked, her eyes wide and scared. She appeared to be holding onto Mel for her own support as well as Mel's.

"I can't talk about it," Mel said, keeping her eyes on the men outside. "But for now...he's not welcome in here."

"Thank heavens."

"DON'T COME BACK HERE," Jensen growled. His hands were clenched into fists and he could barely keep them at his sides. It had nearly driven him over the edge when Mitchell had looked at Mel two days ago. Now that Jensen had caught Micah's father actually touching his girlfriend, all bets were off.

"You can't keep me from coming. It's a public place." Mitchell got in Jensen's face. "Just like you have no business interfering with me and my boy. Stay out of my life, *Mr. Tanner.*" The words might have been formal, but they were anything but a compliment.

"The safety of my students is my top priority," Jensen argued back. "As soon as I have the necessary proof of abuse, I'm taking you down."

Mitchell's jaw tightened and his eyes flashed. "You keep poking into my business and you might just find me in yours." His nearly black gaze shot to the shop, then back. "That girl of yours doesn't look like a satisfied woman. Maybe I oughtta—"

Jensen's fist shot out before he could think twice. His knuckles immediately stung at the contact to the large man's jaw, but he didn't back down. "Don't you dare touch her," Jensen shouted before shifting backward to avoid a flailing punch.

Mitchell grounded himself after missing and glared at Jensen before smiling darkly. "Too late," he whispered. "I already did."

Jensen shot forward, but this time Mitchell was ready for him. His head snapped back and pain ricocheted through his skull and eye socket. There was no way that wouldn't be swollen shut in the next few minutes. Soon both men were on the ground, rolling and throwing punches like wild animals.

When heavy hands finally pulled Jensen off Mitchell, he could barely breathe, but wasn't ready to quit.

"Knock it off, Jensen." Ken's booming voice finally broke through Jensen's angry haze. "You gotta just calm down!"

Jensen finally forced his feet to stand still, though his chest was heaving and sweat poured down his body.

"JENSEN!" Mel's scream completely pulled Jensen from the situation. Her small body slammed into his and Jensen bit back a groan.

He must have taken a couple of hits to his ribs because they were not happy with her touch at the moment. "It's all right," he assured her, his voice raspy. "It's all over now."

Another officer was dragging a still enraged Mitchell to his feet. "I want to press charges," he shouted at Ken while wiping a spot of blood from his lip. "This man attacked me. All these people can witness to it."

Ken sighed before turning to Jensen. "What's this all about?"

Jensen ground his jaw, Melody still buried in his chest. "He threatened Melody."

Ken blinked at him, looked at Melody, then back to Mitchell. "Were you threatening people, Mitchell?"

Mitchell spit blood on the sidewalk. "I did no such thing, Captain. His attack was completely unprovoked."

"Uh...Captain Wamsley?"

The whole group looked to see Darrin standing at the side of the building, shifting his weight from one foot to the other. Now that Jensen was paying attention, there was a large crowd gathered around them, watching the proceedings.

"What is it, Darrin?" Ken asked, putting his hands on his hips.

"Mr. Tanner did throw the first punch," the teenager said, his voice having dropped as if he was worried about outing his teacher. "But Mr. Derringer was saying some really not nice things about Smoothie Girl, I mean. Ms. Frasier." The boy ran a hand through his hair.

Ken sighed. "Looks like you're both coming with me," Ken said, gripping Jensen's arm. "Darrin...you too. We'll need to take your statement." Ken put up his hand to the watchers. "Everyone needs to just go about their business, please. We've got the situation under control."

"You have no right to take me in, Captain!" Mitchell began to scream and pull against the hold on his shoulder. "Talking isn't against the law!"

Ken pulled on Jensen. "You come ride in my car."

Jensen sighed and kissed Melody's forehead. "Hang tight. I'll be back when I'm done."

"Jensen, I'm so sorry," she whispered, her voice breaking at the end. Her shaking fingers rose up and touched a sore spot on his eyebrow. "You need to see a doctor."

"We'll get him taken care of, Mel," Ken promised. "Don't worry about it." He pulled gently on Jensen's arm. "Let's go, man."

Jensen gave Melody one last peck, then headed to the police car, which was blocking the street. He sighed in relief as Ken got him settled in the passenger seat. "Aren't you going to put me in the back?" Jensen asked when Ken was behind the wheel.

"Are you planning to knock me out, steal the car and hightail it out of town?"

Jensen closed his eyes and leaned back against the headrest. "Nope."

"Then I think we're fine." He reached over Jensen's knees and fumbled with the glove compartment. "Here."

Jensen cracked open his one good eye and took the ice pack being offered. He broke the inside and squished it around until it grew cold. "Thanks." The feel of the cold against his swollen eye made him hiss in pain, but after a moment, he relaxed, grateful for the help. After a moment, Jensen realized they weren't moving and he opened his eye again to look at Ken. "What?"

Ken shook his head, turned to the front and started the car. "Just never thought I'd see the day that quiet, calm Jensen took down a guy nearly twice his size." Ken snorted and pulled onto the correct side of the road.

Jensen almost grinned, but his split lip prevented it from happening. "You'd think hanging out with Benny would have done that to me long ago."

"You always keep a cool head," Ken said. "I didn't think you had it in you to break free from the mold."

Jensen didn't respond. Ken's words were just a reflection of everything he'd been feeling the last couple of years. *Until Melody...* That woman seemed to have been the stimulant he needed to kick his life into high gear. Now he found himself looking forward to something every day and smiling more than ever before. His fingers were nearly raw with how many songs he'd been writing lately, and he attributed that to Melody as well. Now that he was rising from the rut he'd been in, his mind seemed to be working in overtime. And most importantly, after their first kiss...Jensen had been able to add the last bit to his song, the one that had started it all. There was something about her that was the perfect complement to his life.

Thinking about his guitar reminded him of the news he had to share with Melody. It was the reason he'd come into Smooth Moves that morning. *Now it'll have to wait.* He sighed and tried to relax for the last couple of minutes to the station. The next few hours weren't going to be pretty, and Jensen just prayed he didn't lose his job or end up in jail or on probation or something. *But at least I'll have one good bit of news to share with her when I get out of here. Hopefully that'll be enough.*

CHAPTER 17

M el had finally retreated to her office. After the fight out front and Jensen being taken into the police station, she's been unable to focus back on work. By the time she'd gotten back inside, her crew had cleaned up the spilled drink and put everything back in order. When the crowd had rushed outside, the tables and chairs had been shoved all over the small space, but now it appeared as if nothing had ever happened.

"You guys are amazing," Mel had whispered to Emily, hugging her friend and every other employee as well.

"It's what we're here for," Emily whispered back. Her eyes were full of tears when they'd been speaking. "Now...go take a moment to pull yourself together, huh? That was crazy."

Mel had pushed the suggestions aside and tried to go back to work, but that hadn't worked, and now she was hiding behind her desk. Her emotions had been too close to the surface and by the time her third tear had slipped down her cheek, she'd handed the cup distribution to Emily and disappeared.

Grabbing a box of tissues from her desk, Melody let all her wild emotions go and broke into sobs. Jensen had been taken over an hour ago and she kept waiting to get the call that he'd been booked into the prison. She felt as if the whole thing was her fault. If Mitchell hadn't been giving her trouble, Jensen wouldn't have gotten into a fight. Even though they'd been outside when the fight broke out, she just knew it had something to do with her. *Well...me and Micah.*

Mitchell's threats just made Mel want even more to get Micah out of that house, but another part of her was terrified. Seeing Jensen getting hurt, and the swelling and cuts on his face as a result, had scared Mel more than Mitchell's threats had. She absolutely couldn't do something that would get Jensen hurt again.

A soft knock came on her door and she brought her head up, sniffling. "Yes?"

The door cracked up and Jensen's broken face came into view. "Hey, Melody," he said with a slight lisp. His bottom lip was split and swollen, obviously making it difficult to speak.

Anything Melody would have said broke on another sob as she jumped from her desk. She rushed the man, then pulled herself back, forcing herself not to touch him. "Have you been to the doctor?" she asked, her eyes taking in every bruise and cut.

He shrugged. "No, but Ken let me wash up."

She could tell the smudged blood and dirt was gone. "I think you should go in."

Jensen shook his head. "Nah. Nothing's broken and nothing needs stitches." His eyes wandered into the room and Mel immediately felt guilty.

"I'm so sorry. Come on in and sit down. You must be exhausted." She paused. "Oh my gosh. I completely forgot about the school."

Jensen sighed as he sank into the cushions of the small couch. "I called them and got excused for the day." He leaned back and closed his eyes. "I'll be off for the next couple of days, actually."

Mel sat back in her seat, perching on the very edge. "I'm sure that's a good idea." She tried to be patient, but when he didn't offer any more information, she had to ask. "What happened at the police station?"

Jensen opened his good eye. "Nothing."

Mel's eyebrows felt like they would jump off her forehead. "What?"

"The charges were all dropped."

"Oh my gosh, thank goodness," Mel gushed, slumping into her seat. "How did you manage that?"

Jensen shrugged, his beautiful brown eye still focused on her. "Once it came out that I could charge him with assault for his threats, Mitchell decided he didn't feel quite so excited about going after me."

Mel put a clammy hand to her forehead. "I was so worried you would end up in jail, or fined a crazy amount, or even lose your job or something." The thought brought tears back to her eyes. "I'm so sorry," she whispered, the words barely audible in the small room.

Jensen stiffened then sat up. "What?"

Her bottom lip began to tremble. "I'm so sorry, Jensen. This is all my fault and I shouldn't have—"

"Don't you dare," he snapped, cutting off Mel's apology. "This is *not* your fault. Not even a little bit." He scooted to the edge of the couch. "That jerk had no business approaching you and causing problems. He's a bully, Melody. He preys on those he thinks he can control. There's a reason he went after you and not me."

She huffed a laugh. "Are you saying I'm weak?"

Jensen gave her a look. "No. But he is stronger than you and if he got physical, you wouldn't stand a chance."

Mel shivered, dropping his gaze. She knew Jensen was right, but that didn't make it any better.

"Come on," Jensen said, patting the couch next to him. "Come over here."

"Jensen...you're hurt," she scolded, even though every part of her wanted to go be next to him.

"I'm more hurt having you so far away," he said, his mouth pulling into a very small smile. "Besides...I have news for you."

Curious now, along with wanting to touch him, she rose from her chair and carefully sat next to Jensen on the couch. "Oof," she huffed as his arm wrapped around her shoulders and tugged her into his chest. "Are you sure this doesn't hurt?" she asked, relaxing into his sternum.

"I'm sure," he grunted, shifting around until he seemed to get comfortable.

"What did you want to tell me?" Mel asked, playing with the button on his polo.

"I got an email today," Jensen hedged.

"About...?"

"My audition reel made it into the next round of that talent show I sent it to."

Mel's breath caught in her lungs. She hadn't thought about the guitar thing for a long time since they'd been so caught up with Micah and his troubles. Her heart sank, but she knew she had been quiet too long. "That's amazing," she squeaked out. "So what exactly does that mean?"

She felt him shrug. "Not much, except that they're still considering me. I'm supposed to know in another two weeks or so. The deadline is coming up soon."

Mel nodded, but didn't turn around to look at him. "Of course they're still considering you...you're one of the best guitar players I've ever heard."

Jensen tugged on her and Mel reluctantly sat up to look him in the face. His knuckles brushed her cheeks. "Well, it's all thanks to you, you know."

Mel frowned. "What?"

He chuckled. "I've discovered that you're my muse. I've been writing music like crazy ever since we got together."

Her hurting heart melted and Mel knew she couldn't allow her own selfish wants to hold him back. "That's the sweetest thing someone has ever said to me."

He grabbed the back of her neck and brought their foreheads together. "Stick with me, baby. I'll sweet talk you all day long."

Mel laughed, even as her heart cracked in two inside her chest. "Always."

JENSEN COULDN'T HELP himself. He pulled Melody in and touched his mouth to hers. The pinch in his lip reminded him to keep things light, but that didn't mean he couldn't enjoy her at all. His knuckles ached as he slid them into her hair, the pleasure outweighing the pain at the moment. He'd been so excited this morning, feeling like life was really going somewhere when he'd gotten that email.

The odds of making it onto the show were pretty slim, but to have been moved ahead was still a bigger accomplishment than he'd expected, and it had only added to his recent happiness of having Melody in his life.

After a few minutes of enjoying her, he could tell his bottom lip was about to split open again and he pulled back. He let his fingers skim along her jawline. Her skin was so soft and unblemished. "You are so beautiful," he murmured, feeling a rush of happiness and joy.

"You have a silver tongue," she teased him back. Leaning in, Melody left feather light kisses against his cheeks, nose and forehead. "And if you ever get hurt like this again for my sake, I'm gonna let Bennett have at you."

Jensen chuckled and leaned back to meet her concerned gaze. "I'd do this a hundred times over if it meant keeping you safe."

Melody shook her head. "No. You can't do this, Jensen. You have to stay away from Mitchell."

His happiness plummeted. "Only if he stays away from you."

Her fingers played with his hair and the soothing sensation made him want to close his eyes and go to sleep. "Maybe we just need to let the police handle it, huh? I thought I was going to die of a heart attack when he hit you."

Jensen's hold on her waist tightened. "And I thought I was going to kill him when he made those lewd remarks about you."

"What lewd remarks?"

He stiffened. *Shoot.* He hadn't meant to say that. *Her fingers make me have a loose tongue.* "Nothing."

Mel scowled. "No. Not nothing. What are you talking about?"

Jensen gave her a look, then winced when it sent his headache soaring. "Why do you think we fought, Melody? He was saying things he shouldn't about you and I did what I needed to make him back off."

Those dang tears were back. "You can't just hit anyone who says naughty things, Jensen."

He shook his head, doing his best to ignore the pain. It seemed to be growing by the minute. "I don't. But he was out of line. You had to notice as well as I did that he was threatening you."

Mel shrugged and dropped eye contact. "I know. But I think he was just trying to scare me. He's afraid we'll manage to get Micah away from him and he doesn't like it."

Jensen took her chin and pulled her back to look at him. "He'd only be scared if he was guilty," Jensen said softly. "But I wouldn't put it past him to do something to you in order to get back at us. Like I said before, he's a bully."

Melody nodded. "I know. And I plan to stay safe."

Jensen nodded, relief flooding his system, which helped ease some of the pain. His entire body was beginning to thrum with pain and as they argued, it had only gotten worse. He moaned and laid his head back.

Melody jumped up from the couch. "Oh my gosh. I'm so selfish. What do you need? A nap? Food? Water?"

"Tylenol?"

Melody rushed to her desk. "Give me a minute and I'll get you taken care of."

He could hear her scrambling through her desk, shoving things around.

"Finally," she breathed. The rattle of a full bottle got closer as she came back to the couch. "Open up."

Without opening his eyes, Jensen opened his mouth and Melody dropped a couple of pills on his tongue and pressed a cold bottle into his hand. Jensen opened his eye just long enough to open it and take a swallow.

"Let me take that," Melody whispered, slipping the bottle from his fingers. "Why don't you lay down? I'll do paperwork and watch over you as you sleep."

Jensen knew he should probably go home, but the idea of Melody playing nurse for him was too enticing. "You sure it's okay?"

"Absolutely." Her hands went to his shoulders and she guided him down to a pillow, his legs hanging over the side of the sofa. "Just sleep, handsome. I'll take care of you."

He liked the sound of that a little too well. "Not so handsome right now," he murmured, his consciousness starting to fade away.

"You'll always be handsome," Melody explained softly. "A black eye and a couple of cuts doesn't change that." Her fingers slid soothingly through his hair and Jensen let out a long, relaxed breath.

Just before he slipped under, she whispered one more thing.

"And that's only part of the reason I'm terrified for us."

His mind was too tired and hurting to understand what she meant, but he figured he could always ask her later. If he remembered.

CHAPTER 18

"You're distracted again."

Mel turned to look at Emily and frowned. "What?"

Emily chuckled and finished wiping the table. "Exactly my point."

Mel turned her brain over, trying to figure out what her friend had said before the words finally clicked. "Oh...yeah. I guess I am a little." Actually, she was more than a little distracted. She hadn't been able to get her head on straight since Mitchell and Jensen's fight three days ago. And now she was also worried about Jensen's news about the audition. She hadn't even been sure he'd sent his music in, and now he was advancing toward the next round.

She wanted to be happy for him, she really did, but every time she thought about him getting into the competition, she *knew* it would be the end of their relationship. She'd pined for him for so long and only had her dream come true for a few weeks. And now it was all about to be ripped away from her. *But how can I begrudge him that happiness? It was obvious by the way he spoke about it that he was excited. I can't ask him to set that aside for me.*

She'd hoped at first that he would grow to love her to the point that he would be content staying in Seaside Bay, but now it looked like that wasn't going to be the case. She only had a couple more weeks before he heard whether or not he'd made it, and it seemed impossible for him to fall in love that quickly.

"I don't think 'a little' even comes close," Emily muttered.

Mel shook her head. "I'm sorry. I guess I'm still a little shaken up about things." She put a chair back under the table and continued sweeping the floor. They had closed up shop a bit ago and were finishing cleaning. Mel didn't always stick around to help, but tonight she'd felt restless and needed something to do. She wasn't going to be able to see Jensen, so she might as well stay busy at work.

A warm hand on her arm had Melody jumping. "Maybe you should go home and get some sleep," Emily said softly. Her concerned brown gaze roved over Mel's face.

Mel knew there were purple bags under her eyes. She hadn't been sleeping well. The nightmares were mostly about Mitchell, but her worries about Jensen certainly didn't help. "I'm fine," Mel said, shaking off Emily's hand. "I'll just finish this up."

Emily sighed but didn't reply. It was clear she wanted to say more, and Mel was extremely grateful that her job as the boss kept her friend from speaking her mind at the moment. She didn't need more coddling. She got enough of that from Jensen and Bennett. Right now she needed courage and a clear direction. Neither of which seemed to be forthcoming.

The small closing crew was efficient and they were done in the next ten minutes.

"Thanks, everyone!" Mel called out with a stiff smile. "I'll see some of you tomorrow!"

Emily stayed in the doorway for a few extra moments, eyeing Mel, then eventually shook her head and left. Once the shop was empty, Mel let out a long breath and leaned against the wall to support her shaky legs. She was so lost. Everything she'd ever dreamed about was in her hands, but she couldn't enjoy it, not when she was so worried about it being taken away.

A couple of tears tracked down her cheeks and she wiped them away roughly. "You're just on edge because of what happened with Mitchell," she whispered to herself. Mel straightened from her place against the wall and took a deep, calming breath. "It's going to be okay. Jensen likes you. He even fought to protect you. You've just got to have faith that it'll all work out."

With no other option but to try and move forward, Mel grabbed her jacket, keys and purse and headed outside. The wind was blowing, causing her ponytail to whip around her head. Mel pulled her collar up and hunkered down in order to try and avoid the worst of the unpleasant weather. She was just about to unlock her car when she heard a noise that seemed out of place.

Mel paused and frowned into the darkness. The hairs on the back of her neck rose up and it suddenly felt as if a dozen eyes were on her. Her already frayed emotions began to completely unravel and Mel found herself in a state of terror. Her hand froze and she could barely breathe past the stiff state of her body. She was sure that if she took in a deep breath, her ribs would shatter from the pressure.

MOVE! Her mind screamed, but her body refused to answer. The sound of footsteps began to penetrate the dark and Mel's shaking grew so strong she barely maintained her hold on her keys. They rattled in her hand and Mel knew for certain this was what a deer felt like when the headlights were bearing down on it.

"Ms. Frasier?"

It was the uncertainty in the voice that finally snapped Mel free from her statue-like position. "Micah?" she croaked, then cleared her throat. She clenched her hand and tried to peer deeper into the alleyway.

Finally the teenager's face appeared under a lone streetlamp. "Ms. Frasier, are you going home?" he asked, his voice still sounding unsure.

"Y-yes," she said, swallowing hard.

"Can I ride with you?" Micah glanced around nervously. His hands were stuffed in his pockets and his usual hood was around his shoulders.

"Of course." Mel blinked rapidly and forced her chest to expand to let in enough air to calm her nerves. "Hop on in."

Micah hurried over and settled himself in her passenger seat. His eyes never stopped roving the alley, and watching him only made Mel's nerves more agitated.

"Jen— I mean Mr. Tanner missed you at school the other day," she said, trying to break the ice.

It wasn't until they were on Main Street that Micah finally relaxed in his seat. "Yeah...I, uh, had a headache."

Mel frowned. Knowing now that their suspicions of abuse were more than likely correct, she was fairly positive he was lying. "I'm sorry," she murmured. "Are you feeling better now?"

Micah shrugged, though his movements were hard to see in the dark interior of the car.

"What're you doing out so late on a school night?" Mel asked. "And do you want me to take you to your home?"

"Nah," Micah said, ignoring her first question. He glanced behind them. "If you'll just drop me off at the entrance to the trailer park, I'll take it from there."

Mel's frown grew. "I don't mind—"

"Just the entrance, Ms. Frasier," Micah said firmly.

"Okay..." she said softly, not willing to argue about it. It took less than two minutes to get there since the traffic was all but gone for the evening.

"Thanks." Micah opened his door and stood up, then paused and leaned back in. "I would make sure you leave with the rest of your employees, Ms. Frasier. Or stick with Mr. Tanner."

Before Mel could say anything, the young man was gone. His dark clothes disappeared into the shadows quicker than Mel would have imagined, as if he knew exactly how to go unseen. Feeling rattled once more, Mel turned around and sped home. She almost never went over the speed limit, but tonight she needed to be in her house with locked doors and windows and a cup of warm tea in her hands.

Micah's warning swam through her head, and Mel wondered what it could all mean. Was Mitchell after her? Was she truly in danger? Was Jensen in danger? What about Micah? Had he been the person she'd heard in the alley? Or was Micah trying to protect her from someone else?

After pulling into her parking spot, Mel grabbed her stuff and rushed inside. She had no idea how she was going to handle all this, but she felt sure of one thing. There was no way she could tell Jensen. If he got hurt again on her behalf, Mel wasn't sure she would ever be able to forgive herself.

JENSEN SIGHED AND PUSHED a hand through his hair as he continued grading the essays on his dining room table. Sometimes it felt as if his kids were kindergartners instead of high schoolers. The current paper he was working on was filled with red marks as he corrected even the most basic grammatical errors.

"Gotta get 'em done," he reminded himself. He would much rather be spending time with Melody, especially if there was kissing involved, but he was behind in his grading. Between missing a few days because of the fight and all his time spent at Melody's town-home, Jensen was behind and had to get this bundle done tonight. Which was why he had told Melody he couldn't see her at all. She was too much of a distraction for him to get any work done.

A soft buzz from his phone was a welcomed break and he grabbed the device quickly.

Hey, handsome!

He grinned. He didn't even have to be with Melody in order for her to make him feel good.

Hello, beautiful! How was your evening? Jensen leaned back on his chair. He'd get to the papers in a minute.

Good. A little slow.

Probably because it was cold today. He hit send.

She sent an emoji of crossed fingers. **Let's hope so!**

Jensen couldn't help himself. He punched the call button. It only rang once before she answered.

"I didn't want to distract you," she said by way of greeting. "I figured by texting, you could easily ignore me whenever you needed to."

Jensen chuckled, enjoying hearing her sweet voice. "You've been distracting me all evening," he admitted. "I can't seem to get you out of my head." She was quiet for a moment and Jensen had a split-second of panic that he'd gone too far.

"Well, what can I do to help, then?"

He sighed in relief. This was definitely the Melody he knew and was falling for.

"It breaks my heart to think of you stuck at home by yourself with only your papers for company." She tsked her tongue. "Have you had dinner? I'll bet you haven't eaten!"

Jensen laughed again. Her desire to look out for him always made him feel adored. "I ate," he defended. *If a handful of Oreos counts as eating, then I totally did.*

"Uh, huh." She obviously didn't believe him. "I remember what you and Bennett used to grab when left to your own. You ate chips for dinner, didn't you?"

"Wrong," he said triumphantly.

"Hmm...then it must have been Oreos."

His jaw dropped. "How the heck would you know that?"

Melody's laugh came through the line and warmed his chest. "I probably shouldn't say," she hedged.

"Oh, no. You gotta spill it now." He shook his head. This woman was always surprising him. How did he overlook her for so long?

"I just have a good memory," she said, her voice having lost some of its humor. "You and Bennett ate Oreos for dinner every time my mom left for the evening." She snorted. "I don't know how you two didn't weigh five hundred pounds."

"A young man's metabolism is a good thing to have," he responded. He found himself frowning as he tried to figure out why she was acting off. "Is something wrong, Melody? What's going on?"

"Oh, no. Nothing. Absolutely nothing," she said a little too quickly.

His frown grew. Something was definitely wrong, but why wouldn't she say? *Maybe she's still upset about the fight.*

"And just for the record...you *still* have a young man's metabolism!" she scoffed. "If I even looked at Oreos for dinner, I'd gain five pounds."

Jensen reluctantly smiled and shook his head. The extra bedroom in the back of his home held way too much exercise equipment and he knew well how much he had to work out in order to stay in shape now that he was older. *Definitely not the same as when I was a teenager.* "I don't think I've ever seen you even come close to gaining weight," he retorted. "All that healthy stuff you eat is part of the reason I have such a hard time taking my eyes off of you."

"Jensen..." she warned.

"Yes?" he asked with fake innocence.

"You can't say things like that and expect me not to come kiss you for such a sweet compliment."

"Why do you think I said it?" Her laugh allowed him to relax. Whatever was bothering her was gone, at least for the moment. His job was done.

She groaned. "Don't tempt me! You practically ordered me to stay home!"

Jensen sighed. "I know. I really do need to get these papers done. It's not fair to my kids to never get a grade or feedback just because you're so wonderful."

"It's no wonder you teach English," she said breathlessly. "You certainly have a way with words. Maybe you should write books. You could be the next Nicholas Sparks."

Jensen snorted. "Not a chance. Any poetry spouting out of my mouth is reserved for you."

"Even better." She gave a loud, dramatic sigh. "I'd better let you go or you'll never get your work done, and then I won't be able to see you tomorrow either."

He eyed his stack of work. "Yeah...I hate to say it, but you're probably right."

"Alrighty then. I lo— have a good night, Jensen."

"You too. I'll see you tomorrow." Jensen stared at the phone. *What was she going to say?* His heart was thudding against his chest. It had almost seemed like she was going to say "I love you", but he was sure that couldn't be right.

They'd only been dating a few weeks. They weren't in that stage of their relationship yet. They couldn't be. His eyes drifted down to his papers, but he didn't see them. If he was being honest with himself, his own feelings had grown much faster than he'd expected. While he wasn't ready to say he loved her, he could easily say he was headed that direction.

When they weren't together, he wanted to be. He enjoyed her voice, her laugh, her touch...her kiss. When she'd been threatened by Mitchell, Jensen had nearly lost his head and had thrown a punch in an angry manner for the first time in his life.

His hands drifted to his ribs without conscious efforts. They were still tender and the bruises dark. He'd been ready to take Mitchell out for treating Melody that way. *Would I do that if I didn't love her?*

Like many times before, his thoughts drifted back to Melissa, his wife. He had loved Melissa, Jensen knew he had. But theirs had been a more...comfortable love. She was a good woman, who had been kind and sweet and treated him well. They'd had similar goals in life and had enjoyed each other's company along the way. This relationship with Melody was brighter, more passionate and definitely a little more volatile.

He shook his head and leaned forward to begin working on his papers again. Right now it didn't matter if he was falling in love with Melody. She was wonderful, beautiful, kind and a mother hen. He enjoyed her and wanted to keep spending time together. That was enough. It wasn't like there was some kind of timeline for their relationship. If things kept going the way they were going, he could see them falling in love eventually, and that would be fine.

The thought of it didn't scare Jensen, he just wasn't ready to say "yes" yet. *There's no hurry. We'll get there when we get there.*

CHAPTER 19

"I'm going to take off early today," Mel announced to Emily as their midafternoon rush began to slow down.

"Good," Emily stated firmly. "You need a break."

Mel rolled her eyes. "I'm sorry. Are you tired of having your boss at work?"

Emily put her hands on her hips and gave Mel a look. "No. I'm tired of having my friend stay busy with work when what she really needs is a good long nap."

Mel's shoulders fell. "You're right. I'm sorry." She hadn't taken a day off since the fight last week and it probably still showed in the bags under her eyes. Mel had worked hard with her foundation, even going so far as to look up tricks on the internet, but nothing quite seemed to cover the evidence of her stress.

Each day that passed peacefully brought a little less worry about Mitchell, but the worry about Jensen getting accepted onto that reality show grew in unnatural leaps and bounds. As long as he wasn't getting a rejection letter, Mel knew the odds of his acceptance were stronger.

Since the frightening night with Micah, things had been quiet in regards to the Derringer household. Jensen said Micah was back in class, but he rarely spoke. The reading club hadn't met last week because of Jensen's injuries, so Mel hadn't had a chance to see him and possibly thank him. She hadn't had the same "I'm being followed" feeling since that night, which made her more suspicious that he was keeping her from harm.

All the information Jensen and Mel had gathered had been turned into Ethan and subsequently Child Services, but Mel hadn't heard if anything had happened on that front. She huffed. *They probably feel like there's still not enough evidence. Why is it that the very program that's designed to protect our children leaves them in the hands of someone who hurts them?*

"You're thinking again," Emily accused quietly.

Mel stiffened. "How can you tell?"

"You get an angry look on your face," Emily whispered. "And it scares the customers."

Mel immediately looked out at the small crowd, all of whom were smiling and enjoying chatting while they waited for their drinks. "What?" she asked, confused by Emily's words.

Her employee cracked up. "Sorry. I couldn't resist."

"Em!" Mel scolded, elbowing her friend. "I can't believe I fell for that!"

"As if you could ever make a face that would frighten customers," Emily said through a sigh of amusement. She wiped at the corner of her eyes. "You're gorgeous and couldn't hurt a fly, even if you tried."

Mel felt a blush creep into her cheeks. "You're too much," she scolded.

Emily shook her head. "For a woman who spends all her time building up others, it's amazing how hard it is for you to take a compliment for yourself."

Mel couldn't help but smile. "You're so wonderful, you know that?"

"See?" Emily pointed at her. "My point exactly."

Well...when you get ignored by the man you adore for enough years, it's easy to feel like you don't matter. The thought made Mel shake her head. She had never really put into words why she did what she did. She liked making people happy. Compliments, smile, smoothies...they all did that. And since she didn't have a family of her own to look after, it made sense to spend that energy toward her friends and customers. But she'd never consciously attributed it to not being able to catch Jensen's notice. And she wasn't sure she appreciated the thought now...especially since he might leave her.

Mel glanced at the clock. "I'm supposed to meet Jensen soon." She looked around. "Are you guys going to be all right? Caleb is coming in to close tonight."

Emily nodded. "You know we got it. Go give your man a kiss or two." She pursed her lips. "Hopefully his mouth has healed, because he certainly deserves a few good smackeroos after standing up for you last week."

"Emily!" Mel cried, covering her cheeks.

Emily rolled her eyes. "Oh, give me a break. I see you look at him. The kisses must be out of this world for you to become gooey-eyed every time he buys a drink."

The blush on Mel's cheeks was growing stronger by the minute. "And on that note, I'm out of here."

Emily laughed.

"See ya later!" Mel called, waving over her shoulder as she headed to her office. Grabbing her purse, she fixed her makeup and hair, trying to look fresh and new rather than like she'd been working since six that morning. She groaned at her limp strands, but knew there was nothing to do about it. Having fine hair meant it was silky, which was nice, but it also refused to keep any volume in it, which was exasperating.

Giving up on her hair, Mel threw on her jacket and took off. With the sun shining high, she decided it was a good time to walk, so Mel put her chin in the air, took in a lungful of salty sea air and began to move toward Jensen's small home. It was a good fifteen-minute walk from downtown, but Mel loved it. She loved being outdoors and exercising her legs. Walks like this always calmed her mind, which she definitely needed right now.

"I've got to learn to just enjoy the moment," she told herself as she walked. Her nose began to run slightly with the nip in the air.

"No one can tell the future. The worst case scenario is that Jensen becomes a big star and leaves me behind, along with Micah being stuck with his father." She blinked as her heart ached at those pictures. "And if that happens, then I'll go back to being Jensen's friend. I've had lots of practice doing that, so it should be a no-brainer." She absentmindedly began to rub at the pain in her sternum. "And if the other occurs, then I'll make sure to be extra watchful for Micah. Free smoothies, lots of smiles and hugs and when he turns eighteen, I'll see if I can help him find a place of his own."

"What's up, sis?"

Mel almost screeched when her brother pulled her out of her pep talk. She'd been so busy talking to herself, she'd missed the sound of his mail truck coming up behind her. "Good grief, Bennett. You nearly gave me a heart attack."

Bennett rolled his eyes. "You're so dramatic."

Mel opened her eyes wide and gave him a look. "Me? The dramatic one?" She shook her head, then cracked a smile and laughed. "Finishing up your route today?"

Bennett nodded. "I'm almost done. Just heading to the last neighborhood." He gave a sly grin. "You might know someone there..."

Mel turned away before he caught her grin. "Oh? Who might that be?"

"A certain lover boy who can't seem to keep his hands off you."

"Bennett!" For the second time that day, she was shocked at what people were saying about her and Jensen. *I don't know why I'm surprised. Most everyone is bolder than I am when it comes to this type of thing.*

"Hop on in and I'll get you there in a jiffy," Bennett said, patting the seat to his left. Mel started to argue, then shut her mouth. It wasn't worth the effort. They arrived at Jensen's in less than five minutes, but instead of getting out, Bennett handed her a stack of mail.

"Here." He pumped his eyebrows. "I'll let you take it in. There just *might* be something special inside."

Mel frowned and glanced down at the few envelopes, immediately noticing that one was thicker and had an official seal on it. Her heart began to pound when she saw the return address, and she snapped her gaze up to Bennett. "Is this...?" She couldn't finish the sentence.

Bennett shrugged. "I'm guessing so, but obviously I don't know for sure." He tilted his head. "Go on. I'll let you do the honors...but just this once."

Numbly, Mel stepped out of the car, her eyes still glued to her hand. With a wave, her brother pulled off. "I'll call and check in later!" He crossed his fingers. "Here's hoping it's good news!"

"Melody?"

Jensen had come out of his house, obviously having heard Bennett's shouts. "Whatcha got?" he asked, coming up to her. He kissed her forehead, then looked down at the mail.

"Here," Mel said, pushing the stack toward him. "I think it's the one you've been waiting for." *And the one that will break me into pieces.*

SHE DOESN'T SOUND HAPPY. Jensen flicked his gaze between the mail and Melody's face. She looked...sad, but appeared to be trying to hide it. "Thanks," he said cautiously, taking the letters. "Why don't we go inside."

"Aren't you curious?" she asked, looking pointedly down at the envelopes.

"About what?"

Melody pulled one of the letters from his hands and held it out again. "You should probably open this one first." Her lips shook a little as she smiled, and Jensen became even more concerned.

He grabbed it and immediately noticed how heavy it was. It only took seconds to notice the return address and his jaw dropped. "Melody! Is it...do you think?" His smile began to fade when her eyes filled with tears. "Sweetheart, what's the matter?"

Melody shook her head and wiped her face. "Sorry. It was a rough day at work." That semi-sad smile was pasted on her face again. "Open it. We've been waiting forever."

Deciding to let it go, Jensen grabbed her hand and practically dragged her inside. "It's too cold to do this out there," he muttered. "Brrr." He closed the door behind them and pulled her to the couch, right onto his lap.

"You can't open the letter like this," Melody protested, trying to get off his leg.

"No way," Jensen protested, holding her tightly around the waist. "I'm scared out of my mind to open this thing and want you with me every step of the way. If I get rejected, I'm planning on having you around to kiss it better."

She paused for a second, then let out a very soft sigh. "Okay." Settling back, Melody settled her back against his shoulder. "Go ahead."

He could still hear something odd in her tone, but his excitement outweighed it at the moment. His fingers were clammy and fumbled as he tore open the envelope. Inside were several pages folded into thirds. Most were held together with a staple, but the front one was loose.

"Dear Mr. Tanner," he read, taking a fortifying breath. "Thank you for your audition. It has been listened to many times by our esteemed panel of judges and we would like to invite you to be on "Our Greatest Talent" this fall." The papers fluttered to the floor as Jensen's hands began to shake. "I did it," he murmured, mostly to himself. "I got in!"

"Of course you did!" Melody said, turning and grabbing his face. "There was no way they weren't going to see how amazing you are." She left a soft kiss on his lips. "Congratulations."

"HAHA!" Jensen cried, grabbing Melody and squeezing her to him. He dipped her to the side in his arm, cradling her like a small child. Melody let out a squeak as he got her settled. Jensen kissed her temple and began to work his way down her cheek. "Are you still my biggest fan?" he asked, enjoying her sighs of contentment. She stretched her head to the side to give him better access.

"Always," she said breathlessly.

"Promise?" Jensen whispered against her skin. He brought his head up and put his lips just above hers. "Promise no matter what happens with this gig, you'll always be my biggest fan." His lips brushed hers as he spoke and the electricity that always erupted when he kissed her began thrumming through his body.

Those aqua eyes were glassy with tears as they darted back and forth between his. Her fingers came up, brushing through his hair, and Jensen closed his eyes, holding back a groan at how good it felt. Everything felt so heightened at the moment. He knew there was no guarantee that anything would come from his being on the show, but it felt like all his dreams were on the precipice of coming true.

He finally had a direction. A purpose. His music was going to be heard by thousands, if not hundreds of thousand, and the idea of it made him feel like he was floating.

"I promise," she whispered thickly.

Those words were barely out of her mouth before Jensen moved in. He held her, cradled her, kissed her and did everything within his power to show her how precious she was and how grateful he was for her support. It was her compliments and ego building that had given him the confidence he needed to send the recording off in the first place. It was everything that made her her. This was as much her victory as it was his, and he hoped she knew that.

Jensen had no idea how long he spent enjoying Melody, but all too soon a loud pounding came on the door.

"Dude!"

Jensen pulled back, his chest heaving right along with Melody's. "Your brother has the worst timing in the whole world."

She laughed through her panting. "Definitely."

The pouding came again. "I want to know what the letter said!" Benny yelled through the door.

"He's gonna bring the neighbors down on your head," Melody said with an eyeroll. She scrambled off Jensen's lap and he mourned the loss. As she tried to straighten her mussed hair, Jensen stared, perfectly content to let Benny stay in the cold a little longer, as long as he could keep watching Melody.

She caught his stare and ducked her head. "Stop," she hissed. "You're making me nervous."

Jensen laughed and finally stood, helping her wrangle the blonde locks into a ponytail. "It can't be helped, sweetheart. You definitely looked like you've been well loved on."

Melody groaned and slapped her hands against her cheeks. "It just had to be my brother outside."

The door opened and the two of them snapped their heads that direction. "Oh, whew," Benny said, wiping his forehead. "When you didn't answer, I was half expecting to find you two making out or something."

"Or something," Jensen grumbled, then grunted when Melody elbowed him in the side.

"Oh!" she gasped. "Did I hit one of your bruises?"

"If I say yes, will you kiss it better?" he asked with a smile. He still felt slightly giddy and didn't even consider their company.

"Oooh." Benny groaned, holding his stomach. "Stop! Or I'm going to puke!"

"Well, you're the one who barged into a house that isn't yours," Melody scolded, putting her hands on her hips.

"Yeah, well, from the redness of your lips, I'm gonna guess you two were celebrating." Benny narrowed his eyes. "What did the letter say?"

Jensen looked at Melody, who smiled softly at him and nodded. He took her hand and gave it a squeeze, then turned back to Benny. "I'm in."

Benny whooped and hollered and grabbed Jensen in a bear hug.

"Easy," Jensen wheezed. His bruises were still hurting and Benny's grip was crushing him.

"Bennett!" Melody pulled Jensen out of Bennett's arms. "You're hurting him."

Benny's wide grin told Jensen he wasn't hearing the lecture. "We gotta celebrate." He rubbed his hands together. "Tomorrow night, at the beach. It's party time!"

Jensen laughed and tugged Melody under his arm. This was going to be amazing.

CHAPTER 20

"Three cheers for the famous guitar player from little ole Seaside Bay!" Caro shouted, raising her sparkling cider in the air.

Mel held back a wince as the group shouted into the night, letting everyone within a half-mile radius know that they were celebrating. The heat from the fire did little to thaw the numbness within her chest. She wanted to be excited for Jensen, but it hurt so badly. The light in his eyes was unmistakable and Mel wasn't sure she had ever seen him smile so widely or be so chatty with everyone.

But despite the easy evidence in front of her, she just couldn't find it within herself to be happy. This was her nightmare come to life. Though Jensen hadn't said anything about them needing to break up or even approached the fact that he would be gone for possibly months, Mel knew it was inevitable. She'd seen the stories and read the headlines. All it took was a little fame and people changed.

When the world got a hold of the handsome, talented man holding her hand, there was no way he would continue to be satisfied dating a girl who made smoothies for a living.

He'll probably end up with some model whose legs are a mile long and has perfect teeth, hair and other womanly...stuff.

A kiss to her cheek had Mel forcing her face back into the same look she'd been holding for days. A brittle smile and wide, doe eyes. "Hey, handsome," she whispered, looking at a beaming Jensen.

"Hey, yourself," he whispered back. His arms wrapped around her, pulling her into his chest. "Can you believe all this?"

Mel shook her head. "Nope. It's all sorts of amazing."

"I know," he gushed. He rested his head on top of hers. "I got a call from the news over in Tillamook. They want to come do a story before I leave."

"Wow," Mel said, doing her best to fake her enthusiasm. "You're going to be famous before you ever set foot in that studio."

Jensen's answering chuckle was smooth and carefree. "Nah. But it's kind of fun anyways, isn't it? I mean...who would have ever thought a teacher like myself could accomplish something like this?"

Mel frowned and pulled back just enough to look him in the eye. "What do you mean, a teacher like yourself? You've accomplished a ton of things in your life, Jensen."

He shrugged, some of the giddiness draining from his countenance. "I don't know. I just..." He blew out a long breath. "I just have felt sort of stuck lately. Like every day is the same and I'm in a rut of nothingness." His low laughter was harsh, lacking any amusement.

Mel felt her smile fade. *He...what? He thinks we're in a rut?*

"Here I had just turned thirty and had done absolutely nothing with my life." Jensen shook his head. "If you hadn't encouraged me to pursue my dreams, I'd probably still be stuck. Now I get to actually try for something big."

Stuck...stuck with me, you mean. She slowly pulled out of his arms. His hold, which was usually so warming and full of comfort, was fading. She knew she was losing him, but Mel had thought their time together these past weeks had been good. She thought he'd been happy. Now to find out that he'd felt stuck with her was almost more than she could bear.

Jensen let her go, but his wide smile came back. "How many people get to try for their dreams like this, huh?"

Mel nodded, taking a sip of her soda to hide the tears forming in her eyes. "Whew..." She fanned her face. "That carbonation gets me every time," she muttered as her vision grew blurry.

He must have believed her because Jensen just laughed and kissed her forehead again. "Want me to get you a water?"

She shook her head. "That's all right. I can get it." Before he could say anything else, Mel slipped into the shadows of the group and walked around the outside, heading toward the coolers, just in case Jensen was watching. Once there, she messed around for a few minutes, but didn't grab anything. Her stomach was churning too hard to put anything else in there.

"Hey, Mel," Rose said softly. She was smiling tentatively and Mel tried to smile back to reassure her friend, but it felt more like a grimace.

"Hey, Rose. We're so glad you could make it tonight."

Rose nodded, toying with her bottled water. "Yeah...tonight was special. I figured it was worth a babysitter." As a single mother who worked full-time, Rose tried to spend as much of her extra time with Lilly as possible. Luckily, the two girls were adored by the residents of Seaside Bay and there was never a shortage of those willing to babysit, be it young or old, when Rose needed one.

"It is," Mel agreed, nodding sagely, keeping her focus on the sand at her feet. "It totally is."

"He's happy." It was a statement, not a question, but Mel nodded anyway.

"Yep."

"And you're not."

Mel jerked her head toward her friend. "Excuse me?"

Rose smiled sympathetically. "It's easy to see when a cheerleader doesn't feel like cheering, Mel."

Mel took a shuddering breath. "Oh." She couldn't think of anything else to say. This night wasn't about her. She already felt guilty for her feelings. But to have Rose say it was obvious made it all the worse. She didn't want to detract from Jensen's big night. This was a celebration. The last thing anyone needed was for Mel to break down and ruin it all with her heartbreak.

Rose's arms wrapped around Mel and she stiffened. "It's hard to see the one you love leave," Rose whispered. "But trust me when I say it would be even harder to ask him to stay."

Mel was trembling when Rose pulled back. Her brows were furrowed and she wanted to ask just what Rose was talking about, but when another cheer went up from the crowd, Mel snapped her mouth shut. *Now isn't the time.*

Rose cupped Mel's cheek and rubbed her thumb over Mel's cheekbone in a maternal gesture. "We're here. We love you." Her beautiful profile became visible as she turned to glance at Jensen before coming back to Mel. "And he loves you too, even if he doesn't know it yet." Rose dropped her voice even more and leaned in. "Hang in there. It'll all work out."

Mel couldn't speak. A rock had settled in her throat and she couldn't get it to move before Rose had dissolved back into the group. Mel stood in the cold shadows, wishing that Rose's last words were true, but feeling caught in a web that said they weren't.

"Hey, hon, did you get that water?"

She blinked rapidly and turned to Jensen. "Oh. No. I didn't." Grateful for the chance to turn away from him, Mel reached down to the cooler and opened it for the drink. "Want anything?"

"Just you," Jensen flirted.

Mel sniffed and pulled herself back together. "Well, you've got me," she responded as she stood up.

"Can't go on without my biggest fan," Jensen said, grabbing her hand. "Oh man, you're cold! Let's get you back to the fire."

Mel followed, knowing the flames would do nothing to warm her up. Despite Rose's advice, every dream Mel had was crashing and she had a feeling she would never be warm again.

SOMETHING WAS WRONG with Melody, but Jensen wasn't sure what it was. His attention had been so caught up in celebrating his invite to the show that he hadn't been able to sit down with her and get everything figured out.

He'd be leaving in a couple of weeks and there was no way he could let things sit as they did now. Their relationship was too new for him to let it go this way. Long distance would be hard enough—her hurting would make it unmanageable.

He tugged Melody down into her seat, then pulled the chair closer to him. "Want to tell me what's wrong?" he asked. He held her hand tightly. Every time he'd tried to get close, she'd put him off. It was starting to worry him.

"Nothing's wrong," Melody said. She smiled, but it wasn't her usual brilliant one.

Jensen shook his head. "Why won't you tell me? You haven't been yourself for days." Melody stiffened and Jensen groaned internally. That probably wasn't the best way to handle it, he knew, but he was running out of ways to get her to open up. He brought their fingers to his lips. "Tell me, sweetheart. I don't like to see you so upset."

She gave him a sad smile. "It's nothing to worry about. I just keep worrying about Micah since we haven't heard anything from Child Services."

Jensen nodded. While he believed her, he wasn't sure it was the whole answer. "I'm worried about him too, but right now, there's nothing we can do. If the opportunity arises to get more information, then we will. Right now, however, we have to leave it in the hands of those who deal with this sort of thing."

Melody's gaze was on her lap. "I know. But that doesn't mean I have to like it."

Jensen chuckled. "That's because you're a nurturer. You don't like to see anybody hurting."

"What's wrong with that?" she asked.

"Nothing," he replied. "It's part of why people love you so much." *Crap.* Those words were a little too close to things he wasn't ready to say just yet. When her eyes widened, he knew she'd caught the reference. Clearing his throat, Jensen turned away for a second. "I'm going to need your help packing," he said, trying to lighten the subject. "If I'm going to be on national television, then I need to look better than my usual khakis."

"I think that's Brooklyn's expertise, not mine," she replied, referring to their friend who owned a clothing boutique in town.

Jensen glanced sideways at Melody, but she wasn't looking at him. Her face had gone back to being melancholy. "Melody..." he whispered soothingly. "Tell me what's going on. Please?" He tucked a piece of hair behind her ear. "You're killing me, baby."

Her eyes glistened in the firelight. "I'm sorry," she whispered thickly. "I'm just not sure how to do this."

Jensen frowned. "This? Do you mean us?"

Melody shook her head. "No. I mean..." She turned away and chewed her lip. "I mean, how to send you away, knowing that you probably won't come back." A tear dripped down her cheek. "It's no secret that I've been in love with you since I was a little girl, Jensen."

"Decided you had to be the big man on campus, huh?"

Melody turned away as Jensen looked over his shoulder and forced a smile for Felix. "Well, if it isn't the captain." He kept his voice light even as his mind fell into dark places. Melody had been about to tell him what was wrong and it didn't sound good.

Felix laughed and walked around so that Jensen wasn't craning his neck. He slapped his friend on the back. "Who'd have thought that the quiet one was the one who would be famous." Felix sipped his soda. "I certainly wouldn't have figured that one out."

Jensen grinned, trying to act relaxed, even though every part of him was wound as tight as a spring. "Truth be told, I wouldn't have either. Dreams are usually that...just dreams."

"Well, it's about time you had one come true," Felix stated. "If anyone deserves to have something good happen to them, it's definitely you." His eyes flitted to Melody and back. "Both of you, actually. You're the two nicest people I've ever known."

"Are you saying mean things about me again?" Charli, Felix's younger sister, asked. She came sauntering up to her brother's side and punched him in the shoulder. "You know what Mom always said."

Felix rolled his eyes. "I didn't say anything mean, Charli." He shrugged. "I just didn't say anything nice about you either."

Jensen chuckled as Charli pretended to be outraged and began to beat on her brother. *I'm going to miss all this while I'm gone.* The thought made him pause. While Jensen had thought about the fact that it would be difficult to be separated from Melody, he hadn't thought about Seaside Bay as a whole. For so long it had felt like he was stuck here. That life was one long monotonous story, and Jensen had always associated that with Seaside Bay.

But now he realized that even though he'd only be gone a month or two, he would miss the bonfires. He would miss eating treats at Caro's shop. He would miss Benny's stupid jokes and insatiable appetite. He would miss Ken giving them all lectures on following the law, only to then wink and let them off the hook.

His eyes went to Melody, who was smiling and chatting with Caro. He would especially miss his mornings at the smoothie shop. Melody's beaming smile that filled him with warmth and her crazy compliments to everyone in the shop. The woman had no idea how special she was. Hopefully they could work out what was bothering her before he left. He didn't want that distracting him when he couldn't do anything about it.

"Did you read through the contract yet?" Felix asked, bringing Jensen's attention back to the conversation.

Jensen nodded. "Yeah. I had Mr. Filchor take a look at it." The elderly lawyer still had an incredibly sharp mind and Jensen had been grateful for his help in understanding the legalese.

"Is there anything weird in it?" Charli asked, stuffing a hot dog in her mouth. The woman did Iron-Mans and could often eat everyone else under the table. Everyone except Benny anyway.

Jensen made a face. "A couple of things. Most of it is about staying away from social media and not leaking any results or secrets of the show."

"Oooh, all hush hush and stuff." Charli nodded slowly. "Can't share anything or they'll lose the ratings."

"Exactly," Jensen agreed.

"Are you allowed to talk to people at all while you're on there?" Felix questioned, tilting his head to the side. "If we shoot you a text, are we gonna be sued or something?"

Jensen noticed Melody's conversation had grown quiet. In fact, the whole group had. He smiled. "Yeah, I can talk to people, but the contract specifically prohibits me from speaking about the show, so I can't give you any updates or anything. And I have to consent to being videoed twenty-four-seven."

"So if you were talking to us on the phone, it could be recorded?" Charli's eyebrows were high.

Jensen nodded. "Yeah...I suppose it could." He turned toward Melody, who looked shocked.

"I guess that limits the mushy things you can say to each other, huh?" Benny shouted across the fire.

Jensen's eyes were locked with Melody's. He felt like he was begging her to understand. "This won't last forever," he said to the group, though he really meant it for her. "Before you know it, I'll be back here teaching and being as boring as before."

"Unless you make it big," Benny pointed out.

The idea of making it big was exciting, but Jensen could tell Melody wasn't ready for that thought when the blood drained from her face. He shrugged at Benny. "I guess only time will tell," he said.

CHAPTER 21

"Tell him we all said goodbye!" Emily called after Mel as she dashed out the back door.

"Will do!" Mel pulled on her jacket as she left. She was supposed to leave ten minutes ago to say goodbye to Jensen before he drove to Portland to catch his plane, but the crowd in the smoothie shop had been bigger than usual and she'd gotten stuck.

The last two weeks had flown by and now Jensen was going to be gone for who knew how long. The only plus side to the passing of time was how quiet things had been with Micah and Mitchell.

Tears once more pricked her vision, but she forced them back. After the disastrous bonfire, Mel had gone home, given herself a stern talking to and forced herself to pull it together. She had years of experience acting happy when she felt broken. It seemed ridiculous that now she would have such trouble.

That's because you didn't truly know what you were missing.

"No," she scolded herself. "No more. Jensen wants this. It's his life and his choice. My job is to support. Even if it means letting him go to do that."

Part of Rose's imparted wisdom the other night had begun to make sense to Mel. Letting Jensen go was hard. But after watching his excitement and how his eyes had pleaded for understanding, asking him to stay would be harder. She couldn't do it. She couldn't cut him off from something that meant so much. And so...she was preparing herself to let him go. Not just to the show, but forever.

Even Jensen had said only time would tell if he came back. The words had been the last bit she needed to completely crush her heart that night, confirming to Mel that it was time for her to prepare for the inevitable. She'd spent plenty of time with him these last two weeks, but had made sure not to let herself get any more deeply involved than she already was. Kisses had been kept light and time spent alone was brief. She just couldn't let herself go on pretending like it would all be okay, because it wouldn't, and it might never be again.

She skidded to a stop on the street in front of his house and jumped out of the car.

"Hey, beautiful!" Jensen greeted her from the side of his car. "I was starting to think you weren't going to make it."

Melody put her fixed smile into place. "Sorry. The shop was busier than normal this morning, so it took longer to break free than I thought."

He held open his arms. "That's all right. I'm just grateful you made it at all."

Melody braced herself, then stepped into his embrace. His warmth tried to penetrate her tight muscles and soothe her every ache, but she wouldn't let it. When he pressed a kiss to the top of her head, she kept the pleasurable shiver from running down her spine and forced her heart to keep its steady beat.

"I'm going to miss you," he whispered against her hair. "Especially how you smell like sweet fruit all the time." He took an exaggerated sniff of her hair and Mel laughed as intended.

She pulled back. "You'll be so busy being famous you won't have a chance to miss me," she said with a grin.

Jensen stepped closer and cupped her face, those beautiful brown eyes searching hers. "I'll miss you by the time I'm a mile down the road," he whispered, all signs of teasing gone. "The hardest part of being gone is going to be you staying here."

She was losing the battle to stay detached as a single tear slid down her cheeks. *Why does he have to say such sweet things? It only makes this harder.* Before she could respond, Jensen had lowered his head and brought their mouths together. This kiss was not like the soft pecks Mel had been surviving on the last couple of weeks. There was a hunger to his actions that she couldn't ignore.

Wrapping her arms around his neck, Mel stood on tiptoe and threw away all her resolutions. If this was her last moment with him, she was going to make the best of it.

One of his hands was splayed across her back, keeping her bound to his chest, while the other dove into her hair, cupping the back of her head. When Jensen moved her for a better angle, Mel did nothing to protest, giving and taking in tandem with his actions.

She had no idea how much time had passed by the time they finally separated, but if their interlude had lasted much longer, Mel was sure she would have fainted. Her chest was heaving as she sucked in air to help with the lightheadedness she was feeling. Considering how much Jensen was panting, she knew he had been in the same position.

He kept his forehead against hers. "That'll have to last us for a while," he whispered.

She nodded. "Considering how amazing it was, it should do the job."

Jensen chuckled and kissed her nose. "Nothing will ever compare with actually having you next to me though."

Mel blinked and nodded. "Be safe," she whispered, her sadness stealing her voice. *I love you! Don't leave me!* The words went unspoken. She couldn't put that burden on him. He'd declared no love toward her, other than a blanket statement about their friend group in general, and now was not the time to ask for it. She had a sick feeling in her stomach that if she pushed for it now, it would only lead to more heartache. *If he loved me, he would tell me. Since he's determined to leave, it's obvious that his feelings for me aren't enough...I'm not enough.*

The realization helped pull her mind out of the clouds and her earlier determination to pull back came roaring back with a vengeance. She forced her shaky legs to back up. "You better run or you'll miss the plane."

"We wouldn't want that, would we?" he asked with a grin. He reached out and caressed her cheek. "Will my biggest fan be watching?"

She nodded woodenly. "Of course. I won't miss an episode."

Jensen opened his mouth, paused, then snapped it shut and smiled. "Right." He took a step backward. "Have a Twinkie for me and I'll talk to you soon."

Mel nodded, backing up onto his lawn so she was out of the way of the car. "You'll do great," she encouraged, swallowing the bile in her throat. "You're too amazing not to win."

Jensen chuckled and gave her a sad smile. "See ya."

She gave a small wave. "See ya." In another minute, the car was out of sight. Putting her hands on her knees, Mel gasped for breath. Her vision grew spotty and she stumbled to her knees. Her hand fluttered to her heart, and Mel realized she was starting to hyperventilate. *Breathe...breathe...*

She closed her eyes and began to count her breaths, forcing her lungs to open and shut on command. After a couple of minutes of focused work, she felt her body begin to calm down and she opened her eyes again. He was gone. Possibly for good. Though the pain felt as if it would rip her apart, Mel knew with a certainty that she had done the right thing. She would never, ever force someone to give up their dreams for her.

If he doesn't love me enough to stay, then we'd never be happy, she reminded herself. *Forced love isn't love at all, and I'd never survive if he resented staying home.*

She groaned as she got to her feet. "Work. I need to work." She realized she'd left her keys in the car and began to stumble in that direction. Staying busy was going to be the only way for her to keep the tears and heartache at bay. As long as she continued to make other people happy, Mel would be able to find solace in her lonely life.

She got in the driver's seat and started the engine before a note in the passenger seat caught her attention. Mel frowned and picked up the folded piece of paper.

Who will protect you now?

The paper fell onto her lap and her breath grew ragged once more. "What is that?" she whispered hoarsely. Her shaking fingers picked up the messy scrawl again and she read it over and over. She glanced to her keychain, noting the mace attached in a small pink canister. "You're fine," she told herself. "Just fine."

Crumpling the paper, Mel tossed it into the small garbage bag she kept in her car. "Was probably left there by mistake," she assured herself as she pulled out onto the street and turned around.

Still, she couldn't seem to help looking around, as if the culprit would be standing nearby. There was no one standing close by who could have left the note in her car. "I'll just be extra careful," she whispered to the quiet car. "That's all I need, is just to be extra careful."

JENSEN HAD SPENT MOST of the day feeling like a young, inexperienced school boy. Nothing in his life has prepared him for what it would be like to be behind the scenes at a major television station.

People were everywhere. Literally. He couldn't turn around without bumping into another body. And the speed at which everyone worked was dizzying. It was nothing like the laid-back, small town he'd grown up in.

I wish Melody could see this. He felt the familiar pinch of pain at his separation from her. It had been more difficult than he'd expected to say goodbye yesterday. Her goodbye kiss had made him want to throw his plans to the wind and never let her go.

But he'd had a day and a night to work on getting his emotions under control and felt like he was in pretty good shape this morning.

The hotel room was nice but nondescript and he hadn't enjoyed his quiet evening since his nerves had been on edge the entire time. Even chatting with Melody hadn't helped his worries. He had been picked up at the airport, driven straight to the hotel and practically locked inside. The only people he'd had face-to-face contact with were the security guards and a couple of assistants from the show.

Today he was supposed to meet the rest of the contestants and Jensen found himself eager to check out the competition.

"Tanner? Looking for Jensen Tanner?"

Jensen shoved his wandering thoughts away and raised his hand. "Here."

The harried assistant scurried over to his side. "You're supposed to be in the conference room," she scolded, grabbing his arm. "All the contestants should be there."

"Sorry," Jensen said, matching her stride. Her high heels clicked on the hard floors, but his dress shoes were quiet. The contrast caught his attention as they left the busiest areas of the building and walked down a hallway. Eventually her footsteps grew quiet as well when they reached carpet. The silence seemed awkward, but he had no idea what to say and the assistant seemed in too much of a hurry for small talk.

They reached a door and Jensen jumped in front of her. "Let me get that," he said, his manners automatically coming out.

The woman looked at him in surprise. "Well, they'll just eat you up, won't they?" She gave a short laugh, then proceeded him into the room. "Here he is, Mr. Timmons. Jensen Tanner."

Jensen's face was hot as he walked in and he noticed all the eyes on him. He really was late.

"Mr. Tanner," the man called Mr. Timmons said casually. "Welcome. Have a seat, please."

"I'm sorry I got lost," Jensen muttered, sitting in the only empty seat in the room. He nodded at the people on either side of him. A young girl grinned back, but the older man to his right looked away without responding. *Okay...*

"Now that we're all here," Mr. Timmons spoke again, "let's start again."

His eyes went to Jensen and he felt his cheeks become even warmer.

"Ms. Sanders, if you would start introductions all over, I'd appreciate it. Your name, where you're from and what your talent is." Mr. Timmons nodded with a small smile.

A young woman who looked like she was about Melody's age preened in her chair. She brushed her hair over her shoulder and put on a perfect pout with her bright red lips. "I'm Victoria Sanders, from San Diego, California."

That explains the blonde hair and tan, Jensen thought. Victoria's hair color reminded him of Melody's, only Melody's wasn't fake.

"I'm twenty-four years old," she continued, "single—" an eyebrow went up as her eyes went around the room—"and I sing."

A small, polite applause broke out around the room.

"Thank you, Ms. Sanders." Mr. Timmons leaned onto the center table. He waved a hand at the man next to Victoria. "Mr. Butterworth."

The man's smirk and wink in Victoria's direction let Jensen know the guy would be difficult to get along with. He oozed confidence, reminding Jensen of some of the football boys in the high school back home. "Tony Butterworth." He gave a crooked grin. "I also sing." His eyes went back to Victoria again. "Maybe we can do a duet sometime."

Jensen barely held back from rolling his eyes. He hoped the company held up the rules about no fraternizing between contestants. It would be all kinds of awkward if people started pairing off.

The introductions went on for a few more minutes before reaching Jensen. Most of the group seemed in awe to be there, making Jensen feel like they would all have something in common. Victoria and Tony had, so far, been the only ones who looked like they would be difficult.

"Mr. Tanner?"

Jensen nodded. "Yeah, I'm Jensen Tanner. I'm a high school English teacher from Oregon." He paused at the snicker coming from Tony's direction. "I play guitar."

"Ooh." Victoria leaned forward. "Guitar players are so fun." Her smile was blindingly white and Jensen simply gave her a nod. No amount of white teeth would ever compare to Melody's warmth.

Ten minutes later, Mr. Timmons dove into the rules of the show and what standards they would be held to during their time at the station.

"All in all, if you'll just do as you're told, we won't have any problems," Mr. Timmons finished, tapping his pen against the table. "I realize this kind of lifestyle will be a shock to many of you, but we've worked with hundreds of people before and know exactly how to make it all work if you'll simply follow directions." His eyes roved the room. "Questions?"

No one spoke up and Jensen gave a small sigh of relief. The meeting had gone on much longer than he'd expected and he was ready to get up and move his legs.

"Great." Mr. Timmons straightened. "Let's get you all to wardrobe and then we'll be doing some publicity shots." He stood. "The show starts next week so we'll be promoting the premiere for the next couple of days and will be using you to do it. And in no time at all, we'll be live." He headed toward the door and Jensen fell into line.

So much for bringing my own clothes, he thought wryly. Brooklyn and Melody would be disappointed that he wasn't going to be wearing the clothes they picked out. *Guess I'll just have to save them for when I get home.*

"In here," Mr. Timmons said, waving them toward an open doorway. "This is the first step to making all your dreams come true." He smiled at each contestant as they began to funnel inside.

Jensen's eyes went wide again at all the clothes and makeup supplies in front of him as he went inside. That excitement he'd felt when he first heard he'd been chosen began to thrum through his veins. He already missed Melody, but with something this grand standing in front of him, he knew he'd have more than enough to keep him busy and distracted. Life couldn't get much better at the moment.

CHAPTER 22

Check these out! Our boy is really doing it!

Bennett's texts were full of excitement and Mel had eagerly clicked the link to see the advertisement, but as soon as the photos had come up, her heart had sunk. Jensen had been glammed up in a way she barely recognized. His hair was styled and cut shorter than usual on the sides, while the longer top was brushed up and over. He wore a collared shirt where the first couple of buttons were undone, showing off just a bit of his strong chest, and a bowtie had been left hanging around his neck. The casual sexiness of his individual picture was mind-blowing and had Mel struggling to catch her breath.

It was the group photo, however, that caused her to stop breathing altogether. Jensen's strong arm was around a gorgeous blonde, who was smiling as if she owned the whole world. White teeth, silky hair, red lipstick and a willowy figure made the woman look like a model. And she looked far too comfortable cuddling into Jensen's chest. *Jensen doesn't look too upset about it either.*

A low whistle came from Mel's right. "Wow. Jensen cleaned up good."

Mel turned to Emily and smiled. "Yep. He always has."

Emily laughed. "True enough. But there's just something about a man with a guitar that screams 'Look at me ladies!'"

Mel forced herself to laugh as well. "No arguments here." Her eyes went back to the screen. This was exactly what she had imagined would happen. The hustle and bustle and wealth of the big city would have Jensen forgetting all about her. Though she had to admit that it was happening faster than she'd planned.

The last text she'd received from Jensen had been last night and he hadn't mentioned anything about the photos or the woman in them. *He can't,* she reminded herself. *He can't talk about the show.*

Mel sighed and stuffed the phone in her back pocket. "Time to get back to work," she said, more to herself than anything, but Emily nodded back.

"Yep. Customers, fruit and smoothies wait for no man."

A genuine smile tugged at Mel's lips for the first time in days. "Good one. We should turn that into our motto."

"I expect full rights and recognition," Emily shot back.

"Deal." Mel walked back up to the counter and began cleaning up. She was letting some of the other workers do the name-calling to-day, though it was Mel's favorite job. Somehow, her heart just wasn't in it at the moment. She spun to look at Emily. "Maybe I'll go work in the kitchen," Mel said. "I wanna try a couple more ideas I had for those smoothie bowls."

Emily nodded. "Go ahead. We've got it covered out here."

Mel knew she did. Emily was a wonderful shift manager and technically, Mel didn't have to be out front at all if she didn't want to be. However, she enjoyed being there. She loved seeing the smiling faces and saying hello to all the locals. At least she did when she was feeling herself. Today just wasn't one of those days.

Setting the towel she was using in the dirty clothes bin, Mel wiped her wet hands on her apron and headed back. She hoped that doing something creative would take her mind off Ms. Model and Jensen.

"He'd tell me...wouldn't he?" she whispered to herself. "Jensen wouldn't drag me along. I mean, it couldn't have happened this quickly, could it? If he's already found someone else, he would let me know that."

Unless he can't.

"Aaargh," Mel growled, shutting the kitchen door behind her. "He can't talk about the show, but he could totally break up with me." She put her hands on the counter and hung her head. "You know him," she reminded herself. "You've known him for years. He wouldn't do that to you. He wouldn't drag you along. He's honest, kind and talented. He also has manners and was raised by old-fashioned, conservative parents. There's no way Jensen would hurt you like this on purpose."

Nodding firmly to build her resolve, Mel set about grabbing some fruit and a blender. "Ice...I need ice." She picked up a large scoop and headed for the ice maker, only to skid to a stop.

Mitchell Derringer stood in the corner of the kitchen with his arms folded over his chest, his shoulder leaning casually against the wall and a triumphant smirk on his face.

"How did you get in here?" Mel asked, her voice coming out stronger than she'd expected. Fear had immediately infiltrated every bit of her body, practically freezing her in place. The fact that her vocal chords still worked seemed like a miracle.

His grin grew. "You really shouldn't leave your back door unlocked." Mitchell clucked his tongue. "You never know what riffraff might find their way inside."

Mel stuck her chin in the air. "Please leave."

"Ooh, please." Mitchel straightened and dropped his arms. "Those are some very good manners you have, Ms. Frasier." He took a step forward.

Mel stepped back and bumped into the counter. "What are you doing here? Ken told you to leave me alone."

Mitchel's eyebrows rose. "Ken? Are you two-timing your little teacher? Does he know?" He laughed as if he'd made a great joke. "I just wanted to talk to you," Mitchell said lazily. "It seems like you have this strange ability to inspire men to protect you." His head tilted to the side and his eyes narrowed. "Just why is that, would you say?"

Mel frowned and took a step to the side when he came her way again. "I don't know what you're talking about." Her voice was beginning to shake.

"You know exactly what I'm talking about," he said quietly. "First, it was the teacher, then it was the cop and lastly, my son." His steps continued, his demeanor predatory. "Just what do you do that causes them to risk themselves for you?" His eyes went from her head to her feet and back, leaving Mel feeling exposed and dirty. "I mean, you're a tasty morsel, but nothing I haven't seen before." His head was still cocked as if she were some curiosity he wanted to figure out.

I knew it! Mel thought. *Micah was trying to help that night.* "It's amazing what kindness will inspire others to do," she said, edging around the counter corner. "Perhaps you should try it sometime."

Mitchell laughed again, shaking his head as he drew closer. "Why worry about being kind when you can just take what you need?"

"Because it's the right thing to do," Mel whispered. She darted to the left, putting the counter between them. It gave her a little bit of relief, but not enough to feel safe. Mitchell needed to leave. Now.

His answering grin made Mel's heart skip a beat. When his muscles tightened, she knew he was about to do something bad. Before he could move, however, her phone began to ring in her back pocket and they both froze.

Mel fumbled for the device, forcing her feet into motion in order to take advantage of his pause so she could answer the phone and gain some distance. "Hello?"

"Melody!"

"Jensen!" she gushed. "I'm so glad to hear from you." Her eyes stayed glued to Mitchell, who scowled, then spun and burst out the back door. Once the door slammed shut, Mel ran over and locked it before turning and putting her back against it.

"How's my favorite girl?" Jensen asked.

Mel's shaky knees gave out and slowly, she slid to the floor. All earlier thoughts of betrayal and heartache were gone with the most recent situation with Mitchell. "I'm fine," she said breathlessly. "How about you?"

"Missing you," he admitted. "But things are going better than I could have ever imagined."

Mel closed her eyes and forced her breathing to slow down. She couldn't ruin that by telling him what had happened. *Support. That's your role right now. Support.* "I'm so thrilled for you," she said, putting extra pep in her tone. "I saw the publicity pictures today and you look more handsome than ever."

His answering chuckle helped her release the bulk of her tension. Letting her legs relax, Mel settled in to chat with her boyfriend, making sure to keep her troubles to herself.

"YOU WANT ME TO WEAR what?" Victoria screeched.

Jensen winced and shook his head. The singer had a major diva problem and liked to share it with the entire cast. The last few days had been a hectic race of make-over and publicity stunts and Jensen was already finding himself wearing thin on patience.

Some of the contestants seemed to eat up the attention, but Jensen wasn't one of them. He didn't mind getting dressed up and playing his guitar, but he did mind spending an hour in a chair getting makeup put on his face and having his hair done.

He also wasn't happy with the style they had decided on for him. His shirts were always undone nearly halfway down his chest and they kept putting ties and bowties on him, only to have them hang there, as if they were some kind of weird necklace. It all seemed so stupid.

A smile tugged at his lips when he recalled Melody telling him how sexy it was, in spite of his reservations. *Suppose that's what they're going for,* he thought. "For Melody," he murmured as he shrugged into the suit coat they wanted him to wear tonight.

His nerves were a little high-strung tonight, since it was the premiere. All the recordings were live events so that the judges and online audience could vote, which made it all even more important that he make a good impression. Two people were headed home right off the bat and Jensen was determined not to be one of them.

He might not have been enjoying some of the aspects of television, but he wasn't about to be the first kicked off the island...or stage as it were.

"Mr. Tanner." Marissa poked her head in the dressing room door. "We need to do your hair and makeup."

Jensen nodded. "Be right there."

The no-nonsense woman nodded and ducked back out.

"No privacy at all," Gary grumbled as he finished doing up his pants.

"I hear ya," Jensen answered. The older man beside him was a harmonica player and from what Jensen had heard during practice, the man was good. Really good. Along with his music skills, the performer also brought the grumpiness that men tended to get in their older years and had ended up becoming Jensen's comic relief in the past few days.

"One of these days she'll get an eyeful of something she can't unsee," Gary continued.

Jensen snorted. "Maybe we'll just learn to dress faster, huh?"

Gary grimaced. "I'm already moving as fast as I can."

Jensen kept his smile and shook his head as he walked to the door. "See ya in a few!"

The man waved him on and Jensen stepped out into the busy hallway. If he'd thought things were busy before, they were downright chaotic now. It was amazing how many people it took to make a show like this run. "It's no wonder the credits last forever," he murmured to himself as he walked down two doors to the styling area.

"Great. Right here, please, Mr. Tanner." Marissa patted her chair firmly. The bright lights set up at each station were blinding if a body looked directly at them, so Jensen made sure to keep his focus on the floor and chair.

"Come to get made up, pretty boy?"

Jensen groaned inside. "Yep," he said, forcing a smile as he finally noticed Victoria sitting in the chair next to his. He lowered himself down and shifted until he was comfortable. "Marissa here can work magic on someone like me."

Victoria snickered. "They've done a good job of taking the small town out of your looks, that's for sure." She looked at herself in the mirror and twisted her head this way and that, much to the frustration of the woman working on her. "Now I just wish they'd learn to stop putting me in those horrid pastels. They wash me out."

Jensen grinned when he heard Marissa grunt in annoyance. "Mm,hm," he said, hoping the egotistical woman would be quiet. During most of the photo shoots, he'd been paired with her. Something about their coloring complimenting each other. The only thing Jensen had really noticed was that Victoria didn't feel nearly as good hanging onto him as Melody did. Soft, sweet Melody was a far cry from whining, entitled Victoria.

A wave of homesickness rushed through him and Jensen found himself frowning.

"Perk up, Mr. Tanner," Marissa snapped. "You'll give yourself wrinkles with that grimace." She began patting foundation on his dark circles.

"Sorry," he muttered, closing his eyes so he wouldn't have to figure out where to stare while she was so close.

"He doesn't stand a chance," Victoria stated loudly, drawing Jensen's attention.

He hadn't been listening to her conversation, one-sided as it was, with her hairdresser. But now he was curious who she was talking about.

"No one listens to the harmonica anymore," Victoria continued, her voice sounding blithe. "I don't know why they brought him on in the first place. Probably just to give the viewers a variety."

"Have you heard him play?" Jensen couldn't help but ask. "He's really good. And just because it isn't as popular as it once was doesn't make his skills worth any less," Jensen continued. "In fact, it probably makes them worth more. Since less people know how to do what he does."

"You mark my words," Victoria snapped. Jensen could hear her anger even though his eyes were still closed. "He'll be the first one gone. He's just a prop."

Jensen sighed and decided it wasn't worth arguing. You'd think he'd know by now not to try and change Victoria's mind. A week in her company was enough to teach him all sorts of things he didn't really care to know.

"Over here, Mr. Smith," another voice said from another spot in the room.

Jensen's eyes snapped open as he realized Gary was there. *I hope he didn't hear Victoria.*

"Don't know why you can't get more comfortable chairs," Gary grumbled. "Have you ever sat in it?" he asked his hairdresser.

Jensen relaxed and let out a long breath as the older man spoke. It didn't sound like he'd overheard Victoria's catty remarks.

"Girl ought to learn to keep her mouth shut," Marissa said tightly in a low voice.

Jensen's eyes met hers in the mirror and he nodded.

Marissa's mouth was pressed into a tight line as she held up a spray bottle. "Close your eyes."

Jensen followed her orders, holding his breath as well as a finishing spray was put on his skin. He had a feeling that the animosity between contestants was only going to get worse the longer the show went on, and as much as he hoped to last for awhile, he wasn't looking forward to that aspect of it.

But Melody and the gang are all rooting for you, he reminded himself. *This isn't just for you anymore.* He took a deep breath. *This is for her. And that'll make it worth it.*

CHAPTER 23

"So what is it you all do exactly?" Mrs. Witherspoon folded her arms over her ample chest and glared at the students, making Mel hold back a laugh.

The woman very clearly did not want to be there, but Principal Nielsen had assigned her to take over for Jensen while he was gone.

"We talk about books," Darrin said, his chair once more settled back on the two back legs.

"Four on the floor, Mr. Stuart," Mrs. Witherspoon snapped. Her shoulders fell and she sighed. "What book have you been working on?"

"Shakespeare!" Eliza shouted.

"*Star Wars!*"

"*How to Train Your Dragon!*"

The room turned to look at Eric, who flushed.

"What?"

"That's like a middle school book," Jack said with a disgusted face.

Eric shrugged. "So? It's awesome."

"The movies were awesome," Darrin agreed. "Eret, son of Eret was like...the man."

"See?" Eric defended himself.

Eliza rolled her eyes. "You boys are all the same."

"Watch it," Darrin sneered. "She'll start spouting old time English, secretly insulting you if you're not careful."

Mel put a fist over her mouth. She couldn't help it. These kids were hilarious and a great distraction from her stress.

Although she spoke to Jensen almost every day, she was finding herself lonelier than ever. Mitchell hadn't been back, thank heavens, since he came into her shop a couple of weeks ago. The biggest worry on that front was the fact that Micah hadn't been back to the reading club. And since she didn't work at the school, Mel had no idea how he was doing in his classes.

As far as her relationship went, however, her short conversations with Jensen weren't quite enough to ease her concerns or to help the fact that she felt like she was losing him. The premiere had gone fantastically and he was already a crowd favorite. His face was everywhere, right along with that blonde singer.

Mel pressed her lips together at the thought of the other contestant. The distance was already killing Mel's relationship. She didn't need a beautiful woman to make it worse, even if Jensen hadn't mentioned her at all.

"So you haven't actually read a book yet?" Mrs. Witherspoon asked, throwing her hands in the air and bringing Mel back to the classroom. "Yes, Ms. Buchanan?"

Eliza sat up straighter. "We've mostly been discussing the books we're working on by ourselves and been picking them apart for themes and symbols."

Mrs. Witherspoon nodded. "Okay. That I can work with." Her eyes roamed the room. "Ms. Torres. What did you read during this last week?"

The shy girl ducked down, her face turning red. She mumbled something under her breath, but Mel couldn't understand what she said.

"Speak up!" Mrs. Witherspoon demanded.

"*Twilight*," Angie said more clearly. She cleared her throat and turned away from the looks of her fellow students.

"Vampires?" Darrin groaned. "You've got to be kidding me." He hung his head backward.

"What's wrong with vampires?" Eliza argued, pushing his shoulder. "Edward could take you out any time."

Darrin rolled his eyes. "Edward is a sparkly wimp who runs at the first sign of danger."

"How do you know?" Eliza folded her arms over her chest. "Unless you've read it?"

"I have sisters," Darrin argued back. He turned to Mrs. Witherspoon. "And there is nothing symbolic about a stupid vampire falling for a stupid girl and the stupid werewolf who wants her."

Mrs. Witherspoon put her hands in the air as the arguments grew louder. "Enough!" she called out. When the room finally quieted, she glared at the offenders. "If we are to have this club, then it will need to be civil. Calling the books someone enjoys stupid is not all right. Do you understand, Mr. Smithfield?"

Darrin sighed and nodded reluctantly.

"Ms. Fisher?"

Eliza huffed but nodded.

"Right. Now...I'm sure we can find some commentary on human frailties if we work hard enough."

For the next half-hour the kids offered their arguments, some insightful, others humorous as they debated the quality of a vampire love story. When it was over, the students rushed out, leaving Mel alone with Mrs. Witherspoon.

"Whew," Mel said, tucking her hair behind her ear. "That was a wild class today."

Mrs. Witherspoon laughed softly. "I'm glad to know that wasn't their usual behavior." She looked up from where she was straightening chairs. "How's Mr. Tanner doing? I'm not one for television or social media, so I'm afraid I have to rely on others for an update. And since you two have been dating, I'm guessing you're the best source of information I can find right now."

Mel's cheeks warmed. *Is it still dating when you barely speak and don't live in the same town?* "He's doing great," she said with a stiff smile. "He's made it past the first two rounds and seems to have a good rapport with the audience."

Mrs. Witherspoon nodded. "As it should be. He's always been easy to get along with."

Mel nodded then brushed her hands together. "Looks like that's about it."

"I suppose so." The older woman made a shooing motion. "Now you go on. I'm sure you've got plenty of things to do."

Mel smiled and waved, then headed out the door. She paused once outside and raised her face to the sun. The weather was getting quite cold, but today was one of those rare fall days where the sun was shining brightly, though it bore little heat.

"Ahh..." She smiled into the sky, enjoying the light on her face. There was just something about nature that was so renewing. Taking a deep breath, she reached into her pocket, withdrew her keys and started toward her vehicle. Right before she reached it, Mel paused. A sixth sense was tickling the back of her mind, just as it had nearly a month ago in the alley behind the smoothie shop. Slowly the hairs on the back of her neck stood on end and she felt the beginnings of fear work its way into her chest.

He's here.

She knew it as surely as she knew her own name. Mitchell was watching her again. Her hand automatically went to her phone in her back pocket while her eyes searched the area. Even though she couldn't see him, Mel could feel that she was being watched, and this time she wouldn't be caught unawares.

Her hand tightened on the keyring, her mace dangling there, and her thumb was posed over the emergency button on her phone. Slowly, she continued to her car, her eyes darting every direction and her muscles coiled and ready to strike.

It wasn't until she was seated in a locked car with the engine running that she finally allowed herself to relax. Sort of. She had no desire for Mitchell to see how much he affected her, so Mel pulled out of the parking lot, quickly drove home and then fell apart.

Her hands shook as she unlocked her apartment and went inside, collapsing on the couch as she forced air in and out of her lungs. "This has got to stop," she whispered to herself.

Jensen was gone, Bennett would blow a gasket if he found out and the police couldn't do anything since Mitchell hadn't ever touched her.

"So what am I supposed to do?"

"HOW ARE THINGS AT THE shop?" Jensen couldn't help the smile playing on his lips as he spoke to Melody. She was still the best part of his day. She always had such good reports of what was happening in town and her upbeat personality gave him help to keep going even though he was growing more and more homesick by the day.

"Fine," she said cheerily. "Things have slowed a little with the cooler weather, but we do that every year, so it's totally expected."

"Come up with any new flavors lately?" Jensen leaned back against the headboard in the hotel he was staying in. The bland room was starting to feel more like a prison than a retreat. He'd made it past the first three eliminations at this point, but each time he survived felt less and less like a victory.

"Nah," Melody continued. "But I have been working on those smoothie bowls and I think I'm ready to start selling them. Plus I've been working with Caro to create a really good homemade granola recipe."

"Caro makes granola?" Jensen asked. "I thought her specialties were candies."

"Yeah, but she actually went to culinary school, so it's not like she doesn't know about making things like granola."

"True enough," he murmured. He closed his eyes as she continued, letting his mind imagine her silky blonde hair and soft pink lips. He could swear he could almost smell the scent of lemons, which always seemed to cling to her like a second skin. "Remind me what a smoothie bowl is exactly?"

Melody's laughter eased some tension in his chest that Jensen hadn't even known was there. "It's exactly how it sounds," she explained. "It's a smoothie, but in a bowl rather than a drink. Then I add things like fresh cut fruit, chia seeds or toppings like granola, depending on what people want."

"Why couldn't you do that before?" he asked, frowning. "Is it really that big of a deal to pour it into a bowl rather than a cup?"

"I had to shift the texture," Melody responded. "In order for it to work well as a meal rather than a drink, it had to be thicker. I was trying to figure out how to do that without sacrificing the integrity of the flavor."

"Well, if anyone could do it, you could," Jensen said. "I've never seen someone so into eating healthy as you."

"You do remember that I'm the girl with the secret Twinkie stash, right?"

Jensen's grin grew. "Oh, yeah. I forgot about that. Have you depleted it yet? You know since you're supposed to be missing me and all?" *My supply would have been gone a hundred times over by now.*

"Too many times," she said softly. "Especially since—"

Her voice cut off and Jensen looked at his cell. "Melody? Are you still there?"

"Yeah. I'm here."

"Well, what were you going to say? Especially since what?" There was silence on the other end for too long and Jensen knew something was up. "Melody...what's going on?"

"Nothing," she hurried to reply. "You just focus on getting those votes."

"I'm not worried about votes," Jensen said firmly, sitting up on his bed. "I'm worried about you. What's going on?" When she still didn't answer, he tried a different tactic. "Mellie...please tell me. I'll worry like crazy until you do." He kept his voice soft and used her childhood nickname, hoping it would get through to her.

"Jensen," she whispered, "I'm not supposed to tell you."

"It's too late," he replied. "You have to now." He heard sniffling on the other side and his heart began to pound. Whatever it was was worse than he thought. "Sweetheart, please. You're killing me."

"I don't want you to worry," she said thickly. "You've got enough going on."

Jensen waited.

"Things might not be as over with Mitchell as we thought," she finally whispered.

"What?" Jensen shouted, leaping to his feet. "What do you mean?"

"See? This is why I didn't want to tell you," Melody said. "I don't want you worrying over something you can't do anything about."

"What has he done?" There was silence again. "Melody...you either tell me or I'm calling Benny."

"No, don't do that." She sighed.

"He doesn't know, does he?" Jensen shook his head as he plopped back onto his bed. "Have you told *anyone*?" He already knew the answer to the question from the way she'd been avoiding talking about it, but he had to ask anyway. As soon as he was off the phone with her, Jensen was calling Benny plus Ken.

"No." Her voice was small and Jensen could tell she was ready to shut down.

He forced himself to stop talking for a second. Pinching the bridge of his nose, he took in a long breath, trying to get his anger under control. "Please tell me what Mitchell did," Jensen said in a purposefully calm tone. "I need to know every detail."

The sentences were broken and he could hear a few tears as she went, but twenty minutes later, Jensen had heard the whole story.

"Why didn't you say something?" he asked, feeling completely useless. He should never have left her. Or at least he should have left someone to take care of her. Instead, he'd walked out to try his hand at an impossible dream and the woman he was falling for was back home fighting off violent men. *What kind of person does that make me?*

"This is why," she argued back. "Because I can practically hear your brain spinning with thoughts of coming back and protecting me. Or worrying that you shouldn't have left in the first place."

Jensen growled and pushed a hand through his hair. He couldn't argue with that. It's exactly where his brain had gone.

"And none of it's true," she continued. "You shouldn't be here protecting me. You should be exactly where you are, pursuing something important to you. Something you've always wanted, but never had the chance to try. I mean...if you didn't do this now, when would you?" she asked.

Her words sunk home. They were the exact argument Jensen had had with himself many times before finally becoming brave enough to send off the audition tape. There was no way of knowing if he'd ever get this chance again. But there were two sides to every coin. "But you're important to me too," he said.

Melody gasped. "Do you mean that?"

Jensen made a face. "Of course. How could you not know that? I thought I made that clear before I left. I told you I would miss you."

"You did," she agreed.

"Mellie." He unconsciously slipped back into the name he used to call her. "Now what?"

"It's just...I mean...you miss everyone here, right? I didn't exactly think I was that special."

Jensen was stunned. *Have I really not let her know how I feel about her?* His mind went over all the times they'd been together and his heart began to sink. While she spent all her time throwing compliments and encouraging him to do what he wanted, he hadn't ever returned the favor. Even when he'd known something was wrong, Jensen had let it go because he was too excited for his upcoming time with the show.

A knock on his door caught his attention and he numbly went to answer it.

"We've got dinner downstairs," Gary said, his hands stuffed in his pockets. "Are you coming?"

Jensen nodded. "Yeah. Give me a minute."

"It sounds like you've got to go," Melody said before Jensen could speak to her. "Good luck this week and I'll talk to you later."

He didn't get a chance to respond before she was gone. Rather than go downstairs, Jensen sat on his bed, brooding. *I did it all wrong,* he thought. *I took and took but never gave back. And now I've left her to the wolves.*

At the moment he was too shaken with his realization to know how exactly to fix the situation, but one thing was for certain. He wouldn't be able to do it alone. Pressing number two on his speed dial, he called the other man in Mellie's life that would want to know what was going on.

CHAPTER 24

M el let out a breath of relief when she got inside the flower shop. She hadn't noticed anyone following her today, but she never knew when the sensation was going to hit. "I'm just being paranoid," she told herself, shaking her head.

Ever since that afternoon in the parking lot last week, she could have sworn Mitchell was everywhere. When she left work, she always felt as if he was watching. When she went to the grocery store. Almost every time she left her house, she felt vulnerable. It was a miracle she hadn't sprayed some innocent bystander with her mace yet.

And after her talk with Jensen this afternoon, she knew she needed to figure out how to get the whole thing stopped. It couldn't continue. Now that Jensen was aware of the situation, it would pull him away from the show and Mel wasn't about to have that guilt on her head. She needed to figure things out and quick, before Jensen did something like come home early in order to try and protect her.

"We're back here!"

Mel smiled. Apparently she'd been standing by the front door for too long and Caro felt the need to remind her of where the women were congregating. Tonight wasn't a meeting of the flower club, just her friends, who all happened to be in the class. Mel, Caro, Rose, Brooklyn and Genni often got together to chat and eat treats, giving them a chance for a girls' night away from their responsibilities. Mel always left feeling lighter and happier, and she was looking forward to that perk tonight.

"Hey, ladies," Mel greeted as she shed her coat and hung it on the back of a chair.

"Hi, Mel," Rose said with a smile. Lilly was sitting on her lap, playing with a tablet. Rose bounced her daughter, then nodded her head toward Mel when the young girl looked up.

Hi, Mel signed with a wide smile. She hadn't spoken to Lilly in forever, and the sweet girl was such a doll.

Hi, Melody, Lilly signed back. ***Did you bring me a smoothie?***

Mel laughed as Rose scolded her daughter. ***Not this time. But stop by soon and I'll make you one of my new smoothie bowls.***

Lilly's eyebrows went up and she began signing rapidly to her mother. It was going too fast for Mel to keep up, but she assumed the little girl was asking to be able to come get the treat.

Rose signed back, then put Lilly on the floor. "I'll be right back, ladies," Rose said, walking with her daughter hand in hand to the stairs, which led to an upstairs apartment.

"That girl is cuter than a porcelain doll at Christmas." Caro sighed, licking chocolate off her fingers.

"Absolutely," Charli added. "Sometimes it's hard to believe she's real. Her skin is so white."

"Yeah...good thing they live in Oregon," Brooklyn added while she dished up a plate full of snacks. "She'd fry like an egg on the sidewalk down in Cali."

Mel nodded.

"So you're selling the bowls?" Caro asked, completely turning the conversation around.

Mel blinked, trying to catch up with the shift. "Oh. Almost. I'm just waiting on a shipment of fruit to come in and then I'll be all ready to go." She smiled. "Thanks again for your help with the granola. I think people are really going to love it."

Caro smiled back. "No problem. I'll just expect to get the first bowl when you open it up." She winked. "For free."

Mel laughed. "Done deal."

"Wait!" Charli hollered. "It'll have to be bowl number two." Charli pointed to the back door. "I'm still not awesome with my sign language, but I think Lilly gets first dibs."

Caro held up a manicured hand. "Heaven sakes, you're right. I get the second one." Her red nail pointed to Mel. "But I still expect it for free."

Mel eyed the table full of food. "I think you've earned that, considering how many treats you bring to our girls' nights. In fact, you can have free forever if you want." She popped a truffle in her mouth and moaned. "As long as you never stop bringing these."

Caro nodded regally. "Sold!"

Brooklyn laughed as she sat down. "If I give you all a free item of clothing, can I get in on the deal?"

"What do you call that silky scarf you gave me last year?" Caro asked, wide-eyed. "I didn't just bring dessert for Melody."

"Ha!" Charli blurted out, settling into her seat. "Don't expect me to come fix your homes for free. I'm totally sending a bill."

The women were all still laughing as Rose came back in. "What's so funny?" she asked, looking around with a confused smile.

"Charli is going to bill us," Caro said happily. "Now...grab a plate and let's spill all the gossip. It feels like we haven't met in forever."

Rose simply shook her head and went back to follow Caro's orders. They all knew better than to argue with Caro. The small, Southern woman always got her way, no matter how difficult it was.

"MELODY!" a deep voice boomed from the front of the shop.

"What in the world?" Caro asked breathlessly. Her hand went to her chest. "Is that Ben's voice?"

Mel jumped to her feet. *Jensen...* He'd called her brother. Mel was sure of it. Her fears were confirmed when Bennett's tall frame blocked the entrance to the room.

"How could you not tell us?" he asked, his voice breaking at the end.

"Us?" Melody's eyes widened when she realized that Ken was standing behind her brother. Her knees shook as she dropped into her chair.

"What's going on here?" Caro demanded, standing up and putting her hands on her hips.

Bennett was glaring at his sister and Ken's expression wasn't much better, but at least he didn't look like he was going to strangle her. "Would you like to tell them, or should I?" Bennett growled.

Mel deflated and tears immediately began to pour down her cheeks. "I didn't want to get you all involved," she whispered thickly.

"I'm your brother," Bennett shot back. "It's my job to protect you."

"And ours!"

Mel turned to look at Caro, who shrugged.

"Just because I don't know what's going on doesn't mean we aren't going to help. If it affects you, it affects us. It's that simple."

Mel shook her head. "I don't want anyone to get hurt."

Bennett walked over and squatted at her knees. "And we don't want *you* to get hurt," he said softly, grabbing her hand. "Now...tell us everything."

The worried and supportive gazes around her finally broke down Mel's resistance and she found she didn't want to fight alone anymore.

JENSEN'S HEART WAS nearly pounding out of his chest and it was all because of the massive crowd waiting in front of the curtains. His clammy hands gripped his guitar and he had to hold tight to keep from pushing a hand through his perfectly styled hair.

He could hear the MC chatting up the judges and cracking jokes with the camera. It all told Jensen that his time was almost here. He was next on the roster, but his mind wasn't in it. It was back in Seaside Bay with Melody.

He was both furious that she hadn't told him that Mitchell was giving her trouble and terrified that the man would hurt her before anything could be done. *They can't even pin the abuse on him. How is Melody safe?*

It wasn't that he didn't trust Benny and Ken. He did. But it seemed like the only way to put Mitchell away would be to let someone get hurt first, and Jensen couldn't handle that. He was the one who had brought Melody into the situation by asking her to help befriend Micah, which made this whole situation Jensen's fault.

His nerves felt twitchy as his mind fought within itself. Go home and fix things with Melody or stay here and pursue his dreams. *But is this really your dream?* He stiffened at the thought. He had to admit that his time on the show hadn't been all he'd hoped it would be.

Yes, his face had been splashed on every television screen and social media page possible, but Jensen had found very little satisfaction in that knowledge. His days were filled with hours upon hours of practice and learning, which was slowly taking the joy out of his playing. His evenings were spent with a group of people who grew more competitive with each week. The smaller in number they were, the more obnoxious and mean those left became.

A part of him wished to be back at the bonfires, just playing for friends and family to enjoy while he made up songs that reminded him of beautiful lemon-scented ladies with long, blonde hair.

Jensen shook his head. *No. I can't think like that. Success requires sacrifice. Melody understood that and told me to come. It'll all work out as it's supposed to.*

"JENSEN TANNER!"

He jumped at the screaming that followed the announcement of his name.

"You're on!" the stage manager hissed, pushing Jensen's back to get him moving.

Jensen almost stumbled as his stiff legs moved, but he caught himself and walked onto the stage, hoping he could remember where he was supposed to stand since the overhead lights kept him from seeing anything.

Once the camera men had calmed the audience down, Jensen turned his gaze to the panel of judges. "Hello, judges," he said cordially.

"Nice to see you again, Jensen," one of them said.

Jensen couldn't see their faces and he didn't know them well enough to separate all the voices yet. He nodded. "I'm grateful to be here."

"You've been a crowd favorite," the male judge continued. They all paused for a moment so the audience could scream some more, and Jensen smiled and waved, ignoring the mental nudge that he was acting like a trained monkey. "Before we get started...why don't you tell us a little more about yourself?" the man asked.

Jensen choked on his words. "Something about me?" He didn't remember this being part of the script.

"Yes," a woman judge purred. "I think our audience, especially the women, would be interested to know more about you. Particularly your love life."

Once more, the audience screamed in response.

Jensen felt his cheeks heat and he rubbed his hot neck. The guitar strap was too hot against his skin, but there was little he could do about it at the moment. "I'm not sure that's of any interest to anybody." Right now he was feeling especially protective of Melody and it didn't feel right to pull her into another shenanigan when she was already struggling.

"Ooh, secretive..." the judge said, as the audience made it known they wanted more. "Okay, then answer just this one question."

"Okay."

"Is there a significant other? Or are you free for the taking?"

Jensen forced a chuckle, anything but amused, but playing it up for the cameras. He leaned into the mic. "I'm afraid I'm taken."

An automatic groan went through the audience, just like Jensen had known it would. It wouldn't have mattered who it was, he knew exactly how the group would respond. There were men and women standing around prompting the entire production, which made the term "reality television" completely ironic.

"As sad as the ladies are to hear that, I, for one, would like to hear your song," one of the male judges pressed.

Jensen nodded and adjusted his neck strap. "Yes, sir."

"What will you be performing for us tonight?" he asked.

Jensen opened his mouth, then paused. He knew what he was supposed to say. He knew what song he'd played hundreds of times over the last week. He knew what background track they were prepared to play, but for some reason, he couldn't do it. The lights, the clothes, the audience, even his newly whitened teeth suddenly felt...fake.

Jensen had spent so long dreaming of doing exactly what he was doing right now that he'd never considered whether or not he should. His life back home wasn't necessarily exciting, but at least it was real. His friendships and students were real. His tiny home with the wood-burning fireplace was real. Melody with her bright smile and encouraging words was real. And so was his love for her.

Admitting those words in his mind brought a clarity Jensen hadn't known was possible and he felt his heart and stiff muscles calm in response to his revelation. He loved her. He loved her and he'd never told her those words. It was time to make an about-face.

"Mr. Tanner?"

Jensen blinked. "Sorry about that. I've got a special song to play for you tonight," he stated, knowing the producers were going to strangle him after he was done. "I wrote it after kissing my girlfriend for the first time."

Right on cue, the audience oohed and aahed.

"I hope you enjoy," Jensen muttered, praying the people running the soundbooth figured out not to play the track they had ready. He strummed the first few chords of the song, the familiar strains washing over him. Closing his eyes, Jensen felt a small smile pull at his mouth and he began to hum quietly along as the song echoed through the theatre.

He'd never known more than he did at that moment exactly where he belonged. Now he just had to figure out how to get there.

CHAPTER 25

The room was silent for several heartbeats after Melody finished telling her story. She chewed on the inside of her cheek, too nervous to say anything else. Spilling her problems for a second time had already felt like running a marathon. But waiting for their reactions was proving to be the worst part.

Bennett whistled low and ran a hand over his hair. "Holy cow, Mel. Why didn't you tell anyone?"

Mel sighed and dropped her gaze to the floor. It was too difficult to meet anyone's eyes at the moment. "I didn't want to burden anyone," she whispered. "Jensen had already gotten hurt once while trying to protect me." She brought her head up, frustration starting to fuel her actions. "I mean...we're lucky he wasn't charged with assault, Ben. It took weeks for all his bruises to heal. I couldn't put him in that position again."

"What about me, Mel?" Ken asked softly. He stood in the doorway with his arms folded over his chest, his shoulder resting against the frame. He was the bulkiest of all their friends and was easily intimidating if a person didn't know just how much of a teddy bear he was. "Why wouldn't you come to me? You knew I would help."

She nodded, trying to hold back her tears. "I know, Ken. But I also knew I had no solid proof. All I have are suspicions and a few creepy conversations. Mitchell has never actually touched me. So what could I ask you to do that wouldn't jeopardize your job?"

"Forget Ken," Bennett shouted. "I'm your brother!" He slapped his chest. "I'm family. Why didn't you say something...anything? How could you keep this to yourself? What do you think I would have done if you'd been hurt? Do you think I wouldn't care?" His eyes were glassy and Mel felt hot shame pour through her body like molten lava.

She'd spent so much of her life taking care of Bennett and his boyish ways that she hadn't considered he would actually step up to the plate in a situation like this. She'd never allowed him the chance to grow up.

"You're right," she croaked. "It was wrong of me not to tell you. But it's always been me taking care of you, Ben. I've always been the protector, the one making sure you eat—"

"Don't give me that," Ben snarled. "Do you really think I'm such a pansy that I can't take care of myself?"

Mel's eyes widened and her mouth hung open. "I..."

Ben huffed. "I *let* you do those things because I know it makes you happy, Mel. You *need* to be needed. You thrive on it. You support and build and take care of everyone around you because it makes you feel good." He sighed and hung his head. "I didn't want to take that away from you."

Mel put a hand over her mouth, trying to stifle a sob, but it didn't work. The sound broke through anyway, followed by a torrent of tears. She had never given her brother enough credit for the man he'd become. He hadn't gone to college, instead staying to become a mailman, which paid the bills, but definitely wasn't anything that afforded him the luxuries of life. He flirted and joked his way from one situation to the next and Mel had automatically jumped into the role of mother, assuming his behavior showed him incapable of doing it himself.

"Ah, Mel," he groaned, walking toward her with open arms.

She jumped to her feet and wrapped her arms around her brother. His shirt soaked up the tears, but she refused to care. Only Jensen had ever made her feel as protected and precious as she did right now.

Mel squeezed her eyes tightly. It wasn't the time to think about Jensen. He was gone, living his dreams, and Mel refused to begrudge him that...no matter what it meant for their future.

Smaller arms came around Mel's back and she opened her eyes to glance over her shoulder at a pair of wide, blue eyes. "I should scold you good for holding out on us," Caro began. Her bottom lip trembled and those beautiful blues filled with tears. "But we love ya too dang much to do it." With a shaky sigh, Caro turned her head sideways and laid it on Mel's back, essentially sandwiching her between her brother and her sassy friend.

The sound of shuffling feet immediately moved closer and soon Mel found herself in the middle of a massive pile of arms and tears.

"Get over here, ya big lug," Caro hissed.

Mel followed her gaze, grinning when she saw Ken still standing in the doorway, looking uncomfortable. "I don't think he's into group hugs," Mel whispered, the tension softening with their laughter.

Caro rolled her eyes. "Men and their fear of emotion. It's so dumb."

"Hey!" Bennett argued. "I'm here, aren't I?"

"I guess you're just more manly than Mr. Police Officer over there," Charli answered with a smirk.

This time it was Ken who rolled his eyes. "You can't guilt me into joining," he said dryly. "I know that trick." His eyes were focused intensely and Mel tried to look around to see who he was staring at. To her surprise, Rose was meeting his gaze head on, a challenge in them. *Whoa. What's going on there?*

As Mel continued to watch, Rose's cheeks grew to a fiery red and she eventually turned away from Ken's stare, though Ken never moved from the doorway.

"Ah, forget about him," Caro said, squeezing Mel tighter. "We're going to take care of you, Mellie girl. Just like you've taken care of all of us over the years."

Mel opened her mouth to argue, then snapped it shut again. This was exactly the problem. She tried to help everyone, but never took anything in return. Instead of responding that she was fine, she laid her head back down on Bennett's shoulder and whispered, "Thank you."

The hug fest went on for a few more long moments before people started to pull back. "I hate to break it all up," Caro stated as she leaned back and straightened her shirt, "but we need to figure out a plan here."

She went back to her seat and sat primly on the edge. "All right, Mr. Cop. What rights do we have?"

Ken raised an eyebrow. "What?"

"What can we do to protect her without getting ourselves thrown in your slammer?" Caro clarified.

Rose snorted. "Slammer? Caro, I swear that you speak like a gangster sometimes."

Caro grinned and pumped her eyebrows. "I always knew being a CSI fan would pay off someday."

Bennett chuckled and Mel bounced against him. They were the only two still standing together, but Mel wasn't ready to pull away. She looked up at him. "I'm sorry," she whispered.

Bennett gave her one more tight squeeze. "Forgiven. Now let's just get this situation fixed before someone else gets hurt."

Mel nodded. It was time to go on the offensive. She wasn't alone any longer and she refused to continue to be a victim. And maybe, just maybe, if they played things right, they could also help Micah along the way. Heaven knew he needed it more than she did.

"WHAT WERE YOU THINKING?" Mr. Timmons shouted. His fist hit the table and curse words flew from his mouth. "It was LIVE television, Mr. Tanner. LIVE! Do you understand what that means?"

Jensen nodded calmly. He fought the urge to bounce his foot. Now that he had decided it was time to go, he was eager to get moving. It wasn't just that Melody needed him, though she definitely did. But once his mind had settled on the fact that he didn't enjoy or want any part of this flashy, fake world, he was struggling to keep from walking out the door. For right now, however, he had to wait out the ranting and raving of the show's producer, who obviously wanted to punish Jensen before sending him home.

Mr. Timmons pushed a hand through his hair. "Stupid rogues who think they can just do whatever they want." His face was nearly purple as more unsavory words flew from his lips.

Jensen tried to hold back a wince. He'd never been a fan of cussing. *Maybe that's just another thing that makes me unfit for this lifestyle.*

Mr. Timmons threw himself into a chair, and it spun a little to the right before he caught himself on the table. "You've presented us with a major problem, Mr. Tanner."

Jensen's eyebrows shot up. "Why? Just cut me and send me home."

A dark chuckle came from the woman at Mr. Timmons's right side. "It's not that easy," Ms. Snyder said in a snarky tone.

"Why not?" Jensen asked, leaning forward and showing interest for the first time in the meeting. "I broke the contract. Send me packing."

Her heavily lashed eyes narrowed. "So you planned all this? You wanted to get sacked?"

Mr. Timmons threw his hands in the air, practically breathing fire. Then he turned and pointed a gnarled finger at Jensen. "I'm afraid your plan failed. While I want nothing more than to sue you within an inch of your life and call it quits, you've put us in a difficult position."

"What are you talking about?" Jensen asked warily. His worry inched up a notch when Ms. Eyelashes smirked.

"Your little stunt hit our viewers right between the eyes," she sneered. "Or at least between their thumbs. Your votes nearly broke the internet last night."

Jensen fell back in his seat. "No," he breathed.

"Yes." Mr. Timmons stated. He sighed and pushed at his hair again. It was a wonder the man wasn't bald. "If we get rid of you, the fans are going to riot."

Jensen shook his head. "I want out. I'm done."

"You have a contract."

"But it's not unbreakable," Jensen pointed out. "I can leave."

"But we have to agree to it," Ms. Snyder snapped. "And I don't know how you do things in your small town, but here we don't let business investments go." She tilted her head and gave him a harsh grin. "You don't get to the top by playing nice."

"I won't perform," Jensen threatened. "I'll blow the next one."

Mr. Timmons snorted. "With the way the female demographic is eating you up, I don't think it would matter. They'd probably just chalk it up to nerves about your mystery woman."

Jensen was barely controlling himself at this point. He wanted to go home. He *needed* to go home. "You can't keep me here."

"And you can't leave without losing everything," Ms. Snyder said succinctly.

Closing his eyes and pinching the bridge of his nose, Jensen forced a long, slow breath into his chest. Then he sat back and faced his judgment crew. "Surely we can come to some kind of compromise here. I did what I did to give you an excuse to throw me off the show. I've gotten news from home that requires my attention and I need to go. It's an emergency."

"An emergency...how convenient," Ms. Snyder said dryly. She rolled her eyes and shook her head, clearly not impressed with Jensen's arguments.

"It's the truth," Jensen insisted, his frustration growing. His hands were clenched in his lap as he tried to stay under control, but he felt like it was all slipping from his grasp. He had been so sure of his path, and now it was blowing up in his face. "She needs me," he ground out.

Mr. Timmons paused and narrowed his gaze. "She?"

Jensen pressed his lips together. He didn't want to drag Melody's name into this. She was his, and he felt incredibly protective of her name and image.

Mr. Timmons leaned over the table. "If you want to convince us to let you out of this contract, you're going to have to give us something." One side of his mouth pulled into a crooked smile. The devious edge of it gave Jensen pause. "A good sappy story just *might* be enough to let you out...provided we have rights to the story."

"She is not a *story*," Jensen argued. "I don't want anything about her drug through the media."

"But you're willing to humiliate our station by going against your contract on live television?" Ms. Snyder scoffed and leaned back in her seat. "Maybe I've been wrong this whole time." She whacked her colleague on the shoulder. "Where do I find myself one of these guys?"

Jensen held in his own eye roll.

"The point here," Mr. Timmons said, getting them all back to business, "is that you have to give us something. I'm not willing to just drop you, not when you're such a hit. But if we had something we could continue to capitalize on when you were gone...then it would be worth my time."

Jensen sighed and rubbed at his forehead. He hadn't had a migraine in ages, but he could feel one coming on now. "Okay, look..."

He held out a hand to the producers. "What if we agreed on a partial story? I'm not willing to give you all of it, but I think I've got a way we can spin it and give you enough to make it worth your while."

The station employees looked at each other, then back at him. Ms. Snyder leaned back in her seat and tucked a pen in her black hair. "We're listening..."

Jensen swallowed hard and his heart pounded against his ribcage. He was taking a huge leap of faith by telling them this, but it seemed like the only way to get him back home. If it paid off, it would totally be worth it, but if it fell through, he'd be humiliated enough to leave the country forever.

"Right." He took a deep breath. "Let me tell you a story."

CHAPTER 26

Melody sighed heavily and let herself fall onto her couch. She was exhausted both mentally and physically. But before she could relax and get comfortable, her phone buzzed.

Did you make it home okay?

Mel smiled. Her brother seemed to have grown up overnight and was proving to be a little too good at parenting her. He'd been checking in constantly ever since their talk a couple nights ago.

I'm fine. Thanks. Just gonna grab some dinner and crash.

He sent back a thumbs up emoji and Mel set the phone on the coffee table. It had been a difficult day even though she'd never felt as loved and supported as she did right now. Her friends had rallied around her after her confession and were doing their best to think of all sorts of ways they could help keep her safe.

Ken had "wandered" into the smoothie shop almost a dozen times over the last two days. He had even sent a deputy by tonight to see her safely to her car, the whole fifty feet that it was. But Mel wasn't going to complain. She hadn't felt Mitchell's eyes on her once today and it had been glorious. She wasn't naive enough to think the problem was gone so quickly, but at least she could breathe a little easier at the moment.

Jensen's situation, however, was a little more difficult. He'd nearly killed her when he'd confessed that the song he had played for her had been inspired by their first kiss. Tears had streamed down her cheeks and her heart had squeezed so tight she could barely breathe. The internet had exploded with praise for his tender heart and loyalty to a woman the media didn't know. Her ache from his absence had been almost uncontrollable and for the first time since this all started, Mel had thought about hopping a plane and going to meet him at the television station. Only common sense and the thought of being arrested as a crazy person at the studio had held her back.

Mel had chosen to stay off social media since Jensen had played the song. She was sure that her feed was probably flooded with everything from well wishes to threats at the moment, and she wanted no part of it. Jensen could have the limelight. Mel would stay in the supportive shadows.

Her stomach grumbled and she scrunched her nose. "Probably should grab that dinner I told Bennett about." She sighed and forced her tired body off the couch. For it nearly being winter, the smoothie shop had been overwhelmingly busy today and since Mel didn't like to be a hands-off boss, she had been just as hopping as the rest of her staff.

Scrummaging through the fridge, Mel grabbed some leftovers and decided just to heat it up and make do. She wasn't in any mood to stand at the stove and cook for a while.

Humming Jensen's song, Mel waited for the timer to buzz, then grabbed the hot plate and planted herself in front of the television. She flipped through the channels, finally settling on an old movie she'd seen enough times that she didn't have to pay attention to know what was going on.

Just as she was scraping the last of her plate clean, her phone rang. Mel smiled. She hadn't spoken to Jensen in two days and was hoping he would call tonight. But the caller ID didn't say his name. It was a number she didn't recognize.

Mel paused. She didn't usually answer calls from people she didn't know, but the number appeared local, so she pressed the accept button. "Hello?"

"Ms. Frasier?" The voice was low and raspy.

"Yes...who's this?"

"I-I'm sorry, Ms. Frasier..." His breath shuddered. "I didn't know who else to call..." The person on the other side of the line coughed and it didn't sound normal.

Mel sat up, her brows furrowing. "Who is this? Do you need help?"

"It's...Micah..."

"Micah!" Mel jumped to her feet. "What do you need? Are you hurt? Where are you?" She began to grab her keys and jacket, preparing without thought to help the young man.

"I'm so sorry, Ms. Frasier." A sob broke through the line and Mel felt her heart lurch in response. "I'm at the trailer park entrance...I'm so sorry."

"Don't you worry, Micah," Mel said, doing her best to keep her voice steady. "I'm going to come pick you up, okay? Hang on. It's going to be okay."

"I'm so sorry...I'm so sorry..." His voice trailed off until the line went dead.

Panicked that he was unconscious or worse, Mel darted out of her townhome and rushed to her little sedan. She hopped behind the wheel and gunned it out of the parking lot, paying very little attention to her surroundings. All that mattered right now was getting to Micah and getting him safe.

It seemed to take an eternity to get to the road that led to the trailer park. The evening was dark and chilly, and traffic was almost nonexistent on this side of town, but none of it gave Melody any pause as she hurried to the rescue.

Parking her car on the side of the road, she jumped out. "Micah? Micah, where are you?" She frowned when no one came forward immediately. *Maybe he's too hurt to answer me. Or maybe he really did pass out.*

Mel slammed the door shut and hurried to the entrance, walking around. She turned the flashlight on on her cell phone and paced the area. The single streetlamp was nearly useless. "Where are you?" she muttered, walking around the bushes and trees that created a thin landscape for the entrance. "Micah?"

A rustle in the bushes caused her to stop and turn around. A lanky silhouette stumbled out of the dark directly toward her and Mel stepped back with a gasp. "Micah?"

He fell to his knees. "I'm so sorry, Ms. Frasier."

"Oh my gosh." She rushed over and dropped down at his side, wrapping her arms around his back. "How bad is it, Micah? Where do you hurt the most?" She shifted him so she could see his face and broke into tears at the bruising and bleeding on his lips, nose and eyes. "We have to get you to the hospital, Micah. Can you walk?"

He shook his head. "I didn't know who else to call...I'm so sorry." His words were broken and had a slight lisp as he spoke through his fat, swollen lip.

"You did the right thing," Mel assured him. "I'm going to get you help." Without warning, the hairs on the back of her neck stood up and Mel froze. *No...*

Gravel crunched behind her and she couldn't breathe as the heavy steps drew closer. They were uneven and stumbled once, leading Mel to assume he was either hurt or impaired in some way.

"I'm so sorry," Micah whispered again and Mel finally realized what he was talking about.

"You brought me here on purpose?" she asked, betrayal striking her chest like a hot iron.

Micah let out a sob and fell limply against the ground. "I didn't know what else to do. I'm so sorry. He wanted...he told me—"

"Well, well, well...look who we have here." Mitchell's words were slurred.

So...he's drunk. Mel filed the information away. She would need to use every advantage she could find.

"And all without a protector," Mitchell spat from behind her.

"So sorry..." Micah moaned.

Mel squeezed where she held the young man's shoulders. "This isn't your fault, Micah," she whispered, leaning down low. "You're a victim here and I don't blame you for anything." She tenderly brushed the hair out of his face. "You rest." She tried to stand, but Micah grabbed her hand, his grip bruising. Even in the dark, Mel could see the bright whites of his eyes as he looked on in fear. Mel shook her head. "This has to end, Micah. Let me go." With a tug, she broke free from the terrified boy and stood up. She wasn't about to face Mitchell on her knees.

JENSEN FROWNED AS HE sat in his car, his thumbs drumming on the steering wheel as he sat at the stop sign. He could have sworn that Mel just sped past him headed to the outskirts of town. But it was pretty late in the evening and he couldn't imagine what she was doing heading that direction at this time of day. Her home, the shop and all their friends lived in the other direction.

He yawned and scrubbed his face. "Maybe I'm just seeing things." He'd been up for almost two days, making deals and getting himself out of the show. He'd just gotten off a long flight and was ready for sleep, but he had hoped to see Melody first and make sure she was okay.

However, as he'd pulled into town, he'd slowed down for a stop sign and a small car, just like hers, with a blonde woman inside had gone racing past him, and now Jensen was confused on how to proceed. He picked his phone up off the passenger seat and considered his options. He had wanted to surprise Melody, but maybe that wasn't a good plan.

"But if she's driving, I can't exactly call her either." Jensen groaned and punched the number for Benny.

"Jensen?" Benny's excited voice came through the line.

"Hey, Ben."

"What the heck are you doing calling? Aren't you like three hours ahead over there?"

Jensen chuckled and checked his rearview mirror to make sure no one was waiting behind him. "No, I'm actually home."

"WHAT?"

Jensen held the phone away from his ear. "I wanted to surprise Melody—"

"Oh, she's going to be surprised, all right." Benny laughed, then paused. "Have you spoken to her since we figured out our plan to keep her safe?"

Jensen frowned. "No. It's been a couple of busy days."

Benny sighed. "Well, since you're back, it'll probably be easier to talk it all out in person anyway. Why don't you and Mel come over for dinner tomorrow and we'll let you in on the plan." He gasped. "Oh man! Does this mean you got voted off the show?" Benny groaned. "I could have sworn you were winning!"

"Hey..." Jensen tried to calm his friend. "The show is a long story, and I'd be happy to talk about it at dinner tomorrow, but..."

"But what?"

"Do you know where Melody is tonight?"

Silence came through the line for a moment. "What do you mean? Have you gone to her house and she's not there? She told me she went home!" There was an edge of panic to Benny's voice and it brought Jensen's protective instincts roaring forward.

"Not yet," he said carefully. "I'm just pulling into town, but I'm at the stop sign at Oak and Main and could have sworn that I just watched Melody drive past, going way above the speed limit, and she was heading out of town."

Benny cursed and Jensen raised his eyebrows. That wasn't something his friend normally did.

"Are you sure it was her?" Benny asked quickly. Jensen could hear shuffling in the background, followed by the slamming of a car door.

"No...yes...I don't know. I've been up for a couple of days and I'm exhausted, but it sure looked like her." Jensen pressed his thumb and pointer finger into his eyes to massage them.

"Okay, you follow her," Benny commanded. "Better safe than sorry, here. I'll go to her house and double check there."

"On it." Jensen glanced behind him again, then put on his blinker and prepared to drive.

"Hey, Jens?"

"Yeah?"

"Where do Mitchell and Micah live?" his friend asked.

Jensen froze, then he let out his own curse word and hit the gas. "The trailer park!" Jensen shouted into the phone before dropping it to the side. He didn't need the distraction right now. His tired mind put together all the puzzle pieces that had been floating through his head when he saw Melody drive by and his foot pressed the gas pedal all the way to the floor.

The neighborhood he sought was only another five minutes down the road on a normal day, but even the two minutes it took Jensen to skid into the gravel at the entrance of the park seemed like eons. Melody's car was off to the side and Jensen could see people standing in the entrance to the park. One was on the ground and two were facing off. It didn't take a genius for Jensen to figure out who was who.

He didn't even bother to shut off his engine before jumping out and rushing across the street. "HEY!" he bellowed, getting everyone's attention.

One sickly yellow beam from a streetlamp gave just enough light for Jensen to see Melody's jaw drop open. "Jensen?" she breathed.

Before Jensen could answer, Melody screamed and was yanked backward into Mitchell's chest. His large paw gripped her neck and the sound she'd been making was cut off, causing Jensen's heart to skip a beat.

"Let her go," Jensen shouted, skidding to a stop. His eyes dropped to Micah, who was curled up on the gravel in the fetal position. "Micah? You all right?" Jensen put his gaze back on Mitchell and left it there.

Micah whimpered, but didn't move, and Jensen knew it was worse than he thought.

"He's hurt," Melody managed to croak, but she began gasping for air when Mitchell tightened his hold.

"Shut up," he hissed in her ear, pulling her back into his chest.

"Mitchell," Jensen said, putting his hands out like he was trying to calm a frightened animal. "You have to let her breathe."

Fat tears began rolling down Melody's cheeks as she was jerked again, and Jensen's panic grew.

"She can't breathe, Mitchell. Please."

Mitchell's eyes narrowed and he brought his head down next to Melody's. "You can breathe just fine, can't ya?" he said, grinning maniacally at Jensen.

Jensen's jaw clenched as Melody shrank away from Mitchell's face. "Look, your problem here is with me. I'm the one who called Child Services, on multiple occasions. I'm the one who's been pressuring Micah to tell me how you treat him. I even started the after school school club so I could get the truth from him."

Mitchell chuckled in that deep voice of him and it sounded menacing. "You think I don't know that already?" He shook Melody like a rag doll. "But you aren't near as much fun to play with as your little girlfriend here." Mitchell began to toy with Melody's hair that had escaped her ponytail.

Jensen held his breath to keep from tackling the man. Melody was too close and he couldn't risk her getting hurt any more than she already was.

"I had figured to just have my fun with her, seeing as you're supposed to be out of town, but since you're here, suppose we strike a bargain."

"Anything. What do you want?"

Mitchell's dark gaze gleamed triumphantly in the barely-there light. "Sounds like tonight might turn out to be better than I expected." He laughed again and Jensen felt his chances of coming out the victor begin to shrivel. He was terrified that he would have to make a choice. Micah or Melody?

CHAPTER 27

The air wheezing in and out of Melody's lungs was not enough. Her vision was starting to blur and she squirmed against Mitchell's grip, desperate for more.

"Hold still," he hissed in her ear, shaking her again.

The movement did nothing to help her swimming head. Her fingernails dug into Mitchell's hand and for the first time ever, she wished she was the type of girl who got those long, sharp, fake nails.

He chuckled in her ear and wrapped his second arm around her waist, nearly hoisting her off the ground with his grip. "I'll be happy to leave the little miss alone, *Mr. Tanner*," Mitchell sneered. "But you have to agree to leave me and my boy alone. No more home visits. No more after school clubs. No more questions."

Mel coughed. "No. Micah..." She couldn't speak anymore and jerked against the large man.

Jensen's face was barely visible, but his despair was easy to read. His eyes went between Micah, who was still on the ground, and Mel. She could see him weighing his options, but the thought of letting Micah go on living with this bully was more than she could stomach.

Deciding she had to do something before Jensen responded, Mel quit worrying about breathing and let go of Mitchell's hard grip on her neck. Instead, she reached over her head for his face and began to claw at his eyes and nose as best she could, blinded and weak as she was.

"ARGH!" Mitchell roared and threw her to the ground.

The little bit of remaining air in her lungs was gone as Mel hit the gravel on her back, her head banging on the ground and sending a sharp pain through her entire body. She couldn't move as the man above her looked down with murder in his eyes. His hands reached for her just as another body slammed him onto his back.

Mel found herself being kicked to the side as Jensen and Mitchell fought again. It was like the scene in front of the shop all over again, except this time she was in the way. More than one boot managed to land on her shoulder or rib cage before she was able to move her limbs enough to drag herself to Micah's side.

Her vision had come back, but her limbs still felt weak as she tried to cover him with her own body, doing what little she could to protect him from the wrestling men. When a siren pierced the air and lights began to flash in the trees and parked cars, Mel jerked her head upright.

Relief began to replace the adrenaline flooding her system as she realized help was arriving. "It's gonna be okay," she whispered hoarse-ly to Micah. "It's gonna be okay." She couldn't continue talking, since it felt like her throat was sandpaper, but she rubbed his back more to soothe herself than the shaking boy. It gave her something to focus on as Mitchell and Jensen continued to throw punches.

Mel winced at the sound of flesh hitting flesh, not knowing who was being more wounded. Jensen was here, back in Seaside Bay, and the first thing that happened was him getting hurt again. That same feeling of shame and guilt she had felt before tried to make its way into her chest, but she was too emotionally overwrought at the mo-ment for them to take root. She knew it would be something she would have to deal with later, however, and tried to brace herself for it.

"MELODY!"

Her head snapped to the side and she winced at the pain in her neck from the movement. "Bennett!" she tried to answer, but her voice was almost non-existent, so she waved an arm instead.

Bennett rushed over, not even glancing at Jensen and Mitchell as he slid to his knees at her side. "Oh my gosh, Mel, what were you thinking?" he moaned as he examined her face and neck.

"Micah," she croaked, grimacing at the pain it took to speak. Shuffling back, she showed Bennett the boy, who now had his head in her lap and was breathing easier than he had since Melody had arrived.

Bennett gasped once he saw Micah's face and then his jaw clenched. His head turned to the side where Jensen had been. "If Ken wasn't already shackling the guy, I'd kill him," Bennett growled.

Mel patted his arm, getting his attention again, and pointed to Micah.

Bennett took a deep breath and nodded. "The ambulance is on its way. We left before it took off, figuring you might need our help."

"How?" Mel croaked.

Bennett shook his head. "It's a long story. Right now you just stay quiet." He examined her neck again. "You're not going to be calling names at the shop for awhile."

Mel nodded, her eyes drifting to where Ken was putting Mitchell in the back of the squad car. She perked up and searched for Jensen. *Ken better not be arresting him!* Her eyes landed on a dark form sitting on the gravel over where the fighting had taken place. She started to rise, then realized that Micah was still in her lap. She looked down and the relief on Micah's face wouldn't let her move. Right now the young man needed her. She would have to see to Jensen in a minute.

"There they are," Bennett stated as more flashing lights hit the scene.

Mel sighed and her shoulders relaxed. It only took a moment for her to begin to ache from the crown of her head to the tip of her toes. Apparently just seeing the ambulance was enough to have her body recognize every injury it had sustained that evening. She turned toward Jensen again, worried about how hurt he was, then jumped when a dark figure was standing right beside her.

"Melody..." Jensen's voice was raw with emotion and hoarse from his exertion. He practically fell to the ground, his knees landing on the rocks.

Tears once again flooded her vision as she took in his swelling right eye and bloody nose. Blood dribbled from the corner of his mouth and along the cut on his cheekbone. "Oh, Jensen," she whispered, her trembling hand coming up to touch him, only to stop short. She was worried about causing him even more pain than he was obviously already in.

When she paused, he leaned in and brought her hand to his cheek. Then turned and kissed it. "What did he do to you?" Jensen asked.

"Excuse us," a man in a paramedic suit said.

Mel, Jensen and Bennett all turned to look at the group.

"Uh..." The man looked at Micah, then Jensen, then Melody and back again. "Who should we see first?" he finally asked.

"Micah," Jensen said, pointing to the boy. "He needs a hospital. His father has been abusing him and he's been hurt for awhile." He took Mel's hand and helped raise her to her feet as the paramedics slipped the teenager from her lap and began to examine him.

Mel's knees shook and she almost went down again, but Jensen's arms wrapped around her waist, bringing her into his chest and helping her stay upright.

"Other than your neck, did he hurt you in any way?" Jensen asked. The tremor in his question made his thoughts on the matter more than plain and Mel found herself shivering at the tone.

She shook her head gently, not wanting to speak again. A headache pulsed at the back of her head from where she'd hit the ground, but she didn't think it was serious.

"Thank heavens," Jensen breathed, bringing their foreheads together.

Mel sighed at the contact and held onto his shoulders with both hands. She had no idea why he was home or how he had come to find her at the trailer park, but right now that didn't matter. All that did was the fact that he was here and he was holding her. She was going to soak up every bit of strength and comfort she could for however long it would last.

MELODY WAS SHAKING against him and Jensen's mind couldn't seem to grasp the fact that she was now safe in his arms. He squeezed his eyes shut and pressed her against him, burying his face in her hair. His body was shaking almost as hard as hers was, but he couldn't bear to let her go.

This was not how he'd imagined their reunion. Seeing the life of the woman you love being threatened was every man's nightmare and Jensen couldn't get the image out of his head.

"I almost lost you," he murmured, more to himself than her. He brought a hand up to cup the back of her head. "He had you...your throat." He moved his face down, kissing her bruised and tender skin just under her jaw.

The touch seemed to ignite something within him, and he found himself unable to stop. "Melody," he whispered against her cheek. "Melody..." He said her name over and over again, as if to assure himself that she was truly there. That she was living and breathing in his arms.

"Tell me you're okay," he rasped, still kissing her skin. "Tell me everything will be all right..."

"Jensen," she said in a barely audible voice. Her hands were all over him. Running through his hair, over his face, gripping his shoulders, then moving down his back. Her movements were jerky and frantic, reflecting his own emotions perfectly.

Before she could hurt herself speaking another word, he took her mouth and stole any words she had been about to speak. His grip on her tightened as the sizzling chemistry that always accompanied their kisses sprang to life. He ignored the stitch in his side and the sharp pain in his ribs. The inside of his cheek was shredded from a hit to his face, but Jensen ignored it all. Nothing mattered at the moment but Melody.

She was alive. She was his, and she was kissing him just as energetically as he was kissing her. This woman was perfect. She'd been so brave during the confrontation with Mitchell. Right before she had started to scratch the abuser's eyes out, he had seen the determined look in her gaze. She knew he was struggling with leaving Micah at the hands of his father. Given the time to respond, Jensen definitely would have chosen to save Melody, but that didn't mean it was an easy decision. The words had stuck in his throat as he'd tried to agree to Mitchell's terms.

Then Melody had taken matters into her own hands and distracted the large man just long enough for Jensen to come tackle him away from the victims. The two had fought hard and Jensen was going to be hurting for a couple of weeks from the hits he'd taken.

"Jensen?" A loud cough broke through the dreamy haze that Jensen was caught in.

He pulled back from Melody and gasped in a breath. Then tucked her under his chin before he was tempted to go back to kissing her and forgetting the entire mess they were in. "Benny," he greeted hoarsely.

Benny was giving Jensen a smirk and shaking his head. "That's my sister, you know."

"Maybe so, but I'm not sure why you think that will stop me from kissing her."

Benny chuckled. "It sure wouldn't stop me if our places were re-versed."

Jensen smiled back and squeezed Melody a little tighter.

Benny grew serious. "The paramedics are ready for her," he said softly. "And you need to be seen as well."

Jensen nodded and leaned back so he could see her face. "You ready?"

Melody nodded. She was sagging into him and Jensen knew she wouldn't be able to walk on her own, so he wrapped an arm around her waist and began to walk her toward the ambulance.

It was another three hours before Jensen was able to walk Melody to her door. Every step hurt as they went up her front steps and his body seemed to grow heavier with each movement. *When the heck is that pain medication going to kick in?* he wondered as he stumbled into her front room.

Melody grabbed his arm, helping him along. The doctors at the emergency room had instructed her not to talk for a few days. The swelling would probably last several days in her throat and speaking would not only hurt, but probably cause it to continue to stay raw.

He groaned as he collapsed on the couch. His head flopped back and then he winced as his skull began pounding even harder.

"Here," Melody rasped, offering him a pillow.

"Don't talk," Jensen reminded her, not bothering to open his eyes. He took the pillow from her and set it in his lap. He would use it in a minute. Right now he needed to stay awake long enough to talk to Melody. He patted the cushion next to him and felt it dip as Melody sat down. Jensen brought his hand up her back, wrapped it around her shoulders and brought Melody into his chest.

Only after he was holding her did he relax. He knew it was going to be awhile before he would be ready to let her go.

Melody sighed and relaxed against his chest.

He let his hand rub her back as they sat and just caught their breaths for a few minutes.

"You never said why you're home," Melody whispered.

"You've got to stop talking," Jensen scolded, cracking open an eye.

Melody sat up and Jensen mourned the loss of her closeness. But when she glared at him, he sighed, knowing they had a long talk ahead, despite her hurt throat.

He shifted himself on the couch and grimaced. "I left the show."

Melody gasped, her eyes wide. "Why?"

He pushed a stiff hand through his hair. "I couldn't stay, Mellie. Not after I realized something."

She raised her eyebrows, clearly waiting for him to continue.

This wasn't exactly how Jensen had pictured saying this, but the opportunity was in front of him and he'd waited too long to say it, so he wasn't about to wait again. He brought his tired arms up and cupped her face. "Melody Ann Frasier. I love you."

Her eyes slowly widened.

"I love you more than I ever could have imagined." Jensen's throat began to close up as his emotions rose to the surface. "I thought I needed adventure. A chance to see more than our small town." Jensen dropped her gaze and shook his head. "I felt held back and like I'd never had the chance to be my own man. When my music began to take off, it felt like the chance I'd been waiting for. I could do something important with my life. I've been in a relationship before," he said, his voice growing quieter and his mouth dry. "And it didn't feel like it added anything to my life." Jensen sighed and dropped his hands, turning away slightly. The next words he had to say were going to be difficult. "Melissa was wonderful, but our marriage wasn't exciting or life changing. It simply...was." He looked back at Melody, hoping she could understand what he was trying to say. "She was a good woman and I'll always miss her. But she wasn't you." He turned to face her more head-on. "I didn't crave to touch her skin or need her kiss to start my day and it took me too long to realize I had those things with you." Jensen shook his head, gently wiping away the tears tracking down Melody's cheeks. "You were always there," he whispered. "You supported and took care of me even when I didn't recognize it." He swallowed, trying to move the lump in his throat. "It took almost losing you before I realized how I felt and what it would cost me if you weren't in my life." He framed her face again. "Melody...I don't deserve you, but I desperately want to have you as part of my life. Can you forgive me for leaving? Can you let me back in, knowing that I never plan to let you go?"

Jensen had much more he wanted to say, but unfortunately it had to wait, due to the cost of coming home. Right now, he was simply setting the stage, and as soon as all the details could be worked out, he would make Melody's his, permanently.

Her head began to move slowly at first, up and down, then more steadily until she began to cry in earnest and wrapped her arms around his neck, burying her head in his neck.

He held her close and rocked them back and forth, murmuring words of love and comfort as she cried into his shoulder. By the time her tears had calmed down, they were laying back on the couch, arms wrapped around each other, both exhausted.

His hand absentmindedly stroked her hair while his eyes remained closed. Soon, he felt her breathing slow down and steady, and Jensen knew she had fallen asleep. He also knew he should wake her up and leave, but he couldn't bring himself to do it. Instead, he let his own hand fall to the side, and after letting out a long breath, gave into his own call to the darkness.

CHAPTER 28

Quiet whispers woke Melody from the best sleep she'd had in years. She was warm and comfortable and content. She frowned, realizing she was more upright than usual and after a second, her brain caught up with the fact that she lived alone. There shouldn't be any whispers.

Her eyes snapped open and Mel jerked upright when she found almost a dozen faces in her family room. "Wha—" she croaked, only to stop and put a hand to her throat.

"Don't speak, sweetie," Caro said, walking in from the kitchen with a steaming cup. "Here. This'll help cure all your ills."

Mel took it with a nod and inhaled the lemony aroma. The faintly sweet edge let her know it was laced with honey as well.

"Should I ask how you guys got in?" a gravelly voice asked from her right.

Mel slowly turned to see a very disheveled Jensen leaning back on her couch. His eyes were barely open and his hair was squished on one side of his head, looking adorably boyish. Her eyes widened when she realized she'd been laying on him while sleeping. *Oh my gosh...What have I done?*

One side of his mouth pulled up into a darling grin. "Just now realizing that you trapped me here last night, huh?"

"Watch it," Bennett growled from his recliner. "You're lucky I didn't black out your other eye this morning when I let everyone in."

Melody set the cup on the coffee table. Her hands were starting to shake as everything about last night came flooding back into her mind. Too many nightmarish visions were wreaking havoc on her brain and she squeezed her eyes tight, trying to fight them back.

A massive hand cutting off her air supply.

Micah's bruised and battered face.

Jensen flying over her head to tackle Mitchell.

Paramedics feeling her throat and shining a light in her eyes.

Strong arms wrapped around her shoulder and she found herself tucked back into Jensen's strong chest. "Breathe, sweetheart," he whispered in her ear. "Just breathe. You're safe, you're loved, nothing is going to happen to you now."

His words were exactly what she needed to hear, because they brought to mind the conversation they'd had *after* the nightmare. The one where Jensen declared his love and loyalty to her. It was every dream Mel had ever had wrapped up in a few easy words. She found her breathing calming down to normal and her racing heart dropping to an easier pace.

"I hate to be the one to interrupt such a wonderful moment," Caro began, "but would someone please tell us exactly what happened last night?"

Mel looked over to see her standing with her hands on her hips.

"Our love birds look like they lost a battle with a baseball bat!"

"Easy, Caro," Bennett interceded. "Let her breathe a little," he said, waving toward Mel. "It wasn't an easy night for any of us." Bennett stretched and rubbed his neck. "This recliner is not meant for sleeping," he muttered.

"You've been here all night?" Jensen asked, voicing the same question Mel had.

Bennett raised a sarcastic eyebrow. "You think I wouldn't come check on her?" he asked, again referring to Mel. "When I peeked in to see you two on the couch, there was no way I was leaving." He settled back in the chair. "This thing was fine, for the first hour or so."

"I'm sorry," Mel whispered, wincing at the pain in her throat.

"Drink your tea," Jensen encouraged her, pushing Mel upright.

She nodded and followed his orders. Its soothing warmth was perfect on her shredded throat.

"Sorry I'm late," Ken said as he came in the front door. Murmured greetings went around the room as he came to stand at the edge of the group. "It looks like you're in good hands, but I thought you might appreciate an update." Dark circles sat under Ken's eyes, letting Mel know he probably hadn't slept at all.

Guilt, mixed with gratitude, swirled through and she gave Ken her attention while Jensen leaned forward, one of his hands resting on Mel's thigh.

"Mitchell has admitted to everything with Mel and even to hitting his son," Ken said. The sad tone in his voice was unexpected. It was amazing he could still care with all the junk he saw in his job. Ken pushed a hand through his hair. "He'll be heading to court for a sentence, but it always takes a while for that to go through."

"Why would he admit to everything?" Jensen asked. His arm came around Mel's back, hugging her into his side. "He went to so much trouble to try and get us to back off. It seems weird he'd let it all go now."

Ken shrugged. "Not much choice, really. We had him red-handed. Micah has agreed to testify, a police captain personally saw him hurting an innocent bystander, and I'll bet Mel, here, would be willing to share her own witness, if necessary."

Mel nodded.

"So he felt backed into a corner and just gave up?" Jensen scoffed, his grip tightening.

"His attorney convinced him to work with us," Ken added. "Usually men like him will get off easier if they appear sorry for what they've done and eager to reform."

The room erupted in anger and frustration, but Mel didn't say a word. There was nothing to add that wasn't already being expressed. She may not like how their system ran exactly, but she had no power to change it. The important thing was that Mitchell would be put away. And hopefully it would be long enough that he forgot all about her.

"I'll be doing my best to see the full extent of the law put down," Ken said over the noise, causing it to dim. "I'm even looking into the possibility of attempted murder, which will have a much higher sentence."

All eyes went to Mel's neck and she shrank back into Jensen's hold, a weak hand coming up to cover her throat.

"Well...if anyone can get it taken care of, I'm sure it's you, Captain Wamsley," Rose said softly. She stood and brushed off her pants, not looking Ken in the eye, though he was beaming from her compliment. "I need to go open the shop." She looked at Mel. "Is there anything I can do for you before I go? I left you an arrangement in the kitchen. It has jasmine, lavender and roses. They all have healing properties plus help with strength." Rose was looking at her sympathetically, but Mel shook her head, giving her friend a small smile.

Rose's way of loving people with flowers was unique and amazing. Mel knew the blooms would help brighten her day.

"What about Micah?" Bennett asked.

Mel nodded, wanting to know as well.

Ken gave a sad smile. "He's still in the hospital, but Child Services are here and plan to place him in a home. They already have someone in mind who had a good record of helping kids just like him."

Mel let out a relieved sigh. That was more than she had hoped for for the troubled teenager. She sent a prayer heavenward that his new home would give him everything he needed.

"I'm glad that's all worked out," Rose said. "But I really do need to run."

"Wait," Jensen said. "There's something I need to say and I'd like you all here to listen."

Rose paused, then nodded and sat back down.

Mel turned to Jensen when he took both her hands in his.

"Melody, I know I only told you last night for the first time how much I love you, so this is probably going to sound crazy and rushed…but I can't imagine my life without you." He took a deep breath. "Will you do me the honor of being my wife?"

MELODY'S FACE WAS COMPLETELY shocked and Jensen didn't blame her. He hadn't really prepared her for this. Any of them. No one had any idea what had happened while he was over playing the part of a musician on television. All they knew was that he'd left, saying only time would tell and now here he was proposing marriage.

He wasn't regretting doing this, but if left to his own devices, Jensen would have handled it a little more tactfully. He wanted to marry Melody, but he didn't have time to take their relationship the way he normally would have, or else those television execs would ruin everything.

"Are you going to answer him?" Charli snapped. "For heaven's sake, Mel, you've been in love with him since we were kids!"

Melody's face turned bright red and she dropped his gaze as if embarrassed, but Jensen wasn't about to let her out of answering. This was the only way to do things on his terms…on both their terms. He put a knuckle under her chin and brought her face back up to his. He hoped his eyes conveyed his love and determination to have her. "I love you," he whispered, sliding his fingers along her skin, careful to avoid the bruises of last night's encounter. "It took me leaving to see just how much. You're amazing and wonderful and kind and caring. You take care of every person you come in contact with. You fit in my arms as if you were made to be there and I don't think I'll survive if I have to walk out of here without knowing what will happen." He gave her a sad smile. "Please don't make me live my life alone,

Mellie. I've experienced that and it has only taught me how much I need you."

"What about..." She swallowed. "Your music?"

Jensen shook his head. "I'll get to that in a minute, but know that I'm not going pro any time soon."

When her brows furrowed, he reached up and smoothed the lines on her soft skin. "Please, Melody. Please forgive me for being such an idiot before." He leaned in and began to kiss her face. Her temples, her cheekbones, her nose...she laughed lightly as he peppered every bit of skin with his lips. "Please," he begged.

Melody pushed against his shoulders and leaned back, still smiling widely. "Yes," she whispered.

Jensen held himself tight, ready to launch, but he forced himself to wait. "You're sure?" His hands began to slide behind her back. "Because if you're really saying yes, there's no going back. I won't let you go."

"Charli was right," Mellie said softly, her voice still raspy. "I've loved you for years. Now that you've finally caught up, I'd be stupid to turn you away." She tilted her head, a small frown on her face. "You're right though, this is sudden. Are *you* sure? I don't want you to do anything you'd regret."

"I've never been more sure." He could handle no more. Amidst the clapping and hollering of their friends, Jensen brought Mellie's mouth to his and showed her just how sure he was. In fact, he would have been content to show her for much longer than their friends allowed, but Jensen contented himself with the idea that he could kiss her like that any time he wanted now.

"Welcome to the family," Benny said, offering his hand to Jensen. Benny shrugged. "I mean, you practically were anyway, but it's nice to make it official."

Jensen grinned and shook his friend's, soon to be brother-in-law's, hand. "I'm just glad you didn't pull out a shotgun or something."

Benny snorted. "Don't tempt me."

Felix came over with a narrowed gaze. "Not that I'm not happy for you, but I would like to know why you were in such a hurry for this. You just got home last night and all the social media sites said you were the favorite."

"Story time!" Caro shouted, putting her hands in the air. "Everyone pipe down so we can hear it all."

Jensen and Mellie settled back on the couch, tucked close to each other as Jensen tried to figure out how exactly he could explain everything that had happened in his life for the last couple of months.

"As much as I want to stick around for this, I have to get back to work," Ken offered. "But I'll be expecting a full accounting soon." He raised an eyebrow at Jensen, who nodded in return.

After everyone offered their goodbyes to both Ken and Rose, the eyes of the group landed back on Jensen and he could feel every one of them.

"Why don't you start with what happened last night," Genni offered quietly from the back where she stood with Cooper. "Then we can backtrack to your time on the show."

"I can help with that," Benny offered, much to Jensen's relief. He let his friend speak for the next ten minutes about the night before, only offering a few tidbits to answer questions that occurred along the way.

"That's crazy," Brooke said, rubbing her hands over her upper arms. "Our town always seems so safe, but we've got things like this going on right under our noses."

Jensen nodded. A heavy quilt of sadness had settled over the group, ruining the light mood of celebration from only moments before.

"You're turn," Felix said, folding his arms over his chest. He spread his legs and stared Jensen down. "What brought you home early, and especially with marriage on your mind?"

Jensen glanced at the beautiful woman under his arm and kissed her temple before telling them about the realities of being on television.

"So you came home because the people were all jerks?" Caro asked with a frown.

Jensen shook his head. "No. I wanted to come home because I realized it wasn't the life for me. The lights, the makeup, the costumes and yes, the jerks. I hated it. All of it." He turned to Mellie again. "And I realized that where I really wanted to be was at your side," he whispered. "There were nights I could barely breathe from aching for you."

"Moving on," Benny said dryly.

Jensen rolled his eyes but obeyed. "So on last week's show, I had a moment of clarity. I wanted out and with Mitchell's threats, I wasn't willing to wait. So I breached my contract by playing that song I had written rather than the one we had practiced."

"That wasn't planned?" Charli asked, her jaw dropping.

Jensen shook his head. "Nope. My hope was to bomb out there and be sent packing because I broke the rules."

Benny snorted. "I think that backfired. Everyone loved it."

Jensen nodded. "Yep. The producers actually refused to let me go because they said the system nearly went offline with all the voting going on."

"You won the heart of every grown woman in America," Caro said with a smirk. "Nicely done."

"That wasn't the plan," Jensen grumbled, smiling when Mellie grinned up at him. His smile fell when he realized what he would have to tell them next.

"So how did you get home, then?" Felix pressed.

Jensen sat up, pushing Mellie to do the same. "I have something to tell you and you're not going to like it, so please just agree to hear me out, okay?"

Mellie looked concerned but nodded.

"They told me that in order to go home, I had to give them something else that would be just as lucrative as keeping me on the show." Jensen took a deep breath. "So, I offered them the chance to record me proposing to you, saying they could tell the story of how playing your song made me too homesick and I couldn't stand to be parted any longer." He squeezed her hand when she started to try and pull away. "They agreed it held just enough schmaltz for them to turn it into an epic love story."

"Can I give him the other black eye now?" Felix asked, his hands clenched at his sides. "How could you do that to Melody?" he asked, then spun on Benny. "And you? Her brother? Why aren't you more upset?"

Benny sat languidly in his chair. "Because Jensen spilled it all to me last night." His eyes turned to Mellie's, which were filled with tears. Jensen refused to let go of her hands, despite her pulling. He knew if she would just listen, she would understand.

"Why do you think he proposed to you this morning?" Ben asked, sitting upright. "After the show the other night, he already had plans to ask you to marry him, but was caught in a contract. So, he gave the studio what they wanted." He grinned and lay back again. "But he thwarted them again by proposing before they were ready. Now you get your real proposal and we'll do a fake one for the cameras."

The room was silent for a moment as Melody and the others digested what he was saying.

"Sneaky..." Caro said in a low tone. "I like it."

Melody's worried gaze met Jensen's. "Is that the truth?" she rasped. He winced slightly, knowing it must hurt to be speaking so much. "You're not proposing out of some weird sense—"

"No," Jensen snapped, then took a deep breath to calm himself. "Absolutely not," he said more tenderly. "I figured out days ago that I want to marry you, Mellie. The only thing that changed was the timeline. If I wasn't under contract, I would have given you time to get used to the idea rather than springing it on you," he explained. "But either way, I'd have asked for your hand." He smiled. "I've spent too many years being blind. I don't want to waste any more."

"But you were so excited when you heard from the television station," she argued. "Your music is a part of who you are and it's clear to anyone watching you play that it comes from here." She patted his chest, over his heart. "I'm selfish, Jensen. I don't want to leave Seaside Bay and I don't really enjoy sharing you with everyone." She shook her head, tears tracking down her cheeks. "I don't know if I'm the right woman for you because I don't know if I can go through it all again if you find you miss it."

He cupped her face and brought their foreheads together. "Melody Frasier," he breathed, sliding one hand to the back of her neck. "I have given in to the urges to run after stardom. I've performed in front of thousands, I've been on television, I've been patient through makeup and wardrobe and everything else they could throw at me." He took in a deep breath through his nose. "And none of it...not a single second, compared to you. None of the elation, the fame, adoration or even possible wealth made me feel the same way you do with just one look, one touch..." His voice dropped to a rough whisper. "Or one kiss."

With a quiet sob, Mellie threw her arms around his neck and kissed him. Jensen, not about to waste an opportunity, returned the embrace and the affection. He barely noticed when the front door opened and their guests filed out. They weren't important at the moment. The only thing that was, was holding Mellie in his arms, and their future laid out before them in all its unadventurous glory.

Though, he had a feeling that with Mellie at his side, nothing would ever be boring again.

EPILOGUE

"Thank you," Jensen mumbled as the audience in the smoothie shop clapped for the song he'd just finished.

Mel stood behind her counter, smiling widely and pretending not to be nervous about the half a dozen cameras that were floating through the shop. No one could walk without bumping into someone else as they tried to fit every person who'd come to listen to the "famous Jensen Tanner" play back in his hometown. *The fire marshal would have a fit if he saw this,* she thought.

Jensen's brown eyes met hers and he winked, sending Mel's heart rate into overdrive. This was it. The moment they'd been prepping for.

"If it's all right with you, I'd like to play an extra special song," Jensen said to the crowd. "It's one that I finished after I met the love of my life and kissed her for the very first time."

The crowd screamed before quieting down to listen to the beautiful tune.

Emily gripped Mel's hand, her skin just as clammy as Mel's was. "This is it," she squealed quietly.

"I know," Mel whispered back. "But I'm gonna need my hand back."

"Touchy, touchy," Emily snapped. She let go, but stayed put. "I put on extra makeup tonight, so you better be sure I'm making it in at least one of those camera shots."

Mel couldn't help but laugh, even though her nerves were jumping all over the place. She and Jensen were already engaged, but no one else knew that. The news that he was *going* to propose, however, was fairly common knowledge. With the addition of the cameras to their normal routine, it had been hard to keep it a secret and that only made Mel even more grateful for Jensen's quick proposal a couple of days before. He had known she wouldn't enjoy being surprised on camera, or sharing the moment with the world, so he'd gone behind the producer's back and proposed on his own so they could share the intimate moment with friends and loved ones.

Mel would forever cherish his thoughtfulness. Now, however, she had to pretend to be surprised when he popped the question when he...

"Melody?"

She jerked her gaze toward Jensen. He was standing, the guitar hanging from his neck. "Yes?" Her heart fluttered like a jackrabbit.

Jensen smirked and began to pluck the strings again, playing the sweet melody from their song. Slowly, he strolled toward her, the crowd parting like the Red Sea under Moses' hands, until he stood directly in front of her. His playing stopped and he lifted the strap over his head, handing the instrument to a nearby patron. "I have a question for you..."

Unbidden, Mel found her eyes filling with tears. She hadn't expected for this moment to mean so much to her, since they were secretly already engaged, but it did. She felt flushed and too warm, and her hands began to shake as he took them in his.

"Melody Frasier," Jensen said in a low tone, "you are the most amazing woman. You love everyone and they love you, and I know exactly why. Your smile lights up the room and I must be selfish because I want that smile to light me up every single day." He brought one of her hands to his mouth and kissed her palm. "You're my heart, my muse and my life." He dropped to one knee and pulled a velvet box from his back pocket. "Will you bless me with your sweet presence all day every day by becoming my wife?"

Tears tracked down her cheeks and Mel laughed as she wiped them away. "Yes," she said softly, then nodded her head for emphasis.

Her injuries still kept her from speaking too loudly and Jensen's black eye was caked with makeup to hide it from the cameras as best they could, but nothing was going to stop them from moving ahead in this moment.

She bounced on her toes, dragging him up to his feet and leaping into his arms. "Yes!"

The crowd went wild, but Mel tuned them all out. Jensen had quickly cupped the back of her head and brought their mouths together, ruining her for paying attention to the cameras, her friends or the customers. Nothing else existed but him.

He had been her dream since she was young and now he was finally, officially hers. The hole in her heart that she had given up hope of ever filling was overflowing at the moment and Mel didn't think she would ever be happier.

"Thank you," he whispered against her lips. "I had no idea that everything I'd ever wanted was here the whole time." He kissed her again before Mel could answer, but that was fine. There were no words to describe how her life had changed for the better in only a few weeks' time.

Her relationship with her brother, her friends and now her fiance had all shifted into something...more. And despite the difficult journey that brought it about, Mel found she wouldn't change any of it for any amount of fame or fortune. The second chance she'd refused to dream of was here...and it was perfect.

Thank you for reading
Melody and Jensen's story!
I hope you enjoyed reading it
as much as I enjoyed writing it.
Not quite ready to be done yet?
Want to read the stories for the other
members of the Bulbs, Blossoms and Bouquets group?
Don't miss any of the romance!
Her Unexpected Roommate[1]
Her Unexpected Second Chance[2]
Her Unexpected Partner[3]
Her Unexpected Rival
Her Unexpected Catch
Her Unexpected Star
Her Unexpected Delivery
Her Unexpected Protector

---

1. https://www.amazon.com/Her-Unexpected-Roommate-Blossoms-Bouquets-ebook/
   dp/B08PPXK15R

2. https://www.amazon.com/gp/product/B08T63NT34

3. https://www.amazon.com/gp/product/B08WJJ3FQH

Other Books by Laura Ann

lauraannbooks.com[1]

BULBS, BLOSSOMS, AND BOUQUETS
Her Unexpected Roommate[2]
Her Unexpected Second Chance[3]
Her Unexpected Partner[4]
Her Unexpected Rival
Her Unexpected Catch
Her Unexpected Star
Her Unexpected Delivery
Her Unexpected Protector
THE GINGERBREAD INN [5]
Three cousins come to help their grandmother
run an inn during the Christmas season when
mysterious happenings nearly ruin everything.
Book 1-3[6]

---

1. https://lauraannbooks.com/

2. https://www.amazon.com/Her-Unexpected-Roommate-Blossoms-Bouquets-ebook/dp/
B08PPXK15R

3. https://www.amazon.com/gp/product/B08T63NT34

4. https://www.amazon.com/gp/product/B08WJJ3FQH

5. https://www.amazon.com/gp/product/
B08N4JD51P?ref_=dbs_p_mng_rwt_ser_shvlr&storeType=ebooks

6. https://www.amazon.com/gp/product/
B08N4JD51P?ref_=dbs_p_mng_rwt_ser_shvlr&storeType=ebooks

SAGEBRUSH RANCH[7]

When city girls meet cowboys,
true love is on the horizon.
Books 1-6[8]

LOCKWOOD INDUSTRIES[9]

The Lockwood triplets started a personal security company.
Little did they know it would double as a matchmaking business!
Books 1-6[10]

OVERNIGHT BILLIONAIRE BACHELORS[11]

Three brothers become overnight billionaires.
Will they discover that love is the real treasure?
Books 1-5[12]

IT'S ALL ABOUT THE MISTLETOE[13]

---

7. https://www.amazon.com/gp/product/B089YPCF6X?ref_=dbs_r_series&storeType=ebooks

8. https://www.amazon.com/gp/product/B089YPCF6X?ref_=dbs_r_series&storeType=ebooks

9. https://www.amazon.com/gp/product/B083Z49VL3?ref_=dbs_r_series&storeType=ebooks

10. https://www.amazon.com/gp/product/B083Z49VL3?ref_=dbs_r_series&storeType=ebooks

11. https://www.amazon.com/gp/product/B07RJZL29J?ref_=dbs_r_series&storeType=ebooks

12. https://www.amazon.com/gp/product/B07RJZL29J?ref_=dbs_r_series&storeType=ebooks

13. https://www.amazon.com/gp/product/B082F8FTHY?ref_=dbs_r_series&storeType=ebooks

When 6 friends brings fake dates to their high school reunion, mayhem and mistletoe win the day!

Books 1-6[14]

MIDDLETON PREP[15]

If you enjoy fairy tale romance,
these sweet, contemporary retellings are for you!

Books 1-9[16]

14. https://www.amazon.com/gp/product/B082F8FTHY?ref_=dbs_r_series&store-Type=ebooks

15. https://www.amazon.com/gp/product/B07DYCWRQL?ref_=dbs_r_series&store-Type=ebooks

16. https://www.amazon.com/gp/product/B07DYCWRQL?ref_=dbs_r_series&store-Type=ebooks

9 781956 176063